LUKE-ACTS

LUKE-ACTS

NEW PERSPECTIVES
FROM THE SOCIETY OF BIBLICAL
LITERATURE SEMINAR

Edited by
CHARLES H. TALBERT

CROSSROAD · NEW YORK

1984

The Crossroad Publishing Company
370 Lexington Avenue, New York, N.Y. 10017

Library of Congress Cataloging in Publication Data

Main entry under title:

Luke-Acts, new perspectives from the Society of
Biblical Literature seminar.

Includes essays that have grown out of the Luke-Acts
seminar of the Society of Biblical Literature (1979-83)
Companion vol. to: Perspectives on Luke-Acts. 1978.
Includes index.
1. Bible. N.T. Luke—Criticism, interpretation,
etc.—Addresses, essays, lectures. 2. Bible. N.T.
Acts—Criticism, interpretation, etc.—Addresses,
essays, lectures. I. Talbert, Charles H. II. Society
of Biblical Literature.
BS2589.L84 1983   226'.406   83-15254
ISBN 0-8245-0608-1 (pbk.)

CONTENTS

vi • Contents

PREFACE

Since 1972 there has existed a program segment in the Society of Biblical Literature dealing with Luke-Acts. A Luke-Acts Seminar was established in 1979 with a five-year life span. This volume of essays is an attempt to bring together some of the work done between 1979 and 1983 by those related directly or indirectly to that seminar. Some of these papers grew out of the annual programs; others have been produced for other reasons. This volume does not pretend to replace its predecessor, *Perspectives on Luke-Acts* (Danville, VA: Association of Baptist Professors of Religion, 1978) but aims to supplement it. It is hoped that this book, like its predecessor, will serve as a stimulus to further study of the Lucan writings.

Appreciation must be expressed to the Department of Religion at Wake Forest University and to the Graduate Council of the same institution for moneys that have subsidized this volume. Without this assistance, publication would have been delayed.

Thanks should also be expressed to Paul J. Achtemeier, former executive secretary of the Society of Biblical Literature, whose encouragement and initiative served to bring the Luke-Acts Seminar (1979-83) into being. To him we dedicate this book.

Charles H. Talbert
Chairman, Luke-Acts Seminar,
1979-83

ABBREVIATIONS

AB	Anchor Bible
AnBib	Analecta biblica
ASNU	Acta seminarii neotestamentici upsaliensis
ATR	*Anglican Theological Review*
BASOR	*Bulletin of the American Schools of Oriental Research*
BBB	Bonner biblische Beiträge
BDF	F. Blass, A. Debrunner, and R. W. Funk, *A Greek Grammar of the New Testament and Other Early Christian Literature* (Chicago and London: University of Chicago Press, 1961)
BETL	Bibliotheca ephemeridum theologicarum lovaniensium
BGD	W. Bauer, F. W. Gingrich, and F. W. Danker, *A Greek-English Lexicon of the New Testament and Other Early Christian Literature* (Chicago and London: University of Chicago Press, 1979)
BTB	*Biblical Theology Bulletin*
BVC	*Bible et vie chrétienne*
BWANT	Beiträge zur Wissenschaft vom Alten und Neuen Testament
BZ	*Biblische Zeitschrift*
CBQ	*Catholic Biblical Quarterly*
EBib	Études bibliques
ETL	*Ephemerides theologicae lovanienses*
EvQ	*Evangelical Quarterly*
EvT	*Evangelische Theologie*
ExpTim	*Expository Times*
FRLANT	Forschungen zur Religion und Literatur des Alten und Neuen Testaments
GCS	Griechische christliche Schriftsteller
HKNT	Handkommentar zum Neuen Testament
HNT	Handbuch zum Neuen Testament
HSM	Harvard Semitic Monographs
HTKNT	Herders theologischer Kommentar zum Neuen Testament
HTR	*Harvard Theological Review*
HTS	Harvard Theological Studies

IB	*Interpreter's Bible* (Nashville: Abingdon, 1952)
ICC	International Critical Commentary
IDB	*Interpreter's Dictionary of the Bible* (Nashville: Abingdon, 1962)
Int	*Interpretation*
JAAR	*Journal of the American Academy of Religion*
JBL	*Journal of Biblical Literature*
JJS	*Journal of Jewish Studies*
JQR	*Jewish Quarterly Review*
JSNT	*Journal for the Study of the New Testament*
LCL	Loeb Classical Library
LSJ	H. G. Liddel, R. Scott, H. S. Jones, *Greek-English Lexicon* (Oxford: Clarendon, 1925-1940)
MeyerK	H. A. W. Meyer, Kritisch-exegetischer Kommentar über das Neue Testament
MT	Masoretic Text
NEB	New English Bible
NIGTC	New International Greek Testament Commentary
NovT	*Novum Testamentum*
NTAbh	Neutestamentliche Abhandlungen
NTD	Das Neue Testament deutsch
NTS	*New Testament Studies*
NTTS	New Testament Tools and Studies
OCD	*Oxford Classical Dictionary*
PG	*Patrologia graeca*, ed. J. Migne
RB	*Revue biblique*
RevExp	*Review and Expositor*
RHPR	*Revue d'histoire et de philosophie religieuses*
RNT	Regensburger Neues Testament
RQ	*Römische Quartalschrift für christliche Altertumskunde und Kirchengeschichte*
RSV	Revised Standard Version
SANT	Studien zum Alten und Neuen Testament
SBLDS	Society of Biblical Literature Dissertation Series
SBLMS	Society of Biblical Literature Monograph Series
SBS	Stuttgarter Bibelstudien
SBT	Studies in Biblical Theology
SJLA	Studies in Judaism in Late Antiquity
SNT	Studien zum Neuen Testament
SNTSMS	Society for New Testament Studies Monograph Series
SPAW	*Sitzungsberichte der preussischen Akademie der Wissenschaften*
ST	*Studia theologica*
Str-B	H. Strack and P. Billerbeck, *Kommentar zum Neuen Testament* (6 vols.; Munich: Beck, 1922-1961)
StudNeot	Studia neotestamentica, Studia
SUNT	Studien zur Umwelt des Neuen Testaments

TDNT	*Theological Dictionary of the New Testament,* ed. G. Kittel and G. Friedrich (10 vols.; Grand Rapids: Eerdmans, 1964–1976)
TF	*Theologische Forschung*
THKNT	Theologisches Handkommentar zum Neuen Testament
TQ	*Theologische Quartalschrift*
TS	*Theological Studies*
TU	Texte und Untersuchungen
UBS	United Bible Societies
UF	*Ugarit-Forschungen*
VT	*Vetus Testamentum*
WMANT	Wissenschaftliche Monographien zum Alten und Neuen Testament
WTJ	*Westminster Theological Journal*
ZNW	*Zeitschrift für die neutestamentliche Wissenschaft*
ZTK	*Zeitschrift für Theologie und Kirche*

PART I

INTRODUCTORY ISSUES

George Rice

WESTERN NON-INTERPOLATIONS: A DEFENSE OF THE APOSTOLATE

Westcott and Hort state in the introduction to their monumental work that the result of their labor "is an attempt to present exactly the original words of the New Testament, so far as they can now be determined from surviving documents."[1] Because of the complexity of the variations offered by the various witnesses, Westcott and Hort inform us that the "original words of the New Testament" can be identified only by the use of criticism, "that is, of a process of distinguishing and setting aside those readings which have originated at some link in the chain of transmission."[2]

It is well known, of course, that in this attempt to render "the original words of the New Testament," the so-called neutral text was seen as being superior to other text types. Speaking of a comparison of the three "Pre-Syrian" text types (the neutral, Western, and Alexandrian), Westcott and Hort conclude:

> In the vast majority of instances the result is identical: in binary variations the Non-Western reading approves itself more original than the Western, the Non-Alexandrian than the Alexandrian: in ternary variations the neutral reading, if supported by such documents as stand most frequently on the Non-Western and Non-Alexandrian sides in binary variations, approves itself more original than the Western and also more original than the Alexandrian.[3]

Western Non-Interpolations

There is a group of readings that appear in the Western text upon which Westcott and Hort looked quite favorably. Concerning these readings, they said that they cannot doubt their genuineness "in spite of the exclusively Western character of their attestation. They are all omissions, or, to speak more correctly, non-interpolations."[4] There is no secret that the term "non-interpolation" correctly states

1

Westcott and Hort's attitude toward their favorite witness. As Bruce Metzger notes, they just could not bring themselves to speak of interpolations in the "neutral text."[5]

The discussion over the Western non-interpolations has centered mainly on the evaluation of their genuineness. As Klyne Snodgrass has noted in his article "Western Non-Interpolations," "The view of Westcott and Hort on the authenticity of the 'Western non-interpolations' has been widely accepted in the past and is still maintained by many, particularly in the English-speaking world."[6] In recent years, however, some dissenting voices have been heard, for example, J. Jeremias and Kurt Aland. After presenting their views, Snodgrass concludes that "the 'Western non-interpolations' . . . have little claim to authenticity."[7]

One aspect of Snodgrass's article that commends itself is a short analysis of fourteen omissions in the Western text of Luke (seven of which are non-interpolations), one omission in John, seven in Matthew, and three in Mark. In his analysis of these verses, Snodgrass puts forward his views about why the various omissions were made, for example, harmonization with the other gospels, errors of homoioteleuton, the possibility that the omitted statements caused offense, etc.

If the non-interpolations appearing in Luke are examined individually, Snodgrass's explanations are feasible. However, if these omissions are examined along with other variants in the Western text, for example, additions, alterations in persons and tenses of verbs, changes in cases, and word substitutions, it will be discovered that some of the Western non-interpolations make a contribution by either enhancing the original meaning of the text or by making alterations in its meaning to a lesser or a greater degree.

For example, Snodgrass treats one of the non-interpolations, Luke 24:12, with greater detail than the other passages from Luke. This verse records Peter's hasty visit to the empty tomb after hearing the report of the women. When dealing with the possible reasons for the omission of this verse, Snodgrass says, "It is not easy to account for the omission of this verse from the Western text unless it was due to scribal accident or was an attempt to do away with the minor divergence from the Johannine tradition (where Peter was accompanied by another disciple)."[8]

Taken by itself, it is indeed difficult to see a reason for this omission. However, taken together with other Western variants in chap. 24, both the non-interpolations and those that are not non-interpolations, a pattern emerges that I would like to identify as "a defense of the apostolate."

There are seven non-interpolations in Luke 24 identified by West-cott and Hort. Five of the seven lend themselves to this motif. They are all set in the context of the empty tomb and the post-resurrection appearances and include vv. 3, 6, 12, 36, and 40. The two remaining non-interpolations, vv. 51 and 52, are set in the context of the ascension.

There exists in Luke 24 an unbelief on the part of the eleven apostles upon hearing the report of the women that the body of Jesus could not be found and that they had been told by two men in shining clothing (later identified as angels, v. 23) that Jesus had risen. Luke reports that the words of the women appeared as nonsense to them (v. 11). The Western variants tend to explain the reasons for this unbelief and, in the process, to exonerate the apostles, thus providing "a defense of the apostolate."

Method Used

At this point the following observations must be made about the methods used in this study.

1. Variants were identified by comparing the Greek text of Codex Bezae (D) with the text of Codex Vaticanus (B). D was chosen as the representative of the Western text because it is the primary Greek witness to this text type and contains unique readings not found else-where. Other MSS will be noted where they bear witness with D. B was used as a standard of comparison because it is a real text. A critical edition represents a text that never existed in MS form. The letter B will be used when referring to the text with which D was compared.

2. Witnesses supporting the variant readings were taken from the critical apparatuses of the United Bible Societies' 3rd edition, the 26th edition of Nestle-Aland, and the 8th edition of Tischendorf.

3. Minor variations are noted, for they often make a contribution to the development of a variant theme. At times, major alterations, like the Western non-interpolations, do not take on their true signifi-cance until they are set in the context of the minor alterations that surround them.

4. It must also be noted that the scribes of the Western text were not always consistent in their alterations. There are places where one would expect an alteration to be made in order to enhance the development of a theme, or to agree with previous alterations, only to find none.

It is my purpose now to examine the variants at the end of chap. 23 and those running through chap. 24 which develop a defense of the apostles against the charge of unbelief.

The Stone at the Tomb

At 23:53, after the report of the removal of Jesus from the cross and his interment by Joseph of Arimathea (vv. 50-52), is the following:

Luke 23:53

Codex B	Codex D
και καθελων ενετυλιξεν	και καθελων ενετυλιξεν
αυτο σινδονι	το σωμα του ιηυ εν σινδονι
και εθηκεν αυτον εν μνηματι	και εθηκεν αυτον εν μνημειω
λαξευτω ου ουκ ην	λελατομημενω ου ουκ ην
ουδεις ουπω κειμενος.	ουπω ουδεις κειμενος
	και θεντος αυτου επεθηκεν
	τω μνημειω λειθον ον μογις
	εικοσι εκυλιον.

Then he took it down
            and
wrapped it in a linen
shroud, and laid him in a
rock-hewn tomb, where no
one had ever yet been laid.

Then he took   down
the body of Jesus and
wrapped it in a linen
shroud, and laid him in a
rock-hewn tomb, where no
one had ever yet been laid
and when he was interred a
stone was placed upon the
tomb which twenty men
could hardly roll.

αυτο] το σωμα του ιηυ, D
+ εν ante σινδονι, D 440
μνηματι λαξευτω] μνημειω λελατομημενω, D
+ και θεντος αυτου επεθηκεν τω μνημειω λειθον ον μογις εικοσι
εκυλιον post κειμενος, D (0124) c sa

There are some who see a similarity between the size of this stone and the one found in Homer's *Odyssey*, where the Cyclops puts into his door "a stone which not even twenty-two carts might carry away."[9] Whether the Western scribe who originated this variant borrowed the idea from Homer to use an immense stone to block the entrance to the tomb is not our concern here. What we are interested in is the size of the stone.

At v. 55 there is a second addition that has a bearing on this study. We are informed by D and others that *two* women followed Joseph and the body of Jesus to the burial site and beheld the tomb, whereas the B text does not specify the number of women.

Luke 23:55

Codex B	Codex D
κατακολουθησασαι δε αι γυ- ναικες αιτινες ησαν συνελη- λυθυιαι εκ της γαλειλαιας αυτω εθεασαντο το μνημειον και ως ετεθη το σωμα αυτου.	κατηκολουθησαν δε δυο γυ- ναικες αιτινες ησαν συνελη- λυθυιαι απο της αγαλιλαιας και εθεασαντο το μνημα αυτου.
The women who had come with him from Galilee followed and saw the tomb and how his body was laid.	The two women who had come from Galilee followed and saw his tomb.

κατακολουθησασαι] κατηκολουθησαν, D c ff[2] r sa
αι γυναικες] δυο γυναικες, D 29 it
om. αυτω, D 63 pc c
om. και ως ετεθη το σωμα, D

The number two may reflect Matthew and Mark, where Mary Magdalene and the other Mary are reported to have followed the body of Jesus to the tomb (Matt 27:61; Mark 15:47), but in the Western text they remain unidentified. Of significance also is the omission of the words in the B text, "and how his body was laid." We will take note of the omission of αυτω later.

At the conclusion of chap. 23 is the following: (1) two women followed Joseph and the body to the tomb, (2) a mammoth stone that twenty men could barely move was placed over the tomb entrance, (3) according to D, this is all the two women witnessed, for the arrangement of the body in the tomb is omitted at v. 55. The emphasis in the Western text, therefore, is on the size of the stone and the difficulty of its removal, and not upon the arrangement of the body in the tomb.

The Women at the Tomb

Early Sunday morning, according to 24:1, "they" came to the tomb. "They" of v. 1 in the Western text would be the two women of the preceding verses. D, along with a host of other witnesses, adds the information that the two were accompanied by certain others.

Luke 24:1

Codex B	Codex D
τη δε μια των σαββατων ορθρου βαθεως επι το μνημα ηλθαν φερουσαι α ητοιμασαν αρωματα.	μια δε των σαββατων ορθρου βαθεως ηρχοντο επει το μνημα φαιρουσαι α ητοιμασαν και τινες συν αυταις ελογι- ζοντο δε εν εαυταις τις αρα αποχυλισει τον λιθον;
But on the first day of the week at early dawn they went to the tomb taking the spices they had prepared.	But on the first day of the week at early dawn they went to the tomb taking what they had prepared and certain others came with them. And they be- gan to reason among themselves Who will roll away the stone?

om. τη, D
ηλθαν] ηρχοντο, D
om. αρωματα, D it sy^{sc} sa
+ και τινες συν αυταις ελογιζοντο δε εν εαυτοις τις αρα
αποχυλισει τον λιθον post ητοιμασαν, D (0124 c) sa

That the members of the larger party were also women is attested by the feminine pronoun εαυταις in the second addition to this verse.

The conversation among the women concerning who would roll away the stone for them reflects a harmonization with Mark 16:3. However, with the Western addition in Luke 23, which makes the stone placed at the entrance of the tomb one of immense size, the women have a right to be concerned about its removal. The fact that the women found it moved from the entrance gives one reason why the men back in Jerusalem should have believed their report. There- fore, the Western addition concerning the size of the stone and its mysterious removal become a factor, but in an unexpected way.

When the women arrived at the burial site and saw that the mammoth stone had been rolled away from the entrance of the tomb, they entered and found it empty.

Luke 24:3

Codex B	Codex D
εισελθουσαι δε ουχ ευρον το σωμα του κ̄ῡ ῑῡ.	εισελθουσαι δε ουχ ευρον το σωμα.

| But when they went in they did not find the body of the Lord Jesus. | But when they went in they did not find the body. |

om. του $\overline{\text{κυ}}$ $\overline{\text{ιυ}}$, D it

The omission of the words "of the Lord Jesus" is the first Western non-interpolation in chap. 24. F. W. Farrar, as well as Snodgrass, notes that this is the only place in the gospels where κυριος Ιησους ("Lord Jesus") is used, except for the long ending of Mark (16:19).[10] On the other hand, this title is found fifteen times in Acts, and it appears frequently in the epistles. Surveying the passages in Acts, one is impressed that the phrase "the Lord Jesus" is an honorific title given to the resurrected Christ. The omission of this phrase in v. 3 may simply stem from the fact that at this point in time the resurrection of Jesus was not an object of faith as far as his followers were concerned. He is not yet "the Lord Jesus." If this is conceivable, the omission would fit into the overall scheme of the Western variants in this chapter; that is, evidence of the resurrection and belief in the resurrection do not appear until the post-resurrection appearances.

While the women were at a loss about what to think of the removal of the stone and the tomb's being empty, two men in shining clothing appeared and asked, "Why do you seek the living among the dead?" (v. 5). The second non-interpolation results in the removal of a clear declaration of the resurrection.

Luke 24:6

Codex B	Codex D
ουκ εστιν ωδε αλλα ηγερθη μνησθητε ως ελαλησεν υμιν ετι ων εν τη γαλειλαια.	μνησθητε δε οσα ελαλησεν υμειν ετι ων εν τη γαλιλαια.
He is not here but has risen Remember how he told you while he was still in Galilee	But remember as much as he told you while he was still in Galilee

om. ουκ εστιν ωδε αλλα ηγερθη, D it
ως] οσα, D c sy^{sc} geo^{B} Marcion Tatian

The communication of these two men is now as follows: (1) the rhetorical question is asked, "Why do you seek the living among the dead?" (v. 5); (2) an appeal is made to remember what Jesus had said while in Galilee (v. 6); which included (3) the Son of Man would be betrayed into the hands of men (D omits sinful), be crucified, and be raised the third day (v. 7). The one clear statement declaring that the resurrection had indeed taken place is removed (v. 6).

The women returned and reported "all this" to the eleven and "all the rest" (v. 9). The eleven were not impressed, "These words seemed to them an idle tale and they did not believe them" (v. 11). In fact, the eleven apostles were so unimpressed that no one went to check out the report of the women, not even Peter. Thus, the omission of v. 12 is the third non-interpolation: "But Peter rose and ran to the tomb, stooping and looking in, he saw the linen cloths by themselves; and he went home wondering at what had happened" (D it syr[palmss]).

It is of interest that, while v. 9 in the B text has a group identified as "all the rest" being with the eleven, it is upon the apostles that the women repeatedly press the report of their experience (v. 10), and it is the apostles who do not believe (v. 11).

At this point we must make a further observation about the women who followed the body to the tomb. We have already noted that the Western text specifies that they were two in number (23:55). D makes further alterations that result in casting these women in mystery.

At 23:55 the B text tells us that the women (their number is not specified) who followed the body of Jesus to the tomb were those who had come with him from Galilee. D and a few other MSS omit the pronoun αυτω ("with him"). This omission makes the women (specified as two in the Western text) traveling companions who came from Galilee, but they have no association with Jesus.

At 24:10 in the B text, where the women who followed the body to the tomb are identified as Mary Magdalene, Joanna, and Mary the mother of James, D and others omit the words ησαν δε ("they were").[11]

Luke 24:10

Codex B	Codex D
ησαν δε η μαγδαληνη μαρια	μαρια η μαγδαληνη
και ιωαννα και μαρια η	και ιωανα και μαρια η
ιακωβου και αι λοιπαι συν	ιακωβου και αι λοιπαι συν
αυταις ελεγον προς τους	αυταις ελεγαν προς αυτους
αποστολους ταυτα.	αποστολους ταυτα.

They were Mary Magdalene and Joanna and Mary the mother of James; and the other women with them told this to the apostles.	Mary Magdalene and Joanna and Mary the mother of James and the other women with them told this to the apostles themselves.

om. ησαν δε, A D W Γ 1010 1241 al sy^{sch}

τους αποστολους] αυτους αποστολους, D

This omission results in these three women no longer being those who followed the body to the tomb. In the Western text, the group that followed the body to the tomb numbered two. The group in v. 10 numbered three and are known by name; they and the rest who were with them bring the report to the apostles. The two of 23:55 are unnamed and mysteriously detached.

It is this mysterious detachment that helps identify the women mentioned at 24:22 as being the two.

Luke 24:22

Codex B	Codex D
αλλα και γυναικες τινες εξ ημων εξεστησαν ημας γεναμεναι ορθριναι επι το μνημειον.	αλλα και γυναικες τινες εξεστησαν ημας γενομεναι ορθριναι επει το μνημειον.
Moreover some women of our company amazed us. They were at the tomb early in the morning.	Moreover some women amazed us. They were at the tomb early in the morning.

om. εξ ημων, D pc

At this point in the narrative the two Emmaus disciples are recounting to Jesus the events of the past several days as he walks unidentified with them to Emmaus. By the omission of εξ ημων, the women at the tomb as reported in 24:22 are placed outside the known group. Those who are known and named are not included in the account given by the Emmaus disciples in the Western text. Could it be that the two mysterious women in the Western text provide an excuse for the unbelief on the part of the eleven? Consider what the Western text presents.

1. Two women follow the body of Jesus to the tomb (23:53).

2. They are not associated with Jesus even though they have come from Galilee (23:55).

3. They are not from Jesus' close followers, who are gathered in Jerusalem (24:55).

4. These two mysterious women behold the tomb and see the mammoth stone placed over the entrance (23:53).

5. They do not see how the body of Jesus is laid in the tomb (23:55).

6. On Sunday morning the two mysterious women return to the tomb and certain other women with them (24:1), namely, Mary Magdalene, Joanna, and Mary the mother of James, and others who were with them (24:10).

If we have reconstructed the thought of the Western variants correctly, Mary Magdalene, Joanna, and Mary the mother of James now see the tomb for the first time. But when they see it, the mammoth stone has been moved and there is no body. That the stone had been placed at the entrance of the tomb and that the body had been interred rested on the testimony of the mysterious two women only, and even at that D omits the statement that the two saw how the body was laid.

Consequently, when the three women who were known to the group in Jerusalem reported to the apostles what they found (v. 10), they had only the word of two unknown women that Jesus had been interred and the mammoth stone had been placed at the entrance. With the omission in v. 6 of the one clear statement made by the two men in shining clothing that Jesus had indeed been raised, the apostles evidently felt that there was not sufficient evidence, and so they did not believe the report of the women nor did Peter go to the tomb to verify the report.

The Two Emmaus Disciples

Later that day two "of them," that is, two of the men who were in Jerusalem, went to the village of Emmaus (v. 13). The εξ αυτων would seem to indicate that they were present when the women rendered their report, but they were not from among the eleven. This is supported by v. 18, where one of the two is identified as Cleopas.

Along the way Jesus joined them and pretended he did not know what they were talking about, whereupon the two informed him of the events of the past several days. Along with the alteration made at 24:22, which placed the two women at the tomb outside of the known group in Jerusalem, the Western text makes a further alteration at 24:24, which harmonizes this verse with the omission of v. 12.

Luke 24:24

Codex B	Codex D
και απηλθον τινες	και απηλθον τινες εκ
των συν ημιν επι το	των συν ημειν επι το
μνημειον και ευρον ουτως	μνημειον και ευρον ουτως
καθως αι γυναικες ειπον	ως ειπον αι γυναικες
αυτον δε ουκ ειδον.	αυτον δε ουκ ειδομεν.

Some of those who were with us went to the tomb and found it just as the women had said but him they did not see.	Some of those who were with us went to the tomb and found it as the women had said but him we did not see.

+ εκ ante των, D
καθως] ως, D c e
ειδον] ειδομεν, D e

The change from "but him they did not see" to "but him *we* did not see" allows the visit to the tomb as reported in this verse while supporting the omission of v. 12, which eliminated Peter's visit to the tomb. This alteration also identifies those who visited the tomb as being at least the two Emmaus disciples. While the eleven apostles felt the report of the women was not creditable and no one from their group went to the tomb, the two Emmaus disciples, coming from the group identified as "all the rest," had enough interest to verify the women's report.

In response to the account given by the two Emmaus disciples, Jesus chides them for their slowness of heart.

Luke 24:25

Codex B	Codex D
και αυτος ειπεν προς αυτους	ο δε ειπεν προς αυτους
ω ανοητοι και βραδεις τη	ω ανοητοι και βραδεις τη
καρδια του πιστευειν επι	καρδια επι
πασιν οις ελαλησαν οι	πασιν οις ελαλησαν οι
προφηται.	προφηται.

And he said to them O foolish men and slow of heart to believe all that the prophets have spoken.	And he said to them O foolish men and slow of heart concerning all that the prophets have spoken.

και αυτος ειπεν] ο δε ειπεν, D c e
om. του πιστευειν, D

Since the infinitive του πιστευειν is omitted, these men are chided not for the lack of faith that was displayed by the apostles but rather for being ignorant and slow to respond to what the prophets had said. The attitude of unbelief seems to rest with the eleven. At least the Emmaus disciples had enough interest to respond to the report of the women, even though they did not comprehend the meaning of everything that had happened.

After Jesus had made himself known to them and had disappeared, the two disciples realized that they had a veil over their hearts, but the veil was not one of unbelief, as was the case with the eleven, but rather one of misunderstanding, for they had failed to understand what the prophets had said about the passion of Jesus.

Luke 24:32

Codex B	Codex D
και ειπαν προς αλληλους ουχι η καρδια ημων καιο-μενη ην ως ελαλει ημιν εν τη οδω ως διηνυγεν ημιν τας γραφας;	οι δε ειπον προς εαυτους ουχι η καρδια ην ημων κεκα-λυμμενη ως ελαλει ημειν εν τη οδω ως ηνυγεν ημειν τας γραφας;
They said to each other Did not our hearts burn as he talked to us on the road while he opened to us the scripture?	They said to themselves Were not our hearts veiled as he talked to us on the road while he opened to us the scripture?

και ειπαν προς αλληλους] οι ειπον προς εαυτους, D c e
καιομενη] κεκαλυμμενη, D sa^mss

This verse now reads that their hearts were *veiled*, instead of their hearts burning, while Jesus spoke to them on the way.

An addition made to the next verse (v. 33) mentions remorse for their slowness of heart to understand what the prophets had written.

Luke 24:33

Codex B	Codex D
και ανασταντες αυτη τη ωρα υπεστρεψαν	και ανασταντες λυπουμενοι αυτη τη ωρα υπεστρεψαν

εις ιερουσαλημ και ευρον ἐις ιερουσαλημ και ευρον
ηθροισμενους τους ενδεκα ηθροισμενους τους ῑᾱ
και τους συν αυτοις. και τους συν αυτοις.

And they arose	And they arose sorrowing
that same hour and returned	that same hour and returned
to Jerusalem and they found	to Jerusalem and they found
the eleven gathered together	the eleven gathered together
and those who were with them.	and those who were with them.

+ λυπουμενοι post ανασταντες, D c e sa
ενδεκα] ῑᾱ, D

Certainly their "sorrowing" does not result from the post-resurrection appearance of their Lord, but rather from their lack of understanding.

When the two returned to Jerusalem and entered the room, the eleven and those with them greeted the two by saying in the B text, "The Lord has risen indeed and has appeared to Simon" (v. 34).

Luke 24:34

Codex B	Codex D
λεγοντας οτι οντως	λεγοντες οτι οντως
ηγερθη ο κ̅ς̅ και ωφθη	ηγερθη ο κ̅ς̅ και ωφθη
σιμωνι.	σιμωνι.

Who said	[And the two] said
The Lord has risen indeed	The Lord has risen indeed
and has appeared to Simon.	and has appeared to Simon.

λεγοντας] λεγοντες, D

But D changes the case of the participle. The accusative case in the B text indicates that the Jerusalem group told the two Emmaus disciples that the Lord had risen and that he had appeared to Simon. This would then be the first time the two had heard about the appearance to Simon, and it would indicate that the Jerusalem group had come to believe the resurrection on the basis of Simon's report.

D alters the case of the participle from the accusative λεγοντας to the nominative λεγοντες, making the two Emmaus disciples the antecedent of the participle and not the Jerusalem group, thus leaving the Jerusalem group in a state of unbelief. The two now confirm the resurrection of Jesus, "The Lord has risen indeed." They also confirm something else.   They confirm an appearance of Jesus to Simon, which, according to the Western text, would have to be known by all, but not believed. The two Emmaus disciples can now affirm the appearance to Simon because of their own experience.

The fourth non-interpolation, which is in v. 36, is now understandable in the light of the Western defense of the apostles and also in the light of what follows in v. 37.

Luke 24: 36, 37

Codex B	Codex D
36 ταυτα δε αυτων λαλουντων	36 ταυτα δε αυτων λαλουντων
αυτος εστη εν μεσω αυτων	αυτος εσταθη εν μεσω αυτων.
και λεγει αυτοις ειρηνη υμιν.	
37 θροηθεντες δε	37 αυτοι δε πτοηθεντες
και εμφοβοι γενομενοι	και ενφοβοι γενομενοι
εδοκουν πνευμα θεωρειν.	εδοκουν φαντασμα θεωρειν.
36 As they were saying	36 As they were saying
this he himself stood	this he stood
among them and said	among them.
Peace to you.	
37 But they were startled	37 But they were startled
and frightened	and frightened
and supposed that they saw	and supposed that they saw
a spirit.	a ghost.

---

36   εστη] εσταθη, D
       om. και λεγει αυτοις ειρηνη υμιν, D it
37   θροηθεντες δε] αυτοι δε πτοηθεντες, D
       πνευμα] φαντασμα, D

D substitutes φαντασμα ("ghost") for πνευμα ("spirit"), making the appearance of Jesus more of an eerie encounter than it is in the B text. When this substitution is made, the fear upon seeing the risen Lord is more understandable. Except for Peter and, of course, the two Emmaus disciples, the members of the Jerusalem group are still in a state of unbelief.

By omitting the non-interpolation in v. 36, "and he said to them, Peace to you," the Western text presents the appearance of an apparition, silent and ominous, standing in the midst of the unbelieving group. It is not until Jesus speaks for the first time in v. 38, telling them to handle him so that they may be assured that it is indeed he, and then eats before them (vv. 41-43), that their fear and unbelief begin to turn to joy and wonder.

The omission of v. 40, the fifth non-interpolation, is also designed to minimize the apostles' unbelief. Verse 41 states that the Jerusalem group continued in unbelief from joy and wonder even though Jesus had shown them his hands and feet, which is recorded in v. 40 in the B text. By the removal of v. 40, the Western text decreases to a great extent a valid reason why they should no longer be unbelieving. Jesus, in v. 39, says, "See my hands and feet, that it is I myself; handle me and see; for a spirit has not flesh and bone as you see that I have." But Luke presents no record of the apostles' actually following Jesus' directive to touch and handle him. The Western text removes the statement that Jesus showed them his hands and feet (v. 40), and the result is that the απιστουντων ("unbelieving") of v. 41 becomes less objectionable and the disciples are protected from further criticism.

Conclusion

By including the Western non-interpolations in their attempt to render "the original word of the New Testament," Westcott and Hort took the position that these omissions originated with Luke. Numerous scholars since then have disagreed with their conclusion; however, the reasons for disagreement have not always been clear or convincing. This study has attempted to show that the Western non-interpolations in Luke 24, when considered together with other variant readings that surround them, give adequate evidence that they resulted from a bias on the part of Western scribes.

The B text of Luke presents an unbelief on the part of the apostles, an unbelief that persists in the presence of evidence testifying to the resurrection. The Western text, led by D, alters Luke's account of these events and presents reasons for the unbelief, which can be seen in (1) the blocking of the tomb's entrance by an immense stone, (2) the role of two mysterious women, (3) the omission of the clear declaration of the resurrection given by the two men in shining clothing, (4) the omission of Peter's visit to the empty tomb, (5) the role played by the Emmaus disciples, and (6) the post-resurrection appearance to the group in Jerusalem.

As a result of the omissions known as Western non-interpolations and the variants in the Western text found at the conclusion of chap. 23 and throughout chap. 24, the apostles are supplied with a defense for their unbelief. This defense of the apostolate presents us with an altered account of the empty tomb and post-resurrection narratives in Luke.

NOTES

[1] Brooke Foss Westcott and Fenton John Anthony Hort, *The New Testament In the Original Greek: Introduction and Appendix* (London: Macmillan, 1896) 2:1.

[2] Ibid.

[3] Ibid., 172.

[4] Ibid., 175.

[5] Bruce Metzger, *The Text of the New Testament: Its Transmission, Corruption and Restoration* (New York: Oxford University Press, 1968) 134.

[6] Klyne Snodgrass, "Western Non-Interpolations," *JBL* 91 (1972) 372.

[7] Ibid., 376-78.

[8] Ibid., 373.

[9] Friedrich Blass, *Philology of the Gospels* (London: Macmillan, 1898) 185-87. See also John Martin Creed, *The Gospel According to St. Luke* (London: Macmillan, 1960) 292; Alfred Plummer, *A Critical and Exegetical Commentary on the Gospel According to St. Luke* (ICC; New York: Scribners, 1906) 542.

[10] F. W. Farrar, *The Gospel According to St. Luke* (Cambridge: University Press, 1981) 358; Snodgrass, "Western Non-Interpolations," 375.

[11] Because the RSV reflects a variant reading with secondary support at 24:10, the English translation of Codex B is mine and the punctuation follows the UBS text.

Thomas Louis Brodie

GRECO-ROMAN IMITATION OF TEXTS AS A PARTIAL GUIDE TO LUKE'S USE OF SOURCES

The purpose of this article is to widen the discussion concerning the evangelists' use of sources. In particular it seeks to indicate that the Greco-Roman practice of literary imitation provides at least a partial guide to Luke's way of reworking and transforming various texts, especially the Old Testament. The article consists of six parts: (1) the broad context within which imitation is to be examined; (2) the theory of imitation; (3) the practice of imitation; (4) imitation and historiography; (5) the Old Testament and the likelihood of Luke's use of imitation; (6) the synoptic problem and the need to cope with authorial complexity.

Imitation: The Broad Context

There are two fundamental differences between the way literary texts are composed in modern times and the way in which they were composed by Greco-Roman writers. The first difference is largely concerned with content. Unlike modern writers, who usually manifest the romantic "preoccupation with otherness" and who seek a content that is new and different, previous writers, even till around A.D. 1800, were generally extremely careful to preserve, at least in some way, the heritage passed on from preceding generations.[1] Examples of preservation and re-use range from the Babylonian reworking of the Sumerian heritage[2] to Milton's sifting and recasting of the Homer-based epic tradition.[3] The reason for this deep-seated custom of preservation and re-use seems to lie, in part at least, in a feeling that existing knowledge, stored largely in precious handwritten texts, was not to be taken for granted but was to be penetrated and clarified. This feeling lasted until about 1800, that is, until the continued use of the printing press, especially as manifested in the French

Encyclopédie (1751-1772), finally led to a situation in which ancient knowledge was taken for granted.[4] Whatever the full reasons, the fact is that writing, including original writing, involved a strong element of preservation.

Among the Greeks this widespread feeling for preserving was sharpened by a particular appreciation of the value of imitating.[5] The general idea of imitation, *mimēsis,* enjoyed immense prestige, for it was used by Plato to describe the whole world of nature (the natural world is a *mimēsis* of the eternal unchanging world)[6] and by Aristotle, who said that imitation was natural to human beings to describe all of art (art imitates nature).[7] However, it was Isocrates, Aristotle's older contemporary, who used this prestigious word precisely with reference to verbal composition: in verbal composition, said Isocrates, the student should imitate his teacher.[8] Thus it became customary among Greco-Roman writers to speak not of a process of preserving but, more specifically, of a process of imitating. Imitation therefore is not only a question of style; it is, above all, a question of content. It was acceptable not only because the general tendency was to preserve the heritage of the past but also because that heritage was not copyrighted, not individualized, but was rather regarded as common property.[9] What was not acceptable was sheer individualistic invention, the fabrication of plots or myths that were unrelated to the common traditions.[10] One had to show solid roots. Quintilian (ca. A.D. 95) sums up a long tradition when he comments that "although invention came first and is all-important, it is expedient to imitate whatever has been invented with success."[11]

The second difference between ancient and modern writers is somewhat more concerned with form. Unlike modern writing, which is generally geared to the eye, to being seen on the page, previous writing was largely geared to the ear, to being read aloud.[12] This aural aspect, this concern for sound, was a development of the concern for sound that prevailed in times of purely oral communication.[13] There are therefore three periods: that of textless oral communication; that in which writing after its invention continued to be pervaded by the rhythms and formulas of oral communication; and the modern period, which began with people like Samuel Taylor Coleridge and was furthered especially by the New Criticism, in which the text very often loses almost all traces of orality and in which the reader, in order to understand the text, has to see it on the page.[14] The essential point is that until about 1800 writing was significantly oral in form, so that the formulary style of, say, Edmund Spenser's *Faerie Queene* is basically that of oral performance,[15] and Tudor prose style contains many of the traits of oral speech.[16]

Among the Greeks the general pervasiveness of oral rhythms was developed and refined through the precise craft of rhetoric, especially through the rhetorical teaching of Isocrates and Aristotle.[17] Rhetoric of course was directed toward improving oral delivery, especially in the law courts and public assemblies, but since speeches were often written beforehand and since in any case literature reflected oral patterns, the rules of rhetoric became in fact the rules of literary composition.[18] Thus literature became of crucial importance for the rhetorician.[19] Nor was rhetoric confined to one type of literature. On the contrary, to an extent that is now difficult to imagine, rhetoric pervaded the system of education[20] and almost every kind of writing, even poetic.[21] Long after the fall of Rome, it so maintained its influence that eventually it could be said that it "encapsulated the most ancient, central, and pervasive tradition of verbalization and of thought known to mankind at least in the West."[22]

The pervasiveness of oral traits in ancient texts may at times cause confusion: it may lead to the premature conclusion that a particular text is dependent on oral tradition. But that does not follow. All that follows is that the text, whatever its origin, is aural, that it has been composed with a view to oral delivery.[23] Dependence on oral tradition must be shown on grounds other than the orality of the text.

The essential point, from all that has been said, is that Greco-Roman writing, in varying degrees, was both imitative and rhetorical (oral-aural). Nor were these two elements unrelated to one another. Rather, it is through one that we may better understand the other. It was in the context of teaching rhetoric and of learning from other rhetorician-writers that imitation was emphasized and refined. As Cicero said, speaking in the context of imitation: "Let this then be my first counsel, that we show the student [of rhetoric] whom to copy."[24]

Our first and rather general conclusion, therefore, is that in Greco-Roman literary composition the form or forms may have been largely oral, may have followed various traits of oral verbalization, but both the form and especially the content were significantly determined by a desire to preserve the work of previous artists or, more precisely, to imitate previous literature. However, this broad conclusion needs refinement and illustration. It is necessary therefore to examine more closely both the theory and practice of imitation. First, the theory.

Literary Imitation: The Theory
There is no single clear-cut theory of literary imitation. This is due in part to the fact that the subject matter is not always clearly

defined: literary imitation is frequently treated in conjunction with the idea of imitation in general, particularly pedagogic imitation.[25] It is also due to the fact that the subject matter is inherently difficult: insofar as literary imitation is concerned with the translation and interpretation of texts it partakes in the general complexity and elusiveness of hermeneutical theory. We are dealing with an art, not an exact science.[26]

What is found among Greco-Roman writers therefore is not a single coherent theory but a series of descriptions and metaphors concerning various aspects of imitation. These references indicate first of all that imitation is a multi-faceted concept, that it comprises different activities. The activities include:

Imitation of a teacher or of a living artist. This type of living contact was especially helpful to the beginner. Among the Greeks it was emphasized particularly by Isocrates,[27] and among the Romans, by Cicero.[28]

Reading. No single teacher or model could match the store of good verbal composition to be found in books, so reading was regarded as indispensable. Horace, for instance, recommended the incessant reading of the Greeks "by day [and] . . . by night."[29] Dionysius of Halicarnassus emphasized that constant reading imparts affinity of style.[30] Quintilian regarded careful repeated reading as a prelude to imitation.[31]

Paraphrase. Paraphrase was of different kinds, sometimes staying very close to the original and at other times involving considerable changes. Quintilian advised that paraphrase (*paraphrasis*) should have a touch of daring, that it should compress and expand with considerable freedom.[32] Isocrates recommended that the same text be paraphrased again and again in different ways.[33]

Inventive imitation. Most Greco-Roman writing involved a tense blend of *imitatio* and *inventio* (creativity), a combining of old material with new. Thus, while Quintilian took it for granted that a large part of art consists of imitation (*artis pars magna contineatur imitatione*), he also realized that sheer imitation is not sufficient (*imitatio per se ipsa non sufficit*) and pointed out that every art involves *inventio* not only at its inception but also throughout its continuing existence.[34] Much of what Greco-Roman writers have to say about imitation is concerned precisely with this rather unpredictable blending of fidelity and creativity, and it is a subject to which we must return later.

Emulation. From the beginning imitation was accompanied by a certain spirit of rivalry or emulation (Gk., *zēlos*; Lat., *emulatio*), by a desire to transform the subtext or model text into a text that would be as good or even better. Isocrates engaged in rivalry and invited rivalry.[35] Dionysius of Halicarnassus spoke as often of emulation as he does of imitation.[36] This spirit of emulation seems to have been motivated by a desire not so much to destroy as to fulfill, to move from the old text to a text that would be nearer to the contemporary world and to a certain ideal of perfection. Isocrates advised the abandonment of any literary field in which perfection has been attained.[37] Phaedrus stated that in a spirit not of envy but of emulation he brought to perfection the work of Aesop.[38] Quintilian hoped that continued striving would finally result in the birth of the perfect orator (*illum oratorem perfectum*).[39] In addition to this rather idealistic striving for literary perfection, there was also a certain nationalistic rivalry, which impelled Roman writers to equal and surpass their older Greek counterparts.

Contamination. *Contaminatio* consisted of the fusing of several texts or parts of texts into a new unity. The idea was to select and to synthesize the best elements in the tradition. Dionysius of Halicarnassus advocated that the writer isolate and imitate specific strengths of several previous writers.[40] Cicero spoke admiringly of a painter who used five models in order to draw one figure.[41] (Later, however, Cicero felt it better to use only one model.)[42] Quintilian also, realizing that each model has flaws, advocated a process of selection[43] and spoke admiringly of the way Cicero, through constant imitation, had combined in himself "the force (*vim*) of Demosthenes, the copious flow (*copiam*) of Plato and the charm (*iucunditatem*) of Isocrates."[44]

Such, in brief, are the main activities associated with the general practice of imitation. It is necessary now to examine more closely the most crucial of these activities—namely, inventive imitation, the process that combines the basic elements of imitation and creativity.

When Greco-Roman theorists spoke of imitation, they generally referred to inventive imitation. Their comments indicate that such imitation involves two moments: meditation and transformation. "Meditation" refers to the various ways of getting inside the source text(s): Dionysius of Halicarnassus advocated a careful comparative analysis of several authors, and he spoke of inspecting the text.[45] Cicero referred to the wholehearted contemplation (*omni animo intueretur*) of a living model.[46] Quintilian advocated an inspection of the text (*introspectis penitus virtutibus*) that would see beyond its superficial aspect to its underlying qualities.[47] For Longinus, who wrote perhaps around A.D. 80, the source text was something with which one became deeply involved—it is like a body with which one wrestles, like a vapor with which one is impregnated, like a light which opens a path to the self.[48]

"Transformation" refers to the various creative processes by which the text is given a new form, a new kind of existence. The extent of this transformation is often considerable.[49] At least three authors, Cicero, Quintilian, and Horace, explicitly discouraged word-for-word adaptation.[50] Horace furthermore advised the imitator to avoid well-worn paths that are easy or a mode of imitating that is constricted and rule-bound.[51] Far from being a slave, the imitator can be a pioneer, one who uses old material to break new ground.[52] A number of writers compared the work of the imitator to the way the bee collects material from different flowers and transforms it into something new.[53] Seneca used the image of honey-making and also compared the imitated source to food, which has to be totally digested and transformed before it becomes part of the body, and to a father whose likeness to his son is largely hidden.[54] He also compared the blending of many sources with the blending of many voices in a chorus.[55]

The conclusion that emerges from this brief survey is that imitation is not a narrow category of literary dependence. It is, rather, a whole world of transformation, the broad context within which diverse writers combine tradition and innovation. It is not tidy and predictable. On the contrary, since it is a complex arena of artistry, it allows for constant surprises.

Literary Imitation: The Practice

Imitation was extremely widespread. A brief survey of the main categories of literary art shows that it pervaded almost every one of them. In lyric poetry it is found in Rome's leading lyric authors, Catullus (84-54 B.C.)[56] and Horace (65-8 B.C.).[57] As Horace put it, he "made Aeolian song at home in Italian poetry."[58] Yet his way of transmuting that ancient Greek heritage was rather novel. He did it, as he himself says, "by arts not hitherto imparted."[59]

In pastoral poetry forms of imitation are found in the most outstanding Latin work, that of Virgil. His *Eclogues* are significantly indebted to the pioneering pastoral poetry of Theocritus, the Sicilian (ca. 300-260 B.C.), so that it may be said of the eighth *Eclogue*: "out of the Theocritean material Virgil has created something quite new, a kind of didactic pastoral."[60]

In didactic poetry the leading Latin works show complex forms of imitation. *De Rerum Natura* of Lucretius (ca. 94-55 B.C.) involves a fusion and synthesis of several Greek sources,[61] and Virgil's *Georgics* reacts to and reflects the work of Lucretius.[62]

In comedy the leading Roman writers are Plautus (died ca. 186 B.C.) and Terence (ca. 190-160 B.C.). Again there is considerable indebtedness to the Greek precedent, particularly to the comedies of

Menander (ca. 341-290 B.C.). Greek scenes are given a Roman setting or ethos, and different Greek plays or scenes are fused (*contaminatio*) into a new unity.[63]

Within satire, which was primarily a Roman genre, the pioneering work of Lucilius (died ca. 101 B.C.) had considerable influence on the *Satires* of Horace, but Horace regarded Lucilius's work as slow-flowing muddy water that needed to be purified, and so his mode of imitation was crisp and critical.[64] Horace provided a model for some of the work of Persius (A.D. 34-62), and Persius in turn helped, to some small degree at least, to pave the way for the biting satires of Juvenal (ca. A.D. 60-130).[65]

In tragic drama the surviving evidence indicates that Roman writers—authors such as Ennius (239-169 B.C.), Accius (ca. 170-90 B.C.), and Ovid (43 B.C.-A.D. 17)—made massive use of their Greek predecessors. In Seneca (ca. 4 B.C.-A.D. 56), the only Roman tragic dramatist whose work has not largely perished, this indebtedness is powerfully evident: Seneca's plays involve a systematic reshaping of the works of Aeschylus, Sophocles, and Euripides.[66]

In epic poetry we encounter the most esteemed and powerful work of the first century A.D., the apex of Roman literary achievement—Virgil's *Aeneid*. Here the use of imitation is comprehensive and complex. The *Aeneid* synthesizes and reshapes the best of previous dramatists and epic writers, whether Greek, Alexandrian, or Roman, but it involves, above all, a systematic rethinking and Romanizing of the foundational work of Homer.[67]

The list of indebtedness is almost monotonous, but it acts as a corrective to the widespread modern presupposition that literary originality and excellence largely exclude indebtedness.

It is not possible, at least in a few pages, to illustrate in detail the many modes of adaptation used in the widespread practice of imitation. All that can be given are a few samples. At the risk of oversimplifying, these adaptations are here put under precise headings: elaboration, compression, fusion, substitution of images, positivization, internalization, form-change.

Elaboration. When Euripides described Hippolytus's fatal chariot accident, he spent one line on Hippolytus's head:[68]

And his dear head [was] pounded on the rocks.

Five centuries later Seneca elaborated in vivid detail:[69]

The ground was reddened with a trail of blood;
His head was dashed from rock to rock, his hair

> Torn off by thorns, his handsome face despoiled
> By flinty stones; wound after wound destroyed
> For ever that ill-fated comeliness.

Compression or synthesis. Euripides describes in some detail the ominous thunder that preceded Hippolytus's accident:[70]

> When we were entering the lonely country
> The other side of the border, where the shore
> Goes down to the Saronic Gulf, a rumbling
> Deep in the earth, terrible to hear,
> Growled like the thunder of Father Zeus.

Seneca, writing for Romans, omitted the references to Greek geography and gods (Zeus). However he grasped the essence of the text and speeded it up:[71]

> At once a peal of thunder broke across the sea.

A rather different form of compression consists of *distillation*, that is, the procedure of isolating the significant. It is a procedure that is found, for instance, in Ovid's *Metamorphoses*—in his ability to isolate and highlight the crucial element in old narratives.[72]

Fusion. More complex than simple compression is the process of turning two or more elements into one new complex element. As the news of Hippolytus's death is announced, Euripides speaks of different people, some of whom (the chorus) are *tearful* and another of whom (the messenger) has a *sorrowful face.*[73] Seneca omitted the outmoded convention of the chorus but attributed to the messenger a *tearful sorrowful face.*[74] Where Homer had spoken of two characters one of whom (Menelaus) *broke his sword in combat* and the other of whom (Diomed) *left his sword,* Virgil spoke of a single character (Turnus) who mistakenly *left his own sword* and *broke in combat* the sword he took.[75] A more general form of fusion is found in the fact that Virgil, in large part, combined in Aeneas both the battles of Achilles (the *Iliad*) and the wanderings of Odysseus (the *Odyssey*).[76]

Substitution of images. Catullus followed Sappho closely yet felt free not only to add and omit but also to substitute new images of his own. Thus, where Sappho had spoken of a jealous passion,

> Which has made my heart (*kardia*) flutter in my breast

Catullus substituted:

> Which robs me of all my senses (*omnis sensus*);

and where Sappho had said,

> I see *nothing* with my eyes,

Catullus wrote:

> The light of my eyes is covered with "twin night."[77]

Positivization. The *Iliad*, from its very first line, is largely dominated by the theme of the anger of Achilles. At one point he
promises to maintain his quest for vengeance

> As long as breath remains in my bosom
> And my good knees have their strength.[78]

In place of this permanent vengefulness Virgil put the permanent
devotedness of Aeneas: he promises to honor the memory of his love
of a woman (Dido):

> While I remember who I am
> And while the breath still governs this frame.[79]

This radical rewriting is an example not only of positivization—
turning something negative into something positive (a fairly frequent
procedure in Virgil)[80] but also of internalization—replacing emphasis
on something external (the knees, symbols of physical strength) by
emphasis on the internal (the memory and sense of identity).

Internalization. A more complex example of internalization is
found in Seneca's version of the reaction of Hippolytus's angry father
to the news of the accident. Where Euripides had written,[81]

> For hatred of the sufferer I was glad
> At what you told me. *Still he was my son.*
> *As such I have reverence for him and the Gods:*
> I neither sorrow nor rejoice at this thing.

Seneca wrote,[82]

> *O potent nature,*
> *How strong a bond of blood is thine to tie*
> *A parent's heart* Even against our will
> *We know and love thee.* As my son was guilty,
> I wished him dead; as he is lost, I mourn him.

The italics have been added in order to clarify the complex relationship of the texts. Seneca has taken the central section of the father's

reaction—his recognition, despite his anger, of his relationship to his son and his consequent *reverence* both for *sonship* and the *gods*—and changed it into an *awe-filled recognition* of nature and *parenthood*, and in doing so he spelled out some of the basic internal factors of parenthood: a bond of blood, a heart that is tied, and—despite the opposition of the will—knowledge and love. Then in the last line and a half Seneca gathered and synthesized the opening and closing lines of Euripides' text: the gladness at Hippolytus's suffering (Euripides) becomes "I wished him dead"; and the rather mechanical "I neither sorrow nor rejoice" becomes the more deeply-felt "I mourn him."[83]

Form-change. In *Epode X*, Horace wishes an evil omen on the voyage of his critic Maevius: "With an evil omen (*mala . . . alite*) the ship is unmoored and departs, carrying the stinking Maevius: South Wind, remember to lash each side with wild waves. . . ." Not only does Horace's colorful curse seem to involve a careful transformation of a somewhat similar curse written centuries earlier by Archilochus (ca. 700 B.C.), but it involves also a careful adaptation of a particular poetic form called the *propempticon*, which consisted of a farewell with words of *good omen*. Horace's procedure was radical, subversive almost, but it was typical of the way in which imitation combined careful continuity with bold novelty.[84]

These examples are useful but limited. In order to get a better idea of the richness and complexity of imitation it is necessary to examine the total procedure of particular authors. Virgil and Ovid, for instance, particularly in their epic poems the *Aeneid* and the *Metamorphoses*, show an extraordinary capacity for combining a variety of sources and methods of adaptation. It is a matter for further research to isolate particular examples of the way sources were used and to ask if such examples cast light on particular Lucan texts.

The conclusion that emerges from this brief survey of poetry and drama is that imitation was widespread and varied. It was used on authors who were contemporary or recent, but among the Romans it was used particularly to appropriate and reinterpret the texts that were often considered normative—those of ancient Greece. It seems reasonable, in fact, to accept G. Kennedy's conclusion that "all of Latin literature is in origin an imitation of Greek."[85]

Imitation and Historiography

Is it possible that what applied to literature in general did not apply to history and to the related subject of biography?[86] After all, it is a fact of modern studies and a presupposition of most modern readers that literature and history are usually quite distinct disciplines, taught by different university departments and discussed at different conventions. It is also true that, unlike many poets and dramatists, historians such as Thucydides and Livy spoke of real historical events and characters. Furthermore, even though most ancient historiographers did not discuss sources and source criticism, there were a number of writers who stressed the need for adherence to precise facts and to trustworthy sources. Lucian of Samosata (ca. A.D. 120-180), for instance, emphasized that "the historian's sole task is to tell it as it happened (*hōs eprachthē eipein*). . . . He should for preference be an eyewitness, but if not, listen to those who tell the least impartial story."[87] Arrian (ca. A.D. 140), in writing his history of Alexander, told that he chose two sources that seemed to narrate "what actually happened" (*hōs synēnēchthē*) and where these two sources were in conflict he selected the one that seemed "most trustworthy and most worth telling" (. . . *pistotera . . . axiaphegeto-tera*).[88] Philostratus (ca. A.D. 200), in prefacing his life of Apollonius, claimed to aim at giving a precise chronicle of the man's words and deeds and claimed also to have chosen his sources with discrimination, rejecting unreliable accounts, and combining various reputable sources into a stylized synthesis.[89]

But even though real events often were recorded and someone like Lucian could call for factual reporting, the general practice of history was heavily influenced by factors other than the bare events. These other factors, sometimes overlapping, consisted particularly of poetry, rhetoric, and drama.

Poetry. In a world where poetry and history writing are so separated, it is difficult to imagine to what extent the two were frequently interwoven in ancient times. Poetry in fact was linked with several areas of knowledge: it was through what is known as didactic poetry that Hesiod (ca. 700 B.C.) sought to communicate his far-reaching message of justice, that Empedocles (ca. 493-433 B.C.) taught his doctrine of the four elements of the universe, that Aratus (ca. 315-240 B.C.) taught astronomy, and that Lucretius (ca. 95-55 B.C.) gave new life to Epicurean philosophy.[90] But poetry had a special link with history. The two outstanding works of Greco-Roman literature, the *Iliad*-and-*Odyssey* of Homer and the *Aeneid* of Virgil, consisted precisely of an extraordinary blend of history and poetry. Herodotus (ca. 450 B.C.) was known as the father of history, but his work consisted largely of Homeric-type stories. When Ennius (239-169 B.C.) wrote a history of Rome, he did so in poetry. In fact Lucian's call for factual reporting was largely a protest against blending poetry and history: "Every single person is writing history. . . . Such writers seem unaware that history has aims and rules different from poetry and poems. In the case of the latter, liberty is absolute and there is one law—the will of the poet."[91] Indeed Lucian felt so overwhelmed by the pervasiveness of the poetic approach that he compared himself to the lonely and cynical Diogenes.[92] It is possible of course that Lucian overstated the problem, but the frequent intermingling of history and poetry seems undoubted, and it is in this context that one understands better Quintilian's statement that history is close to poetry and is a kind of prose poem: *Historia . . . est enim proxima poetis et quodammodo carmen solutum.*[93]

Rhetoric. Given the pervasiveness of rhetoric, it is not surprising that it should be found in the writing of history. It is found first of all in a close follower of Isocrates, Timaeus of Tauromenian (ca. 356–260 B.C.). It reappears in some Roman writers, and does so with particularly questionable effect in Valerius Antias (ca. 90 B.C.), who "fully observed the Isocratean canons of (in fact) plausibly detailed mendacity."[94] And the history of Valerius's contemporary, Q. Claudius Quadrigenarius, "had as its primary purpose the entertainment of the reader."[95] Coelius Antipater's influential monograph on the Second Punic War (written 120 B.C.) is strewn with rhetoric and fiction.[96] Particularly significant is Cicero's linking of rhetoric and history and his declaration that history demands, above all, a rhetorical treatment: *historia . . . opus unum oratorium maxime.*[97] It is the teaching of Cicero that inspired the method of Livy, and even though Livy often worked from the careful Polybius he also drew on the plausibly detailed scenarios of Valerius Antias.

Drama. The mingling of drama and history may be discerned at the very roots of the recounting of Greek history—in the opening book of the *Iliad* (1:53–303, the bitter confrontation between Achilles and Agamemnon) and again in Herodotus, particularly in the scene in which Xerxes is depicted as debating the question of invading Greece (vii, 4–19). Something similar may be found in Ctesias of Cnidos (ca. 400 B.C.), a writer who depended on Herodotus, but it is in later writers such as Duris (ca. 340–260 B.C.) and Phylarchus (born ca. 210 B.C.) that history, in large part, is turned into dramatic tragedy, in other words, into a narrative specifically designed to evoke pity and horror.

It seems reasonable therefore to conclude that a considerable portion of Greco-Roman historiography was governed largely by the norms of rhetoric, poetry, and drama.

It is within this general context that it is useful to look more closely at a front-rank historian such as Livy. Though he sometimes shows a fairly close verbal similarity to the sober Polybius[98] he generally exercised considerable freedom. In particular he tended to idealize and to dramatize. Thus where Polybius had reported that after the Trasimene defeat both people and Senate were in confusion, Livy drew a sharp and dramatic contrast between the panic (*terror ac tumultus*) of the general population and the cool counsel-taking of the Senate.[99] P. G. Walsh summarizes his literary methods:[100]

> He utilizes one main source, reorganizes the structural arrangement, and introduces new material to achieve more dramatic effects. He compresses or omits the less interesting content, using as criteria the purpose of his work and the interests of his audience. Then in addition to these literary aims of *enargeia* [graphic presentation to achieve dramatic effect] and *syntomia* [compression], he seeks to fulfil his historian's duties of *saphēneia* [clarification] and *pithanotēs* [credibility in narration].

His affinity with poetry is particularly clear in his opening books. At that point "his narration . . . has poetical colour and style: it is the prose epic of Rome, ranking with the *Aeneid*."[101] Livy, therefore, no less than historians who were more obscure, lived in a world that was heavily influenced by rhetoric, drama, and poetry.

It is also useful to look at a front-rank biographer such a Plutarch. Like Livy he seems to have drawn on sources of very different quality. His lives of Agis and Cleomenes, for instance, were largely based on Phylarchus, a writer who himself had drawn heavily on the sensationally dramatic accounts of Duris.[102] Again like Livy, he seems, despite his wide reading, to have used one basic source at a time,[103] but he felt free to employ bold processes of adaptation: compression and rephrasing; conflation (or fusion) of similar items; compression and rearrangement of time sequences; transferral of an item from one character to another—a procedure akin to the fusion of characters already noted in Seneca and Virgil; elaboration or expansion of an underdeveloped source through fabrication of a context or of circumstantial detail[104]—a procedure which is quite similar, for instance, to that found in the poetry of Lucretius,[105] and which is somewhat akin to Cicero's way of providing a new context for traditional mythical material.[106] Plutarch also felt free to interpret an event and its motivation now in one way, now in another, so that it suited his general argument, and when he was describing a defeat, such as that of Pompey at Tharsalus, he turned it in some ways into a tragic drama.[107] In general, therefore, Plutarch's method of composition showed considerable freedom, a freedom that at times resembles that of a poet or dramatist.

Is it possible that, within the general idea of historiography, there was one stream of writing, that of Thucydides and his later admirers —Dionysius of Halicarnassus, Polybius, Sallust, Tacitus—which was exempt from the pervasiveness of rhetorical and literary considerations? After all, when Lucian of Samosata appealed for matter-of-fact reporting, he expressed his admiration for Thucydides.[108] Were Thucydides and his followers different then; were they a breed apart?

To some extent they were. As one analyst put it: "Thucydides and Polybius . . . untypical and exceptional."[109] They usually avoided excesses. But they were not exempt. The difficulty is seen first of all with regard to Thucydides himself. He wrote of contemporary events and there can be little doubt that from some points of view he was well informed. Yet while Lesky insists that Thucydides was scrupulously accurate,[110] he concedes that at times he was concerned with what was typical rather than with what actually happened, and that Pericles' magnificent oration over the fallen, for instance, was Thucydides' own composition, a work of art that contrasts in ideal images the traditions of Sparta and Athens.[111] But Cornford's *Thucydides Mythistoricus* is much more radical: it contends that as Thucydides watched the terrible Peloponnesian War drag on and on he began, increasingly, to depict it as a tragedy, and so his history is written as though it were a Greek tragic drama.[112] Cornford's criticism, though possibly overstated, seems to be essentially accurate. Thucydides' style furthermore "has a poetical and archaistic flavour."[113] Nor was he free of rhetoric. In fact during the two centuries following his death, it was primarily his more lavish rhetorical traits that were noted and imitated.[114] And his later admirers also knew rhetoric. The historical work of Dionysius of Halicarnassus has been called "a vast exercise in *mimēsis*."[115] Sallust rejected the rhetorical methods of Cicero but not rhetoric as such, and in fact his historical works, modeled largely on Thucydides, may be characterized as "rhetorical monographs."[116] In this context it is understandable that he should indulge in imitation. He thought little of taking a speech that Demosthenes had delivered against Philip and using it, in adapted form, to condemn Sulla.[117] And he indulged also in the sophisticated literary procedure of deliberately using a rather archaic vocabulary—a procedure, incidentally, which was "a significant feature of much of Roman historiography."[118]

An example not only of Thucydides' dramatic style but also of the way he was imitated by subsequent historians may be found in the recurring image of the battle spectators. Just as Thucydides, in describing the momentous sea battle in Syracuse Harbor (413 B.C.), suddenly launched into an elaborate description of the intense emotion of the spectators on the shore,[119] so Polybius, when describing a daring naval escapade in a Sicilian harbor (250 B.C.), suddenly switched attention to the intense emotion of the spectators,[120] and so in turn Tacitus, when describing the decisive clash in the Roman Forum between the supporters of Galba and those of Otho (A.D. 69), suddenly switched the attention to the onlooking populace:[121]

> The basilicas and the temples around were packed with
> spectators of the woeful scene (*lugubri prospectu*). No
> word was uttered either by the people or the plebs; dismay
> sat on every face, and every ear was turned to listen.
> There was no uproar, there was no calm, only a silence like
> that of some great terror or some mighty passion (*magni
> metus et magnae irae*).

As in Polybius's text, the spectators consist of the mass of the city's
population (*populi aut plebis*, "the people or the plebs"), and the
picture is quite compact. But the quality of the emotion has been
further simplified, so that the population is like an audience watching
a tragedy. In describing an earlier stage in the day's tumult, Tacitus
had explicitly compared the city's entire population to a clamorous
circus crowd,[122] but now that same audience is, as it were, gripped in
tragedy. Furthermore, Tacitus's description, when compared with
those of Thucydides and Polybius, involves a process of internalization: the crowd makes no sound and the ultimate focus of the
narrative is on what goes on inside a person.

The essential point is not only that Thucydides painted a highly
dramatic picture of battle spectators but also that subsequent writers
adapted that picture to their own circumstances. There are several
other examples of the same procedure. We find varied but related
pictures of warnings against tyrants, exhortations before battle, the
way a nation wins friends, the bad conscience engendered by tyranny,
the ravages of civil war.[123] One could add further examples,[124] but
the full extent and complexity of the practice of reworking sources
are simply not known. Thus in the case of Tacitus, while some critics
believe that he weighed his evidence as carefully as a modern historian, others hold that he "has done little more than transmute by
stylistic alchemy a pre-existing literary source."[125] The truth, as
Martin suggests, may be midway between these extremes,[126] but
what is certain is that the question of the origin and nature of
Tacitus's text may not be studied in isolation from preceding histories
and from the general practice of imitation. It is also useful to bear in
mind that Tacitus's *Dialogue on Oratory*, which explicitly claims to be
a report of a factual conversation (chap. 2), filled with lifelike pictures of the speakers concerned, turn out, on analysis, to be an artistic composition that is largely if not entirely a work of fiction,
modeled considerably on the writings of Cicero.[127]

Summing up, one may say that the ancient practice of "history"
was something quite distinct from the modern discipline that bears
the same name. In varying degrees it was governed by practices that
were literary rather than "scientific": rhetoric, poetry, drama, the
invention of speeches, pragmatic instruction or moralizing, and

archaizing. Hence, even though ancient history by and large contained a wealth of factual information, it was not exempt from the norms of the composition of literature, one of which was imitation.

It seems reasonable, therefore, when inquiring about the composition of an ancient work—even one that is history-like—to ask whether, to some degree at least, it is the result of a process of imitation. It is in this context that we turn to the question of whether Luke-Acts involves a process of imitating the Septuagint.

The Old Testament and the Likelihood
of Luke's Use of *Imitatio*

There are two distinct arguments that seem to indicate that Luke-Acts does not involve the use of *imitatio*.

1. In the course of history Luke-Acts and the other New Testament texts have enjoyed unparalleled popularity and power and have been "canonized" in a way that sets them apart from most other writings of the first century A.D. This general apartness, this uniqueness, might seem to indicate that the New Testament documents are not to be grouped with other ancient writings, that they were not governed either by the prevailing general rules of literary composition or by the specific practice of imitation.

Neo-orthodox theology, particularly as propounded by Karl Barth, so emphasized the transcendence of the Word of God and its discontinuity with the human word that further attention was given to the idea of the uniqueness and apartness of the Bible. When this idea of *theological* apartness was taken over by Rudolf Bultmann it contributed to his idea of *literary* apartness, that is, to the idea that there is a considerable discontinuity between the gospels and the other literature of the first century. Such discontinuity does not encourage the idea that the gospels were composed according to prevailing literary methods.[128]

2. Hermann Gunkel's theory of oral traditions and forms, a theory taken up by Bultmann and reinforced apparently by his general theology of the Word and particularly of the spoken word which engenders faith, suggested that the origin and composition of the gospels is to be sought in an oral rather than a literary context. Redaction criticism, much as it emphasized the work of the final author, has done little to deny the formative influence of oral tradition.

But these arguments cannot stand. The uniqueness of the New Testament texts, as emphasized by the first argument, does not mean that they did not share the basic literary traits of first-century writings. After all, it may be contended that the uniqueness of Christ among humans is rooted in a basic solidarity with positive human traits and therefore that it is altogether appropriate that the basic

Christian literature should be rooted in a solidarity with the positive traits of human literature.

As for Gunkel's theory of oral tradition, it has been shown to have been built on an anthropology that is fundamentally flawed. [129] It is not surprising, therefore, that form criticism, which tries to build on a presupposition of oral tradition, should sometimes be severely criticized. [130] It is also significant that B. Gerhardsson, one of the very few New Testament scholars who have tried to articulate how oral tradition actually functioned in the first century, has been quite unsuccessful in convincing those who have examined his work. [131] Hence, however appealing the simple notion of oral tradition may be, it is no longer possible simply to assume that the development of a gospel text is to be sought in a way that is primarily oral rather than literary. The literary explanation deserves an equal hearing.

There are in fact some positive indications that Luke's text involves imitation of previous texts or at least imitation of parts of the Old Testament. There is, first of all, considerable evidence not only that Luke was a litterateur but also that he employed specifically Hellenistic modes of writing, including various techniques of Hellenistic rhetoric. [132] But it would have been almost impossible to receive a literary and rhetorical training that did not include the practice of imitation. Imitation, as already indicated in this article, was a basic starting point, often *the* basic starting point, of rhetorical and literary composition. It is probable therefore that Luke was practiced in imitation.

Second, it appears that Luke regarded the Old Testament in general as being in some basic sense a normative text. At crucial points he emphasizes the fundamental continuity between the Old Testament and his own narrative: in the programmatic Nazareth speech (Luke 4:16-30), in the climactic chapter 24 (24:25-27, 44), and in the culminating Roman speech (Acts 28:17-29, esp. 28:23). Since writers of the Roman period tended to use normative texts (i.e., classical Greek texts) precisely as objects of imitation, it is not a priori unlikely that Luke should have imitated the Old Testament.

Third, there are, de facto, signs of literary continuity between Luke and the Old Testament—continuity of literary genre, [133] of narrative technique, [134] and of vocabulary and style. [135] In fact, Luke's style has been described as a *mimēsis* of the style of the Septuagint. [136] More specifically, it has been contended that large areas of Luke's text show a relationship to various prolonged Old Testament narratives, a relationship both of systematic detailed dependence and of careful consistent adaptation. [137] In other words, there is evidence that Luke's acceptance of the Old Testament as normative is not just a general assent to some disembodied theological ideas but involves also a close and creative interaction with the body of the Old Testament, with the text as text.

Altogether, therefore, there is on Luke's part both an a priori probability of having practiced imitation, and a de facto practice of adapting a normative text in a way that corresponds, broadly at least, to the actual practice of imitation. Such a combination of prior probability and de facto similarity constitutes a noteworthy case. It does not mean that everything Luke did with the Old Testament is to be explained exclusively in terms of imitation—allowance must be made, for instance, for midrashic practices—but it establishes at least a significant probability that the practice of imitation is an important clue in unravelling Luke's use of the Old Testament.

The Synoptic Problem and the Need to Cope
with Authorial Complexity

The question of Luke's use of sources cannot, of course, be isolated from the synoptic problem, and the question arises whether the use of sources within the context of the synoptic problem (e.g., Luke's apparent use of Mark and his possible use of Matthew) bears a consistent relation to Luke's use of the Old Testament. For instance, does Luke *always* employ greater freedom in adapting the OT than in adapting Mark? It would be extremely helpful for tracing particular processes of imitating or using sources if we could decide beforehand that there are, say, four basic techniques Luke is likely to have employed and if we could specify further, say, that two of these techniques were used on ancient texts (the Old Testament) and the other two on more recent sources. If we could pin Luke down to one precise genre of history or biography and if writers in that genre always used sources in one of four precise ways (two for ancient texts and two for texts that were relatively new), then these four ways or techniques could guide our investigation. On a question of whether a particular Lucan passage involved dependence on a particular Old Testament passage, we could simply ask if either of the two relevant techniques of transformation could account for the possible relationship in question. If they could not, then we might conclude that those particular texts probably did not involve literary dependence. And in the same way, the techniques for transforming more recent sources could be tested on the question of whether a particular Lucan passage involved literary transformations of, say, a particular Matthean or Pauline passage.

But we do not have a tidy genre and a clear-cut field of possibilities. This is the core of the problem that faces us. The fact that Luke-Acts has affinities not only with ancient historiography and biography but also with the ancient novel[138] is an indicator of the complexity of its genre. The novel was particularly complex, a mixture of fact and fiction that "acted as a literary collecting-basin and admitted features from other genres."[139] And with regard to modes of adaptation and composition, Dionysius of Halicarnassus (ca. 60-5 B.C.) provides a reminder of the individuality of each author:[140]

> I assert without any hesitation that there are many specific differences of composition and that they cannot be brought into a comprehensive view or within a precise enumeration; I think too that, as in personal appearance, so also in literary composition, each of us has an individual character.

Or as George Steiner says about the various ways of reusing texts in literature as a whole: "We find innumerable formal possibilities. . . . The [artist] need not cite his source text. . . . *It is up to us to recognize and reconstruct the particular force of relation.*"[141]

Thus, it is quite inadequate to approach the problem of Luke's sources and the larger question of the synoptic problem with a narrow list of preset categories based on some rather narrow selection of, say, historiographical narratives. The difficult task of recognizing and reconstructing the particular relationship between two texts is best undertaken by someone who is aware of the startling variety and complexity that may be employed in the use of sources. Discovery is rarely the result of working with rules that are clear and well established.[142]

At this point the synoptic problem is its own worst enemy. Since the problem is largely stated, or laid out (e.g., in Aland's *Synopsis*), on the basis of the obvious verbal similarities among the first three gospels, and since many students of the New Testament receive their formative training in text comparison on the basis of a synopsis like Aland's, there often develops an implicit expectation that whatever progress is to be made on the problem is to be made on the basis of comparing texts that show obvious verbal similarity. But obvious verbal similarity, useful though it is, is only one of several possible relationships between texts. The fact that the evangelists sometimes used sources in a way that retained a considerable amount of obvious verbal similarity does not mean that they did not also use methods that were complex and subtle, ways that removed almost all verbal similarity, ways that correspond to the degree of transformation implied in the descriptions and metaphors that are used concerning imitation: inspection, contemplation, following a light, pioneering, wrestling, impregnation, honey making, chorus making, digestion, generation, emulation, and contamination. There is not much point in rendering homage to the literary artistry of the evangelists unless an effort is made to articulate the full dimensions of what is meant by literary artistry. Such articulation must take account of many different ways of using sources.

As New Testament sources stand at the moment, there is a tendency when the comparison of texts proves difficult to "explain" the difficulty by appealing to some unknown quantity—an oral tradition that is not defined or a document (e.g., Q, a Signs Source) that is lost. These hypotheses imply a complexity of sources rather than a complexity in the authors' methods. They may have a certain validity, but part of the reason they seem relatively successful is precisely because, being unknown quantities, they can be made to fill almost any gap in any solution. Furthermore, the question arises whether they represent a process both of unwittingly avoiding the analyzing of authorial complexity and of reasserting a rather simplistic view of the evangelists' literary artistry.

Allowance for authorial complexity opens the way to the linking of extant texts. It would appear, for instance, when account is taken of such modes of adaptation as compression, internalization, and form-change, that the triple "call" of Luke 9:57-62 involves, among other things, a pithy synthesis of the different kinds of calls found in 1 Kings 19.[143] But are there no categories of adaptation that would cast light on Luke's possible use of Matthew? If, for instance, so sensitive an artist as Ovid could subvert and compress his revered older contemporary, Virgil,[144] why could not Luke's Sermon on the Plain be a subversion of or, at least, a compressed revision of Matthew's Sermon on the Mount? As already suggested one of the main effects of postulating Q and oral traditions is to drive so many wedges between the two gospels that the literary solution is never fully investigated. In other words the postulating of Q and of oral traditions has helped to isolate Luke from the other canonical material. For a long time the formulation of the synoptic problem was so narrow that it even isolated Luke from Acts. That has to some degree been rectified—studies on Luke-Acts are now fairly common—but the problem of isolation continues, particularly with regard to John and the Johannine epistles. John's gospel is left out of the problem largely because it does not conform to the criterion of obvious verbal similarity. But is there no category of poetry, fiction, or historiography that could resolve the question of John's possible dependence on Mark? And is there no category of adaptation that would clarify G. Volkmar's contention that Mark renders Paul's theology into narrative form?[145]

To suggest the possibility of a direct literary link between the gospels and the epistles may at first seem far-fetched. However, given the fact that secular writers did not work in isolation from one another and from their predecessors but rather that it was accepted as "expedient to imitate whatever has been invented with success,"[146] it seems unlikely within the relatively small but communicative Christian body that writers should have been unable or unwilling to imitate and emulate the Old Testament and one another. This is particularly true of Luke, one who was so conscious both of the Old Testament and of the need for gathering sources (see Luke 1:1-4) and who is regarded as a writer in the Hellenistic mold. Would a researcher like Luke who wanted to highlight Paul and his preaching set to work without bothering to get copies of Paul's epistles?[147] In what corner was he marooned that he did not know of these documents? In what literary impoverishment did this elegant writer live that he could not get copies of them? The general lack of obvious verbal parallelism between Luke and the epistles proves nothing. As Cadbury remarked once about the relationship between two writers: "the material of one writer is transferred to another without any acknowledgement and with almost complete change of diction."[148] Nor does Luke's different theological emphasis prove anything. In a world of literary artists there is room for—indeed, there is need for—complementariness and variety. Perhaps the relationship of the epistles to Luke may yet be explained, in significant part, through such concepts as positivization, digestion, and emulation. And perhaps it is through similar imitative concepts that progress may be made on the synoptic problem as a whole.

Conclusion

Poetry and drama may seem peripheral to the search for Lucan sources and New Testament sources in general. Perhaps they are. But we do not know. What we do know is that sustained efforts to unravel New Testament sources on the basis of appeals to hypothetical lost documents and traditions have largely failed. Some basic dynamic seems to be missing. Since the New Testament documents, *to a degree not yet defined*, consist of artistry and poetry, it is surely not outlandish to suggest that that dynamic has something to do with poetic inventiveness and imitation. Authors such as Livy and Plutarch may indeed provide partial guidance to unraveling the New Testament use of sources, but to confine oneself to such models is to prejudice the basic question—the nature of the New Testament text.

Obviously the only effective way of showing the relevance of poetic methods of imitation and transformation to the writings of Luke is by giving concrete examples. These I have tried to provide elsewhere.[149] Space dictates that this essay be limited to that of suggesting a wider context of research and greater variety in modes of transformation.

Apart from thus suggesting categories of adaptation that may lead to the recognition of sources, Greco-Roman literature also gives certain negative indications, warnings against using a rather superficial aspect of the text as a guide to the nature of its source. Archaic language (e.g., Semitisms or the use of Hebrew words) is not a reliable indicator of an old or a Semitic source, since archaizing was a well-known feature of Hellenistic historiography. Nor is detail a reliable indicator of historicity, for the careful describing of vivid details, whether details of narrative, topography, or personality, is as much the sign of a poet or dramatist as of a factual historian. Seneca and Tacitus were both capable of writing detail that was striking but fictitious. And of course, as already explained, orality is not a reliable indicator of dependence on oral tradition.

As a general conclusion, therefore, it may be said that just as the history and sociology of the Greco-Roman world have much to impart to New Testament studies so does a study of Greco-Roman literature. Ultimately of course each literary relationship must be examined on its own. As Dionysius of Halicarnassus suggested, each author's mode of composition is as unique as one's personal appearance. Hence, while a study of Greco-Roman literature may broaden the mind and suggest possibilities, the decisive step consists of being able to bring to the comparison of two particular texts an appropriate blend of sympathetic imagination and scholarly control, a sensitivity that allows for each author's artistic individuality.

NOTES

[1]W. J. Ong, *Rhetoric, Romance and Technology* (Ithaca, NY: Cornell University Press, 1971) 255-83, esp. 255-61.

[2]See W. G. Lambert (*Babylonian Wisdom Literature* [Oxford: Clarendon Press, 1960] 2, 6): "The ancients constantly rewrote old texts. . . . The (Babylonian) *Descent of Istar*, to take the obvious example, is nothing but a free rewriting of the Sumerian *Descent of Inanna*."

[3]See T. M. Greene, *The Descent from Heaven. A Study in Epic Continuity* (New Haven and London: Yale University Press, 1963) 363-418; C. M. Bowra, *From Virgil to Milton* (London: Macmillan, 1945) 194-247, esp. 195-97.

[4]Ong, *Rhetoric, Romance and Technology*, 276-79.

[5]The study of imitation has been rather in abeyance in recent times. The *OCD* (*Oxford Classical Dictionary*) does not deal with it directly, and the *Princeton Encyclopedia of Poetry and Poetics* (1975) begins its treatment of imitation by noting that it is only now that the term is coming back after its banishment in the nineteenth century. The following studies are particularly useful: G. C. Fiske,

Lucilius and Horace: A Study in the Classical Theory of Imitation (Madison: University of Wisconsin Press, 1920; reprinted, Westport, CT: Greenwood Press, 1971) 14-63, 476-91; H. O. White, *Plagiarism and Imitation During the English Renaissance* (Cambridge: Harvard University Press, 1935) 3-19; A. Reiff, "Interpretatio, Imitatio, Aemulatio: Begriff und Vorstellung Literarischer Abhängigkeit bei den Römern" (Diss. Cologne, 1959); T. M. Greene, *The Light in Troy: Imitation and Discovery in Renaissance Poetry* (New Haven: Yale University Press, 1982) chap. 4. (I am grateful to Professor Greene of Yale for providing a section of his manuscript before its publication.) See also D. L. Clark, "Imitation: Theory and Practice in Roman Rhetoric," *Quarterly Journal of Speech* 37 (1951) 11-22; G. Steiner, *After Babel: Aspects of Language and Translation* (New York and London: Oxford University Press, 1975) 253-55; G. Kennedy, *Classical Rhetoric and its Christian and Secular Traditions from Ancient to Modern Times* (Chapel Hill: University of North Carolina Press, 1980) 116-19. E. Auerbach, *Mimesis* (Princeton: Princeton University Press, 1953), is not immediately relevant to this study.

[6]On *mimēsis* in Plato, see R. McKeon, "Literary Criticism and the Concept of Imitation in Antiquity," *Modern Philology* 34 (1936) 1-35, esp. 3-16. See esp. Plato *Republic III*, 392D-394C, VI 500C-E.

[7]On *mimēsis* in Aristotle, see McKeon, "Imitation in Antiquity," 16-26. See, e.g., Aristotle *Physics* 2.2.194a22, 2.8.199a15-17; *Poetics* 9.1451b9; on imitation as natural to humans, see *Poetics* 4.1448b4-23.

[8]*Against the Sophists* 17-18.

[9]See esp. Isocrates *Panegyricus* 8-9; Horace *Ars Poetica* 131. See Fiske, *Lucilius and Horace*, 39-40; White, *Plagiarism and Imitation*, 6-7.

[10]Isocrates, for instance, praises "not those who seek to speak on subjects on which no one has spoken before" but those who speak on established subjects in a new and better way (*Panegyricus* 10). And Callimachus (hymn 5 ["On the Bath of Pallas"], 56) proclaims: "The account (*mythos*) is not my own; it is from others." See Fiske, *Lucilius and Horace*, 33-34; White, *Plagiarism and Imitation*, 6.

[11]*Institutio Oratoria* (trans. H. E. Butler; LCL; Cambridge: Harvard University Press, 1960) 10.2.1.

[12]Ong, *Rhetoric, Romance and Technology*, 1-22, esp. 1-4.

[13]W. J. Ong, *Interfaces of the Word. Studies in the Evolution of Consciousness and Culture* (Ithaca, NY: Cornell University Press, 1977) 214-16.

[14]Ibid., 213-29, esp. 216.

[15]See J. Webster, "Oral Form and Written Craft in Spenser's *Faerie Queene*," *Studies in English Literature* 16 (1976) 75-93; Ong, *Interfaces*, 195-99.

[16]Ong, *Rhetoric, Romance and Technology*, 23-47.

[17]On rhetoric, see Kennedy, *Classical Rhetoric*, 3-160.

[18]See A. Lesky, *A History of Greek Literature* (2d ed.; New York: Crowell, 1966) 590: "Isocrates achieved his strongest influence in the realm of Greek literature through his perfection of attic literary prose."

[19]Thus the rhetorician's reading matter as outlined by Quintilian (Inst. Orat. 10.1) consists of the whole range of Greco-Roman literature.

[20]For a summary of the way rhetoric pervaded Greco-Roman education, especially in the first century A.D., and for references to the key works on education by M. P. Nilsson, H. I. Marrou, and D. L. Clark, see W. S. Kurz, "Hellenistic Rhetoric in the Christological Proof of Luke-Acts," CBQ 42 (1980) 171-95, esp. 192-94.

[21]On the supremacy of rhetoric, see J. F. Dalton, Roman Literary Theory and Criticism (New York: Russell and Russell, 1962) 438-524; C. S. Baldwin, Ancient Rhetoric and Poetic (New York: Macmillan, 1924) 224-25.

[22]Ong, Interfaces, 214.

[23]The orality of the Mishnah, for instance, does not prove that the text depends on oral tradition. As J. Neusner comments: "The sole fact in our hands is that Mishnah has been so formulated as to facilitate memorization" (Method and Meaning in Ancient Judaism [Brown Judaic Studies 10; Missoula: Scholars Press, 1979] 59-75, esp. 66). Nor does the orality of Hebrew poetry prove its oral origin; see the review of D. K. Stuart's Studies in Early Hebrew Meter (HSM 13; Missoula: Scholars Press, 1976) by A. Cooper, BASOR 233 (1979) 75-76. M. Parry (The Making of Homeric Verse: The Collected Papers of Milman Parry [Oxford: Clarendon, 1971]) and A. B. Lord (The Singer of Tales [Cambridge: Harvard University Press, 1964]) have rightly pointed to the profound orality of Homeric verse, but their conclusion that such orality indicates an origin that is oral and not written is much disputed. R. Lattimore, for instance admires Parry's work but does not know what conclusion to draw; see Lattimore's The Iliad of Homer (Chicago and London: University of Chicago Press, 1951) 37. A. Lesky (History of Greek Literature, 73) shows even greater ambiguity.

[24]De Oratore 2.21.90.

[25]See Quintilian Inst. Orat. 10.2.2-4.

[26]For a study of the inherent artistry and complexity of language and interpretation, see Steiner, After Babel, 110-470, esp. 110-15, 220-35, 274-301, 460-62.

[27]Against the Sophists 17-18; Antidosis 175, 301-3.

[28]De Oratore 2.21.89-90.

[29]Ars Poetica 268-69.

[30]On Imitation Frag. 6 Us.

[31]Inst. Orat. 10.1.19-20. See Fiske, Lucilius and Horace, 35-36.

[32]Inst. Orat. 1.9.2.

[33]Panegyricus 7-8. See Fiske, Lucilius and Horace, 36-37.

[34]Inst. Orat. 10.2.1, 4-8.

[35]Panegyricus 8.188. See White, Plagiarism and Imitation, 11-12; Fiske, Lucilius and Horace, 40-50.

[36]E.g., see Dionysius Lysias 3-4.

[37]Panegyricus 3-6.

[38]Fables, i, prologue; iv, 20; ii, epilogue.

[39] *Inst. Orat.* 10.2.9.

[40] *The Ancient Orators* 4; see also *Lysias* 13.

[41] *De Inventione* 2.1-5.

[42] *De Oratore* 2.22.93.

[43] *Inst. Orat.* 10.2.14-15, 24.

[44] Ibid., 10.1.108.

[45] *The Ancient Orators* 4; see also Kennedy, *Classical Rhetoric*, 348.

[46] *De Oratore* 2.21.89.

[47] *Inst. Orat.* 10.2.16.

[48] *On the Sublime* 13.2-14.1.

[49] See White, *Plagiarism and Imitation*, 9-11.

[50] Cicero *De Optimo Genere Oratorum* 14; *De Finibus* 3.4.15; Quintilian *Inst. Orat.* 1.9.2; Horace *Ars Poetica* 133.

[51] Horace *Ars Poetica* 131-32, 134-35.

[52] Horace *Epistle to Maecenas* 1.19.21-34; Lucretius *De Rerum Natura* 4.1-5.

[53] Horace *Odes* 4.2.27-32; Seneca *Letters* 84.3, 5. For a history of the analogy of the bee, see J. von Stackelberg, "Das Bienengleichnis," *Romanische Forschungen* 68 (1956) 271-93.

[54] *Letters* 84.5-8.

[55] Ibid. 84.9.

[56] On Catullus, see M. Balme, "Lyric Poetry," *Greek and Latin Literature* (ed. J. Higginbotham; London: Methuen, 1969) 24-62, esp. 46-50.

[57] Ibid., 50-61.

[58] *Odes* 3.30.13-14.

[59] *Odes* 4.9.3. See J. B. Leishman, *Translating Horace* (Oxford: Bruno Cassirer, 1956) 89-110, esp. 102-5.

[60] R. Coleman, "Pastoral Poetry," *Greek and Latin Literature*, 100-123, esp. 117.

[61] A. Cox, "Didactic Poetry," *Greek and Latin Literature*, 124-61, esp. 134-45, 143.

[62] Ibid., 145-53.

[63] R. Harriott, "Comedy," *Greek and Latin Literature*, 195-222, esp. 201, 215-22; see also *OCD*, Plautus, Terence.

[64] J. Higginbotham, "Satire," *Greek and Latin Literature*, 223-61, esp. 227; see also Fiske, *Lucilius and Horace*.

[65] Higginbotham, "Satire," 238-42.

[66] See esp. F. J. Miller, *The Tragedies of Seneca* (Chicago: University of Chicago Press, 1907) 455-96.

[67] On Virgil's general use of sources, see J. Conington, *The Works of Virgil* (Hildesheim: Georg Olms, 1963), vol. 2, xix-xliv; G. Lee, "Imitation and the Poetry of Virgil," *Greece and Rome* 28 (1981) 10-22. On Virgil and Homer, see R. S. Conway, "Virgil as a Student of Homer," *Martin Classical Lectures* 1 (1930) 151-81 (Cambridge: Harvard University Press, 1931); and esp. G. N. Knauer, *Die Aeneis und Homer* (2d ed.; Hypomnemata 7; Göttingen: Vandenhoeck & Ruprecht, 1979).

[68] *Hippolytus*, scene vi, 1238 (trans. D. Grene from *The Complete Greek Tragedies*, Vol. 3 [ed. D. Grene and R. Lattimore; Chicago and London: University of Chicago Press, 1959]).

[69] *Phaedra*, Act 4, 1092-96 (trans. E. P. Watling, *Seneca: Four Tragedies and Octavia* [Harmondsworth: Penguin, 1966]).

[70] *Hippolytus* 6.1199-1203.

[71] *Phaedra* 4.1007-8.

[72] For a summary and bibliography, see *OCD*, Ovid. On Ovid's careful but complex use of sources in *Metamorphoses*, see esp. B. Otis, *Ovid as an Epic Poet* (Cambridge: Cambridge University Press, 1966) 1-3, 45-49, 346-94. According to Otis, "Ovid never imitates literally" (p. 366). Note also W. S. Anderson, *Ovid's Metamorphoses*, Books 6-10 (Norman, OK: University of Oklahoma Press, 1972) 6-17 (on Ovid's plan and sources), and 34-35 (select bibliography).

[73] *Hippolytus* 6.1142-52.

[74] *Phaedra* 4.989-90.

[75] For an analysis, see Conway "Virgil as a Student of Homer," 156.

[76] For a summary of Virgil's fusing of different Homeric characters into single characters of the *Aeneid*, see Knauer, *Die Aeneis und Homer*, 342-43.

[77] For primary references and for further analysis and details, see M. Balme, "Lyric Poetry," 47-50.

[78] *Iliad* 9.609 (trans. by Conway, "Virgil as a Student of Homer," 157).

[79] *Aeneid* 4.336 (trans. by Conway, "Virgil," 157).

[80] On Virgil's emphasis on peace (as opposed to Homer's emphasis on war), see G. Miles, "Glorious Peace: The Values and Motivation of Virgil's Aeneas," *California Studies in Classical Antiquity* 9 (1976) 133-64.

[81] *Hippolytus* 6.1257-60 (Grene's translation).

[82] *Phaedra* 4.1119-23 (Watling's translation).

[83] For some further notes on Seneca's internalization of Euripides, see G. Steiner, *After Babel*, 431-33.

[84] For further discussion of Horace's procedure in the *Epodes*, see Balme, "Lyric Poetry," 50-55. On the larger question of form-change in general, see Ovid's *Metamorphoses*, esp. 1.1-4.

[85] Kennedy, *Classical Rhetoric*, 118.

[86] On the relatedness of ancient history and biography, see C. Turner, "History," *Greek and Latin Literature*, 300-341, esp. 328-34. Both C. H. Talbert (*What Is a Gospel? The Genre of the Canonical Gospels* [Philadelphia: Fortress, 1977] 16-17) and M. Hengel (*Acts and the History of Earliest Christianity* [Philadelphia: Fortress, 1980] 15-16) suggest that there is a clear distinction between the genres of history and biography. It is indeed possible to cite individual works that are quite distinct from one another in genre, but on the whole this distinction does not hold. Even Plutarch's *Lives* at times seems more interested in history than in biography; see C. B. R. Pelling, "Plutarch's Adaptation of His Source-Material," *Journal of Hellenic Studies* 100 (1980) 127-40, esp. 136-37. Hengel's contention (*Acts*, 27-

29) that the gospels consist of biographical reminiscences (*apomnē-moneumata*) may at first sound quite plausible, but, apart from the apologetically oriented evidence of Justin, it rests largely on Hengel's own bland assertion—made despite an admission (*Acts*, 22-23) that we do not know how oral tradition actually worked—that Jesus' brief activity in Galilee "provided *a wealth of firmly fixed and permanent impressions*" (*Acts*, 24, emphasis added). In this way, without any significant argumentation, Hengel prejudges a fundamental issue—the nature of the ultimate sources behind the text.

[87]Lucian *How to Write History*, paragraphs 39, 47.

[88]Arrian *Anabasis* 1.1-2.

[89]Philostratus *Apollonius* 1.2-3.

[90]See A. Cox, "Didactic Poetry," 124-45.

[91]Lucian *How to Write History*, paragraph 8.

[92]Ibid., paragraph 3.

[93]Quintilian *Inst. Orat.* 10.1.31. With regard to the Old Testament also it seems to be a mistake to regard poetry as being quite distinct from history. Thus G. von Rad (*Old Testament Theology* [New York: Harper & Row, 1962] 1. 109) believes that "a large part of even the historical traditions of Israel has to be regarded as poetry," and J. L. Kugel (*The Idea of Biblical Poetry: Parallelism and its History* [New Haven and London: Yale University Press, 1981] esp. 302) argues that "the concepts of poetry and prose correspond to no precise distinction in the Bible and that their sustained use has been somewhat misleading about the nature and form of different sections of the Bible."

[94]E. Badian ("The Early Historians," *Latin Historians* [ed. T. A. Dorey; New York: Basic Books, 1966] 1-38, esp. 21) remarks that "the tradition of Roman historiography made plausible lying easy."

[95]R. Martin, *Tacitus* (London: Batsford Academic and Educational Press, 1981) 18.

[96]Ibid., 17.

[97]*De Legibus* 1.5.

[98]On Ctesias, Duris, and Phylarchus, see Lesky, *History of Greek Literature*, 623-24, 764-66.

[99]E.g., compare Livy 33.39-40, and Polybius 18.49-51.

[100]P. G. Walsh, *Livy: His Historical Aims and Methods* (Cambridge: Cambridge University Press, 1961) 190.

[101]*OCD*, Livy.

[102]See *OCD*, Duris (2), Phylarchus.

[103]C. B. R. Pelling, "Plutarch's Method of Work in the Roman Lives," *Journal of Hellenic Studies* 99 (1979) 74-96, esp. 91-96.

[104]On compression and rephrasing in Plutarch, see H. J. Cadbury, *The Making of Luke-Acts* (New York: Macmillan, 1927) 161-63. On the other techniques, see Pelling, "Plutarch's Adaptation," 127-31.

[105]See E. J. Kenney, "The Historical Imagination of Lucretius," *Greece and Rome* 19 (1972) 12-24.

[106]See C. L. Thompson, "Cicero's Editing of Mythographic Material in the *De Natura Deorum*," *Classical Journal* 75 (1979-80) 143-52.

[107]Pelling, "Plutarch's Adaptation," 131-35.

[108]Lucian *How to Write History,* paragraph 139.

[109]E. Gabba, "True History and False History in Classical Antiquity," *Journal of Roman Studies* 71 (1981) 50-62, esp. 50. H. Butterfield (*The Origins of History* [London: Methuen, 1981] 118-37, esp. 136-37) rightly emphasizes the achievement of Thucydides but does not make clear that Thucydides' method was not followed by most subsequent Greco-Roman writers.

[110]Lesky, *History of Greek Literature,* 484-81, esp. 459, 473.

[111]Ibid., 461, 463, 466.

[112]F. M. Cornford, *Thucydides Mythistoricus* (London: E. Arnold, 1907).

[113]*OCD,* Thucydides (2).

[114]Turner, "History," 306.

[115]*OCD,* Dionysius (7).

[116]Turner, "History," 307.

[117]Sulla *Hist.* 1.55.24.

[118]Martin, *Tacitus,* 21. For an analysis of the rationale behind archaism, see Steiner, *After Babel,* 333-53. For a survey and analysis of archaism of style and content as found in works written in Greek ca. A.D. 60-240, see E. L. Bowie, "Greeks and their Past in the Second Sophistic," *Past and Present* 46 (1970) 3-41.

[119]Thucydides *Hist.* 7.71.1-4.

[120]Polybius *Hist.* 1.44.5.

[121]Tacitus *Hist.* 1.40 (trans. G. G. Ramsay, *The Histories of Tacitus* [London: John Murray, 1915] 47-48).

[122]*Hist.* 1.32.

[123]For further details see Turner, "History," 311-21.

[124]Ibid.

[125]Martin, *Tacitus,* 11. Emphasis added.

[126]Ibid.

[127]For a discussion, see J. W. H. Atkins, *Literary Criticism in Antiquity* (Cambridge: Cambridge University Press, 1934) 2. 177-96, esp. 182-85, 194.

[128]For further aspects of this argument, see Talbert, *What Is a Gospel?,* 4-8.

[129]See S. M. Warner, "Primitive Saga Men," *VT* 29 (1979) 325-35; J. W. Rogerson, *Myth in Old Testament Interpretation* (Berlin and New York: de Gruyter, 1974) 57-65; A. Wolf, "H. Gunkels Auffassung von der Verschriftlichung der Genesis im Light mittelalterlicher Literarisierungsprobleme," *UF* 12 (1980) 361-74. On the question of the possible oral transmission of the gospel, see the discussion between A. B. Lord and C. H. Talbert in *The Relationships Among the Gospels* (ed. W. O. Walker, Jr.; San Antonio: Trinity University Press, 1978) 33-102, esp. 99.

[130]E.g., see W. Schmithals, "Kritik der Formkritik," *ZTK* 77 (1980) 149-85; E. Schillebeeckx, *Jesus: An Experiment in Christology* (New York: Seabury, 1979) 92-95.

[131]Despite a favorable review by J. A. Fitzmyer ("Memory and Manuscript: The Origins and Transmission of the Gospel Tradition,"

TS 23 [1962] 442-57) Gerhardsson's work has generally been severely criticized; for references see M. J. Cook's review, *Int* 34 (1980) 314-16; note esp. the critique of J. Neusner, "The Rabbinic Traditions about the Pharisees before AD 70: The Problem of Oral Transmission," *JJS* 22 (1971) 1-18, esp. 6-7; see also W. H. Kelber's review, *JAAR* 48 (1980) 279-80.

[132]For references and discussion, see esp. Kurz, "Hellenistic Rhetoric."

[133]The fact that the genre of the gospels is in some significant respects similar to that of Greco-Roman biographies (see C. H. Talbert, *What Is a Gospel?*) does not take away from the fact that in other important respects the genre of the gospels, and particularly of Luke-Acts, is strikingly close to some of the Old Testament histories; see R. E. Brown, "Jesus and Elisha," *Perspective* 12 (1971) 85-104, esp. 97-99; *The Birth of the Messiah* (Garden City: Doubleday, 1977) 561; T. L. Brodie, "A New Temple and a New Law. The Unity and Chronicler-based Nature of Luke 1:1-4:22a," *JSNT* 5 (1979) 21-45; C. H. Talbert, "Prophecies of Future Greatness: The Contribution of Greco-Roman Biographies to an Understanding of Luke 1:5-4:15," in *The Divine Helmsman: Studies on God's Control of Human Events, Presented to Lou H. Silberman* (ed. J. L. Crenshaw and S. Sandmel; New York: Ktav, 1980) 129-38, esp. 137; M. Hengel, *Acts*, 30-32; D. L. Barr and J. L. Wentling, "The Conventions of Classical Biography and the Genre of Luke-Acts: A Preliminary Study" (paper presented at the SBL/CBA regional meeting, Duquesne University, Pittsburgh, PA, April 1980).

[134]See W. S. Kurz, "Luke-Acts and Historiography in the Greek Bible," *Society of Biblical Literature 1980 Seminar Papers* (ed. P. J. Achtemeier; Chico, CA: Scholars Press, 1980) 283-300; idem, "Farewell Addresses in Luke-Acts and the Greek Bible" (paper delivered at the CBA meeting, Duluth, MN, August 1980).

[135]For summaries of the evidence, see E. Haenchen, *The Acts of the Apostles: A Commentary* (Philadelphia: Westminster, 1971) 72-77; and esp. J. A. Fitzmyer, *The Gospel According to Luke, I-IX: Introduction, Translation, and Notes* (AB 28; New York: Doubleday, 1981) 113-18.

[136]E. Plümacher, *Lukas als hellenistischer Schriftsteller: Studien zur Apostelgeschichte* (SUNT 9; Göttingen: Vandenhoeck & Ruprecht, 1972) 38-72, esp. 63-64; F. L. Horton, "Reflections on the Semitisms of Luke-Acts," in *Perspectives on Luke-Acts* (ed. C. H. Talbert; Special Studies Series 5; Danville, VA: Association of Baptist Professors of Religion, 1978) 1-23, esp. 17-18.

[137]T. L. Brodie, "Luke the Literary Interpreter. Luke-Acts as a Systematic Rewriting and Updating of the Elijah-Elisha Narrative in 1 and 2 Kings (diss., Angelicum University, Rome, 1981).

[138]See S. Praeder, "Luke-Acts and the Ancient Novel," *Society of Biblical Literature 1981 Seminar Papers* (ed. K. H. Richards; Chico, CA: Scholars Press, 1981) 269-308. Note also the view of Gail O'Day Preston that "Acts offers the reader a combination of romance,

biography and historiography" and adapts romance techniques ("Hellenistic Romances and Early Christian Narratives," paper delivered at the AAR/SBL regional meeting, Gainesville, FL, March 1982, esp. pp. 10-11).

[139]*OCD*, Novel (Greek).

[140]*De Compositione Verborum* 21 (trans. from J. D. Denniston, *Greek Literary Criticism* [New York: Dutton, 1924] 145).

[141]*After Babel*, 425 (emphasis added).

[142]For an analysis of the process of problem solving and of discovery, see M. Polanyi, *Personal Knowledge: Toward a Post-Critical Philosophy* (Chicago: University of Chicago Press, 1958) 120-24, esp. 123. On the priority of paradigms over clear rules, see T. S. Kuhn, *The Structure of Scientific Revolutions* (2d ed.; Chicago and London: University of Chicago Press, 1970) 43-51.

[143]Brodie, *Luke the Literary Interpreter*, 216-27.

[144]Compare Ovid *Metamorphoses* 12.39-63 with Virgil *Aeneid* 4.173-97; see N. Zumwalt, "*Fama Subversa*: Theme and Structure in Ovid *Metamorphoses* 12," *California Studies in Classical Antiquity* 10 (1977) 209-22; F. J. Miller, "Ovid's *Aeneid* and Virgil's: A Contrast in Motivation," *Classical Journal* 23 (1927-28) 33-43, esp. 36-39.

[145]G. Volkmar, *Die Evangelien: oder Markus und die Synopsis der Evangelien* (Leipzig, 1870); see also Gary Nolan, "The Influence of Romans and Galatians in Mark's Gospel" (paper presented at the AAR/SBL regional meeting, Gainesville, FL, March 1982); Schmithals, "Kritik der Formkritik," 179-85.

[146]Quintilian *Inst. Orat.* 10.2.1.

[147]For a review of the discussion about Luke's possible use of Paul's epistles, see M. E. Enslin, "Once Again, Luke and Paul," *ZNW* 61 (1970) 253-71.

[148]*The Making of Luke-Acts*, 163.

[149]*Luke the Literary Interpreter*, 128-366; "A New Temple and a New Law," 21-45. I have begun also to develop some examples in considerable detail: see "The Accusing and Stoning of Naboth (1 Kgs 21:8-13) as One Component of the Stephen Text (Acts 6:9-14; 7:58a)," *CBQ* 45 (1983) 417-32; "Towards Unraveling Luke's Use of the Old Testament: Luke 7:11-17 as an *Imitatio* of 1 Kings 17:17-24," *NTS* (forthcoming); "Luke 7:36-50 as an Internalization of 2 Kgs 4:1-37: A Study in Luke's Use of Rhetorical Imitation," *Bib* (forthcoming).

John T. Townsend

THE DATE OF LUKE-ACTS

There is no conclusive evidence that Luke-Acts was written in the first century. In fact, it is not before the last decades of the second century that one finds undisputed traces of the work, although by that time Irenaeus was citing it extensively and by name (*Adv. Haer.* 3.13.3; 3.15.1). The work appears also in the Muratorian Canon and the Anti-Marcionite Prologues, but neither of these works can be dated much earlier than Irenaeus.[1] It is likely that there is also a mention of Acts by Dionysius of Corinth in his letter to Soter of Rome ca. 170 (in Eusebius *Hist. eccl.* 4.23.3), although the "Acts" that he mentions might not be the canonical Acts. After the end of the second century, Christian writers were citing Luke and Acts regularly; yet no definite reference to the work is extant from before 170, even though the references by Irenaeus and his contemporaries imply that in their time Luke and Acts were accepted without question as canonical writings from apostolic times.

That some earlier writers did allude to Luke or Acts is possible but far from certain. The most obvious example is Marcion, whose gospel certainly bears a literary relation to canonical Luke. However, Marcion's gospel is not canonical Luke and may well have preceded canonical Luke.[2] Several possible allusions to the work by other earlier writers are too fleeting to be regarded as more than coincidences in wording. More substantial citations tend to be sayings that may have come from some source other than Luke-Acts, perhaps from oral tradition. The earlier writer most likely to have used Luke-Acts is Justin Martyr,[3] and the possible citation of Luke-Acts is in *Dial.* 105. There Justin cites words of Jesus from the cross that appear in no gospel except Luke (23:46): "Father, into your hands I commend my spirit." Although such words may well have come from canonical Luke, there are other possibilities. Justin could have been citing an earlier version of the third gospel, perhaps similar to Marcion's gospel, which apparently contained the verse (see Tertullian *Adv. Marc.* 4.42).[4] The apologist and the evangelist may both have been drawing upon a saying of Jesus in oral form. Since the saying ultimately comes from Ps 30:6 (LXX = RSV 31:5), the existence of this saying in oral tradition would not be hard to explain.

Whether or not Justin cited canonical Luke-Acts, it is unlikely that the work as we know it was written much after his time. By 170 the work was widely accepted as apostolic and canonical, and it would hardly have achieved that status in much less than twenty years. Thus, the middle of the second century is the terminus ad quem for the final composition of Luke-Acts. A terminus a quo in the early sixties of the first century is determined by the last event mentioned in Acts. Therefore, it is possible that Luke-Acts appeared in its present form at any time during a nine-decade period. Over the years there has been no shortage of critics to date Luke-Acts at one or the other extremity of this period, but today few would argue for a mid-second-century dating of the work. It is the purpose of this paper to test whether so late a dating is probable or even tenable.

Four decades ago, in 1942, John Knox published a work on Marcion and his relation to Luke-Acts,[5] a work that later writers on Luke-Acts have largely ignored.[6] According to Knox, Marcion did not make a radical abridgment of our canonical Luke, as most critics have assumed since Tertullian. Rather, Marcion "edited"[7] an earlier, shorter form of the gospel. In doing so he probably made editorial changes no more radical than those he made in editing his version of the Pauline epistles. Knox uses many pages of linguistic arguments to support his thesis, but, as he himself recognized, all such arguments are flawed. The reason is that we are unsure about the exact wording and extent of Marcion's gospel.[8] There are, however, two facts about Marcion's work that are quite clear. The first is that his gospel is a work that is quite similar to canonical Luke but lacks many sections found in canonical Luke.[9] The second is that Marcion's gospel contains matter that appears to contradict Marcion's own views. This fact is admitted even by Tertullian (Adv. Marc. 4.43), who found it difficult to explain. The only explanation he does offer is that Marcion allowed such passages in his gospel in order to fool his opponents into thinking that he had not tampered with the Lucan text. What seems more likely is that Marcion was producing what he believed to be a legitimately edited text. He had apparently edited the text of Paul from his version of the letters in conformity with his understanding of what the apostle truly believed and therefore probably wrote. Would Marcion not be expected to treat his gospel similarly? The anti-Marcionite passages in Marcion's gospel suggest that he did so.

One way to test Knox's dating of Luke-Acts is to look for other links between the work and what we know of the mid-second century.

Such links may be found in several parallels between Acts and the pseudo-Clementine literature, which probably represents at least one type of Jewish Christianity.[10] While the pseudo-Clementine literature in its present form must come from the third century or later, source criticism indicates that parts of the literature stem from the second century. According to most source critics, the Clementine Homilies and the Clementine Recognitions are based on a Grundschrift, one source of which is a work known as the *Kerygma Petrou* (*KP*). Moreover, it has been possible to extract much of this *KP* source from the Homilies and Recognitions as they exist today.[11] One usually dates the Grundschrift in the third century, and *KP* can easily be placed in the second century, even in the early part of that century.[12]

Perhaps the most interesting similarity between Acts and the pseudo-Clementine literature concerns the Apostolic Decree as it appears in the so-called neutral text (represented by Codex Vaticanus) of Acts 15:19-20, 28-29; 21:25.[13] The decree lists four requirements expected of all Christians, Jewish and non-Jewish. These requirements are the avoidance of

1. idols (15:20), more specifically defined in 15:29 and 21:25 as meat offered to idols;

2. blood, presumably in this context meat with the blood in it;

3. things strangled, that is, meat so killed as by a hunting snare;

4. fornication, a requirement that, on the surface at least, belongs in a different category from the other three in that avoiding fornication has nothing to do with Jewish food regulations and is not even particularly Jewish.

The author of Luke-Acts chose to insert the decree into Acts in two places. First he attached the decree to his account of the Apostolic Council in Acts 15 although even a casual reading of the chapter reveals that the decree does not deal directly with the main subject matter of the council. According to Acts 15 the council concerned circumcision of non-Jewish Christians (vv. 1-5), a subject the Apostolic Decree does not even mention. Rather, the decree treats kosher meat and fornication. In chap. 21 of Acts the decree appears in a somewhat different setting. Here the decree is a decision of the Jerusalem church; and James has to inform Paul of its contents, even though Paul had presumably heard the decree at the Apostolic Council. Moreover, if Gal 2:1-10 is Paul's description of the events in Acts 15, then the fact that the council was concerned with circumcision and not idol meats is confirmed by an eye witness. In fact, Gal 2:11-13 specifically records that the whole problem of table fellowship between Jewish and Gentile Christians remained unresolved. It is therefore unlikely that the Apostolic Decree stemmed from the

Apostolic Council. It is also unlikely that the decree was simply an invention by the author of Luke-Acts. Had he been inventing freely, he would probably have written a decree more specifically concerned with circumcision. What appears more likely is that the author of Luke-Acts based the Apostolic Decree upon a piece of tradition that he valued and felt obliged to add to his work in the best context available.

If the decree came from neither the Apostolic Council nor from the author of Luke-Acts but from some other source, what was that source? The roots of the Apostolic Decree may well go back ultimately to Leviticus 17 and 18.[14] This section of the Holiness Code contains certain prohibitions that were binding not only on Israelites but on the non-Israelite inhabitants of Israel as well, and some of these prohibitions resemble the four parts of the Apostolic Decree. Thus, it is not unlikely that the decree was some kind of special Jewish code for certain non-Jews such as the God-fearers in the synagogue. This decree, however, should not be confused with the so-called Noachian Commandments.[15] These latter are regulations that Jews believed governed all descendants of Adam and Noah. Although different sources have recorded various specific Noachian Commandments, they generally make up a basic moral code about which most societies would agree. The four prohibitions of the Apostolic Decree, or at least three of them, are commandments of special interest only to Jews. Non-Jews would likely agree with Noachian precepts against robbery, murder, blaspheming the divine name, cursing judges, and incest, but they might not feel bound by Jewish dietary laws.

A better parallel is to be found in the ethical summaries that are scattered throughout the pseudo-Clementine writings. The important passages are Recog. 4.36, 6.10–12; Hom. 7.4; 7.8; 8.19; 11.27–30, all of which come from the *KP* source except Hom. 7:4 and perhaps Hom. 7.8. Recog. 4.36 lists the ways in which one might stain the baptismal garment. The list contains three classes of staining sins:

    1. those which pollute *ad mortem* (apostasy and heresy);

    2. those which pollute *in actibus* (murders, adulteries, hatreds, avarice, and evil cupidity);

    3. those which pollute body and soul together ("to partake of the table of demons, to taste things sacrificed, blood, or a carcass[16] that has been strangled").

It is obvious that the third section of this list corresponds to the three prohibitions of the Apostolic Decree that concern diet; but there is no mention of fornication, although the second section mentions adulteries.

The parallel account in Hom. 8.23 lacks the threefold division. Moreover, while there is mention of "the defiled (*miaras*) table," an expression probably equivalent to the "table of demons" in Recog. 4.31.4, Hom 8.23 contains no amplification of the expression suggestive of the Apostolic Decree. However, just before Hom. 8.23, in Hom. 8.19:1 (*KP*), there is an angelic oracle addressed to demons. This oracle speaks of those "worshipping you [demons] and sacrificing and pouring libations and partaking of your table or accomplishing something else improper or shedding blood or tasting dead flesh or the remains of wild beasts or what is cut or what is strangled or being satiated with something else unclean." Again, neither Hom. 8.23 nor 8.19 mentions fornication, although both mention adultery.

An explanation for this neglect of a ban on fornication is suggested in Recog. 6.10-12 // Hom. 11.27-30 (*KP*). Both passages contain ethical prohibitions similar to the second section of the list in Recog. 4.36. Then in both Recog. 6.10-12 and Hom. 11.27-30 there follows a commandment for purity as a special requirement for the church. In Recog. 6.10-12 this purity is defined as abstaining from intercourse with a menstruous woman, washing the body with water, and never copulating for pleasure but only for offspring. The parallel account in Hom. 11.27-30 further defines the washing as a purifying immersion after sexual intercourse (*koinōnia*). Such acts might well fall within the meaning of *porneia* (fornication) as used in the Apostolic Decree. The Apostolic Decree would then have a single focus, and that focus would be not a full ethical code, but only those specifically Jewish commandments incumbent upon all Christians.

A similar situation exists in Hom. 7.8, but here the ethical precepts follow the prohibitions of the Apostolic Decree. First, one is "to abstain from the table of demons, i.e., from meat offered to idols, dead carcasses, things strangled, things killed by wild beasts, and from blood." Then follows the command against impurity, which is defined as washing after *koitē* and, for women, keeping purity laws. Finally there come precepts of an ethical nature. These are quite general. All are "to be chaste (*sōphronein*) do good, do no wrong, expect eternal life from the almighty God, and they are to ask to receive it with continuous prayers and supplications." Thus, in Hom. 7.8 the only specific precepts are those that correspond to the four prohibitions of the Apostolic Decree. Unfortunately, there is one difficulty in using the passage in a discussion of mid-second-century Christianity. Some critics doubt that the passage stems from the *KP* source, although there seems to be little reason for their doubt.[17]

If we look at the ethical requirements of *KP* as a whole, we notice that the only specifically Jewish precepts stressed are those that correspond to the Apostolic Decree. Still, Gentile Christians would have found even these burdensome. For example, the regulations about meat in a pagan society without kosher butchers would effectively eliminate meat from the diet of most Christians (see Rom 14:21), and at least some Jewish Christians of the pseudo-Clementine circle had become vegetarians (Hom. 8.15 [KP]; cf. Recog. 7.6.4 // Hom. 12.6.4).[18] However, one should not overemphasize the burden of abstinence from meat, since meat was relatively rare in the ancient diet apart from feasts.

The whole question of idol meats was a living issue throughout the second century. During the mid-first century the apostle Paul had generally allowed his congregations to eat such meat (1 Cor 8:1-13; 10:19; cf. Rom 14:13-25), but many Christian leaders contested this liberal attitude from Paul's day into the third century. John of the Apocalypse (Rev 2:14, 20), the author of Didache (6.5), Justin Martyr (Dial. 34.8-35.1), Irenaeus (Adv. Haer. 1.6.3; 24.5; 26.3; 28.2), and Tertullian (Haer. 33) all opposed the practice.

Although the prohibition against idol meats eventually found wide acceptance,[19] there is little evidence for acceptance of the other prohibitions of the Apostolic Decree outside of Jewish-Christian circles. Even Acts 15 came to be written in a way that was subject to a more general interpretation. In the so-called Western text (here Codex Bezae) of the decree in Acts 15:29, there are three prohibitions: against idol meats, against blood, and against porneia. To these were added the Golden Rule in its negative form. With these changes the prohibitions of blood and porneia could be interpreted as forbidding murder and ordinary fornication respectively. However, the intention of the change may not have been simply to make the decree less Jewish.[20] There was a similar change in the pseudo-Clementine literature. Hom. 7.4 (not KP) contains an ethical list that begins with the four prohibitions of the Apostolic Decree, but the sexual prohibition is defined as washing from all pollution. Then as in Codex Bezae there also follows the Golden Rule, even though the wording of the prohibitions rules out any interpretation that is not specifically Jewish.

Before reaching a conclusion about the origin of the Apostolic Decree, we must first note that the decree is not the only point of contact between Luke-Acts and the pseudo-Clementine literature. First, there is little doubt that the pseudo-Clementine writings emphasize poverty as a Christian virtue (Hom. 5.7, 9; Recog. 2.28 [all KP]). Moreover, if these writings are indeed Ebionite,[21] the fact that "Ebionite" means "poor ones" (ʾebyônîm) in Hebrew confirms this emphasis. Similarly, Acts 4:32-5:11 regards personal poverty as essential for Jerusalem Christians, who "had all things in common" (Acts 2:44; 4:32). Even Epiphanius (30.17.2), who gives a different derivation of "Ebionite," sees a relation between this sect and Acts 4-5.

Another similarity between Acts and the pseudo–Clementine writings, as well as the patristic descriptions of the Ebionites, concerns an ancient equivalent of the modern Eucharist. According to Irenaeus (*Adv. Haer.* 5.1.3) and Epiphanius (30.16.1), Ebionites used bread and water rather than bread and wine. Likewise, Hom. 14.1.4 (not *KP*) mentions Peter's using bread and salt in connection with a thanksgiving (eucharist). The same practice is mentioned also in the *Contestatio* of James 4:3(4).[22] In both cases the practice appears to be a religious act. It may be more than a coincidence that Acts speaks of Christian fellowship meals in terms of bread only (2:42, 46; 20:7, 11). The same is true of the supper at Emmaus (Luke 24:30, 35).

Regarding the salt, there may be a reference to the symbolic use of salt in Acts 1:4. The key word here is *synalizomenos*. If the word was intended literally in the sense of "eating salt together," then the verse refers to Jesus' eating salt together with his disciples between the resurrection and the ascension. The same word appears also in Hom. 13.4.3 (not *KP*)[23] and in the epistle of Clement to James 15.4.[24] It must be admitted that the word need not imply the actual use of salt, sacramental or otherwise. It is even possible that the word does not refer to eating at all, but such general interpretations are not probable.[25] The pseudo–Clementine contains a dozen quite specific references to salt sharing,[26] and four of these imply that the usage is religious.[27] Also in Hom. 13.4.3 the context of *synalizomenos* suggests that the word is decribing a religious act. In any case, *synalizomenos*, whatever its precise meaning, is a word of extreme rarity, particularly as here in the middle voice. In fact, apart from Acts 1:4 and the few uses in the pseudo–Clementine literature, this verb in the middle voice is not found in the works of any Christian writer of the first two centuries. Such rarity suggests that the author of Acts 1:4 and the group represented in the pseudo–Clementine writings may have shared a special vocabulary not used by Christians generally.

A common designation of Jesus in the pseudo–Clementine literature is "the Prophet," that true messianic prophet promised by Moses in Deut 18:15-18 (Recog. 1.43 [*KP*],[28] et passim). Among the other Christian writings of the first two centuries only Acts 3:22 and 7:37 (cf. *Barn.* 12:1-7) specifically designate Jesus as the Deuteronomic prophet like Moses.

The pseudo–Clementine writings stress the importance of the twelve apostles, men who carry identity cards from James of Jerusalem (Recog. 4.35.1-2 [*KP*]). Surely the evidence of the senses must be superior to evidence from a mere vision claimed by people like Paul, known as Simon Magus in this literature (Hom. 17.13-19 [*KP*])!

In a similar way the author of Luke-Acts also undermined Paul's apostleship by making a physical relation with the historical Jesus essential to becoming one of the twelve (Acts 1:21-22). Acts also subjects Paul to human ordination (13:1-3; cf. 22:12-16) in spite of the apostle's vehement denial of any such ordination in Gal 1:1, 12, 15-16.[29]

The treatment of Paul in Acts as a whole is interesting. The work is clearly pro-Paul; yet, if the apostle himself had read the work, he would have been far from flattered. Acts seems to represent the very views that Paul was busy denying, particularly in Galatians 1-2.[30] Paul denied that he had received any human ordination; Acts 13:1-3 affirms that he did. Paul denied that he had contacted the church immediately after his conversion; Acts 9:10-19 affirms that he did. Paul denied that he had preached to Jews after his conversion; Acts 9:20-22 affirms that he did. Paul denied that he had contacted the Jerusalem apostles sooner than three years after his conversion; Acts 9:19-26 affirms that he did so in a matter of days. Paul described his first post-conversion visit to Jerusalem as a private affair in which he had met only Peter and James the Lord's brother; Acts 9:27 suggests a more formal meeting with "the apostles." Yet, compared with the pseudo-Clementine writings, for whom Paul is Simon Magus the epitome of all heretics, Acts seems to have taken a relatively moderate view of the apostle.

Another similarity between Acts and the pseudo-Clementine literature concerns the importance of baptism. Contrary to what the heresiologists tell about Ebionite practice (Irenaeus *Adv. Haer.* 1.26.2; Epiphanius 30.16.8-9; see also Tertullian *Haer.* 33), the pseudo-Clementine writings stress baptism and not circumcision (Hom. 11.26-27 [*KP*]).[31] Recog. 5.34.2 (*KP*) states bluntly that true worshipers of God need not be circumcised. Rather, baptism alone suffices for table fellowship (Hom. 1.22; 13.4; 11 [none *KP*]). Acts also stresses baptism. In fact, Acts (2:38) and 1 Peter (3:21) are the only New Testament works that specifically speak of baptism as a necessary requirement for salvation.[32]

There is one final similarity between Acts and the pseudo-Clementine literature. That similarity is a common stand against the Jerusalem temple and its cult. Although the author of Luke-Acts has made use of relatively pro-temple material in the early chapters of Luke and of Acts, the speeches he uses in Acts reveal a strong anti-temple bias.[33] The relevant passages are in the Areopagus speech of chap. 17 and in the Stephen speech of chap. 7. The Areopagus speech contains the relatively gentle reminder that it is foolish to provide housing for the God who created the world and rules it as Lord (vv. 24-25).

The Stephen speech is more severe. Acts 7:38-43 appears to regard Israel's sacrificial cult as idolatrous. The passage is commenting on the exodus story of Moses' receiving the law on Sinai. Verse 38 recalls how Moses had received "living oracles" for the Israelites, and vv. 38-41 speak of how Israel had rejected these oracles for the worship of Aaron's calf. According to the exodus account Moses had broken the original tablets with the oracles and later received them anew. However, the author of the Stephen speech apparently assumed that the new tablets contained commandments different from the old. These new commandments were no longer "living oracles" but an idolatrous cult. Thus, vv. 42-43 cite Amos 4:25-27 as proof that Israel's cult was indeed idolatrous, even in the wilderness period.

The attack on Israel's cult is followed in vv. 49-50 by an attack on the physical temple itself. The attack is threefold. As stated in the Areopagus speech, it is ridiculous to suppose that God would dwell in any temple made by human hands. Moreover, this fact is stated in scripture (Isa 66:1-2). Finally, Israel's temple at Jerusalem was erected contrary to what God wanted. Regarding the last point, the speech maintains that Solomon went ahead and replaced the tabernacle, which Moses had constructed from the heavenly pattern, with a temple made by mere humans. In fact, Solomon did so after his father David, who unlike himself had "found favor in the sight of God," had asked vainly for permission to build such a temple.

The only Christian writings that approach the anticult bias of the speech material in Acts 7 and 17 are the *Epistle of Barnabas* (chap. 2) and the pseudo-Clementine literature; and the latter more closely resembles Acts in the assault on the Jerusalem cult.[34] According to Recog. 1.35-37 (probably *KP*), it was because of the worship of the golden calf that Moses felt constrained to allow the Israelites to use an Egyptian-type cult in the worship of the true God. As in the Stephen speech, this attack on Israel's cult is followed by an attack on the temple building as a monument to "regal ambition" of evil kings (Recog. 1.38.5 [*KP* or Strecker's *AJ*]).

All these similarities between Acts and the pseudo-Clementine literature are evidence that the Jewish Christians represented in the pseudo-Clementine literature would have found much in Acts with which to agree. Perhaps most important is the ethical stance that Acts proclaims in the Apostolic Decree. As shown above, it is unlikely that the decree either came from the council described in Acts 15 or was formulated by the author of Luke-Acts, because the decree does not fit the context for which that author used it. What is more likely is that the author of Luke-Acts knew of the decree and added it to Acts 15 and 21 as the most suitable contexts he could find.

What was the origin of the decree, and what was the author's purpose for using it in Acts? A likely origin would be the Jewish-Christian communities from which the pseudo-Clementine literature arose, since the decree corresponds exactly to the special Jewish regulations that this literature in general and the *KP* source in particular would require of all Christians. Regarding the author's purpose in adopting the decree, one need only consider what could result if it were accepted by all Christians generally. Such acceptance would pave the way for table fellowship and intermarriage between Jewish Christians and members of Gentile congregations.

Was there some particular reason that the author of Luke-Acts would have been particularly interested in relations between Jewish and Gentile Christians at this time? If one were to assume late first-century dating of Luke-Acts, then it would be natural to point to the so-called *Birkat haMinim*, a prayer of the synagogue liturgy that curses certain heretics (*minîm*) and, in some versions of the prayer, Jewish Christians (*nôṣrîm*).[35] Such a curse wherever adopted would certainly make Jewish Christians feel unwelcome. According to the *Talmud Babli* (*b. Ber.* 28b-29a), the prayer was arranged in its anti-*minîm* form under Rabban Gamaliel at the end of the first century. However, the parallel account in the *Talmud Yerushalmi* (*y. Ber.* 5:4 [9c]), which seems to be the earlier tradition,[36] lacks the chronological reference to Gamaliel. Therefore, the dating of the prayer is far from certain. Nevertheless, it is unlikely that the arrangement of the prayer took place later than the second century, because the *Yerushalmi* account is told as a *baraita*, a rabbinic form for recording traditions of the first two centuries. Thus, the *Birkat haMinim* may well have been written in the mid-second century.

Whatever the date of the *Birkat haMinim*, it is abundantly clear that there was no complete separation of Jewish Christians from the synagogue in the late first century. There is evidence of Christians frequenting synagogues as late as Chrysostom (Homily 8.8.8-9).[37] However, it is also clear that in the middle of the second century Justin Martyr was concerned about Jews cursing Christians, whether or not the curse was the *Birkat haMinim*.[38] In at least nine places he specifically states that Jews cursed Christ and those believing in him (*Dial.* 16.4; 47.4; 93.4; 95.4; 96.2; 108.3; 123.6; 133.6; 137.2).[39] Of these nine references, three mention that the cursing took place in synagogues (16.4; 47.4; 96.2), and one mentions it in the context of prayer (137.2). Thus, there is little doubt that Jewish Christians were having a difficult time with various Jewish communities in the mid-second century.

If Luke-Acts was indeed written at this time, the work can be seen in part as responding to both the difficulties of Jewish Christians and the challenge of Marcion.[40]   Regarding Jewish Christians, Acts suggests that Gentile Christians welcome them into their fellowship by respecting their sensibilities in dietary and sexual practices. The work also espouses many views that pseudo-Clementine-type Christians would find appealing. In particular, Acts has treated Paul in a way that would make him acceptable to Jewish Christians without alienating Gentile Christians.

As for Marcion, the author of Luke-Acts has a response to him as well.   The author would accept Paul without the theology of his epistles. To do so the author of Luke-Acts replaced Marcion's canon with a two-volume work of his own. He merely expanded Marcion's gospel with added traditions, but he rejected entirely the Pauline epistles as theologically unacceptable. In their place the author of Luke-Acts wrote a separate volume affirming the importance of all the apostles.[41]   In particular he singled out Peter, the Jewish-Christian hero of the pseudo-Clementine literature, and Paul, the hero of Marcion.[42]

There are several objections to be raised about so late a dating of Acts.   First, the fact that Acts nowhere mentions that Paul wrote epistles leads some to believe that the work must have been written before the epistles were widely known. However, as suggested above, the silence regarding Paul's letters may have been deliberate. Besides, in the mid-second century Paul was not as popular as he later became, perhaps because of the association of his name with Marcion. In fact, Justin Martyr was able to write much more extensively than the author of Luke-Acts without reference to the Pauline epistles.[43]

Other objections are that a dating of Luke-Acts toward the middle of the second century would leave little time for the rise of a "Western text" and for the work's becoming accepted as canonical by about 175.[44]   These objections, however, are hardly conclusive. Twenty-five years more or less is almost a generation and would certainly provide enough time for a work to become popular enough to achieve canonical status in an age before careful records were maintained regarding authorship and dates of publication. Similarly the Western text would have needed only a single creative scribe to produce a copy, which others would recopy, reedit, and disseminate.[45]

Two other objections apply more specifically to John Knox's theory of an Ur-Lukas. The objections are (1) that there is not enough evidence for the text of Marcion's Luke for a detailed analysis and (2) that there are no traces of Ur-Lukas in non-Marcionite literature.[46]   Regarding the first objection, it has been shown above that there is considerable evidence for Knox's theory that does not depend upon detailed analysis. As for the second objection, two points should be made. The first is that, if a writer happened to cite Marcion's shorter gospel, it would be difficult to distinguish the citation from a citation of canonical Luke. Second, when Marcion put out his gospel, it confirmed the existence of a shorter version of Luke; before Marcion there was no conclusive allusion to a Lucan gospel, short or long.

There is one final matter, the question of "primitive" titles and other terminology in the speeches of Acts, particularly in Acts 3. R. F. Zehnle has cited several instances of words and titles from Acts 3 that he considers unusual enough to betray the use of "primitive" source material.[47] Most of the instances, however, are to be found in Christian writings from the second century and, in some cases, from the first century as well. As two such unusual titles for God, Zehnle cites "the God of Abraham, Isaac, and Jacob" and "the God of our fathers." But Valentinus (cited in Hipp. *Philos.* 6.31) used the first, and Justin (*Apol.* 1.63.7, 11, 17; *Dial.* 59.2) used both. Zehnle's four unusual titles for Jesus are "author of life," "servant (*pais*)," "the holy one," and "just one." All four are applied to Jesus elsewhere in the New Testament, and all four appear in second-century Christian writings.[48] Zehnle also discusses the description of Jesus as the prophet like Moses; yet, even though Zehnle is fully aware of the pseudo-Clementine use of this concept, he concludes that it must imply usage in an earlier period. Zehnle's two unusual titles for a Jewish audience in Acts are "sons of the prophets and [sons] of the covenant," neither of which can be found elsewhere in Christian literature of the first two centuries. Nevertheless, one must ask how often in such literature outside of Acts situations appear where someone exhorts Jewish crowds by title. Finally, Zehnle lists four unusual terms of which three are found in second-century works. It would seem that such evidence for early source material in Acts would equally suggest that the speech might have arisen during the second century.

In summary, the date when Luke-Acts was written cannot be determined conclusively because of a lack of evidence; however, whatever evidence exists is compatible with a date that approaches the middle of the second century. In such a situation the work can be understood in part as responding to situations faced in the church of that period. Two such situations were Marcion's canon and the problems of Jewish Christians.

NOTES

[1]Both sources, however, may be dated considerably later. On the Muratorian Canon, see A. C. Sundberg, "Canon Muratori: A Fourth-

Century List," *HTR* 66 (1973) 1-41; idem, "Muratorian Fragment," *IDB Supplementary Volume* (ed. K. Crim; Nashville: Abingdon, 1976) 609-10. There is considerably more agreement that the Anti-Marcionite Prologues are later, although they were dated in the latter half of the second century by A. von Harnack, "Die ältesten Evangelien-Prologe und die Bildung des Neuen Testaments," *SPAW* 24 (1928) 322-41. Against Harnack, see E. Gutwenger, "The Anti-Marcionite Prologues," *TS* 7 (1946) 393-409.

[2]So John Knox, *Marcion and the New Testament* (Chicago: University of Chicago Press, 1942).

[3]For a discussion of Justin's possible use of Luke-Acts, see J. C. O'Neill, *The Theology of Acts in its Historical Setting* (2d ed.; London: SPCK, 1970) 29-44.

[4]For a discussion, see Harnack, *Marcion* (TU 45; Leipzig: Hinrichs, 1924) 236*-37*.

[5]*Marcion and the New Testament: An Essay in the Early History of the Canon* (Chicago: University of Chicago Press, 1942).

[6]The work is not mentioned in W. W. Gasque, *A History of the Criticism of the Acts of the Apostles* (Grand Rapids: Eerdmans, 1975). However, Knox's book is discussed by C. H. Talbert (*Luke and the Gnostics* [Nashville: Abingdon, 1966] 108-9) and is listed in A. J. Mattill and M. B. Mattill, *A Classified Bibliography of the Literature on the Acts of the Apostles* (NTTS 7; Leiden: Brill, 1966) #2055.

[7]See Polycarp *Phil.* 7.1. According to Irenaeus (*Adv. Haer.* 3.3.4) Polycarp had addressed Marcion as "the first-born of Satan." Here in his epistle to the Philippians Polycarp used "the first-born of Satan" to designate one who "twists" (*methodeuē*) the oracles of the Lord for his own lusts. Such a verb would hardly describe the kind of abridging that Marcion would have done if he had been abridging canonical Luke.

[8]So also Talbert, *Luke,* 108-9. The same textual problem also casts doubt on linguistic arguments that advance a traditional position, e.g., W. Sanday, *The Gospels in the Second Century* (London: Macmillan, 1876) 222-30.

[9]See Harnack, *Marcion,* 52-61, 177*-240*.

[10]While there seems to be little reason to doubt the basic Jewish-Christian, perhaps Ebionite, orientation of the literature, certain caveats are necessary. Nowhere does the literature use the name "Ebionite"; there is no emphasis on circumcision (see below, p. 55); and Recog. 1.34.4, which comes from a second-century source (*Kerygma Petrou* [KP] or Georg Strecker's *Anabathmoi Jakobou* [AJ] as defined below, pp. 49-50 and n. 28), refers to Christ "the true prophet" as something more than a human messianic figure. He appeared to Moses as preexistent, if not divine. See also the Trinitarian baptismal formula in Hom. 11.26.2, which is probably an interpolation into the KP source. Finally, this literature, in particular the KP source, has gnosticizing tendencies, such as male-female oppositions. See G. Strecker (*Das Judenchristentum in den Pseudoklementinen* [TU 70; 2d ed.; Berlin: Akademie-Verlag, 1981] 137-220), who may go too

far in finding gnostic parallels but concludes "dass die Kerygmen einem gnostizisierenden Judenchristentum angehoren" (p. 213). On the general problem of defining Jewish Christianity, see A. F. J. Klijn, "The Study of Jewish Christianity," NTS 20 (1974) 419-31

[11] On the source criticism of the literature, see Strecker, Judenchristentum; H. J. Schoeps, Theologie und Geschichte des Judenchristentums (Tübingen: Mohr [Siebeck], 1949); O. Cullmann, Le problème littéraire et historique du Roman pseudo-clémentin (Études d'histoire et de philosophie religieuses, 23; Paris: Alcan, 1930); G. Schmidt, Studien zu den Pseudo-Clementinen (TU 46:1; Leipzig: Hinrichs, 1929); H. Heintze, Der Klemensroman und seine griechischen Quellen (TU 40; Leipzig: Hinrichs, 1914); H. Waitz, Die Pseudoklementinen, Homilien und Rekognitionen: Eine quellenkritisch Untersuchung (TU 25; Leipzig: Hinrichs, 1904).

[12] So Cullmann, Roman pseudo-clémentin, 96: "Le cadre général du christianisme primitif ne nous défend nullement de placer la composition des Prédications de Pierre au début du IIe siècle."

[13] For an excellent study of this relationship, see E. Molland, "La circoncision, le baptême et l'authorité du décret apostolique (Actes XV, 28sq.) dans les milieux judéo-chrétiens des Pseudo-Clémentines," ST 9 (1955) 1-39.

[14] E. Haenchen, The Acts of the Apostles (Philadelphia: Westminster, 1971) 469; K. Lake, "The Apostolic Council of Jerusalem," The Beginnings of Christianity (ed. F. J. Foakes Jackson and K. Lake; London: Macmillan, 1933) 5. 208.

[15] Against Schoeps, Theologie und Geschichte, 259; Lake, Beginnings, 5. 208; W. Schmithals, Paul and James (trans. D. M. Barton; SBT 1:46; London: SCM, 1965) 101 n. 24.

[16] The word for "carcass" here is morticinum in the critical GCS edition by B. Rehm, but the PG edition by P. de Lagarde reads morticinium, which specifically denotes a carcass with blood in it.

[17] For arguments that the passage does indeed stem from KP, see Molland, "La circoncision," 31.

[18] Schoeps, Theologie und Geschichte, 188-96.

[19] The matter was still an issue, however, in the time of Justin Martyr; see Dial. 35.1.

[20] For example, see E. J. Epp, The Theological Tendency of Codex Bezae Cantabrigiensis in Acts (SNTSMS 3; Cambridge: University Press, 1966) 107-12.

[21] See above, n. 10.

[22] In the ancient world, bread and salt symbolized the simplest fare. See Philo Contemplativa 37, according to whom the Therapeutae ascetics "eat, nothing very expensive, but cheap bread and salt for a relish . . . , and for drink they have running water." See also Acta Thomae 20 (Bonnet ed., p. 131): "For he fasts and prays without ceasing: he eats only bread with salt, and his drink is water." Similarly ibid. 104 (p. 217).

[23] The word is also retained in the two epitomes.

[24] Because the context of this part of the epistle does not immediately suggest a meal, Rufinus (d. 410) rendered synalizomenoi as

congregandos (although he used *cibum sumimus* in Hom. 13.4.3).
Similarly the Latin version in Cotelerius has *congregati*. However,
C. R. Bowen ("The Meaning of *synalizomenos* in Acts 1, 4," *ZNW* 13
[1912] 250-52) has shown that, in keeping with a general pattern in
this literature, *synalizomenoi* here also should refer to the common
meal.

[25]For alternate interpretations, see the commentary of K. Lake
and H. J. Cadbury (*The Beginnings of Christianity* [London: Macmillan, 1933] 4. 4-6), who themselves prefer to emend the text. For a
full discussion of the problem, see Bowen, "Meaning of *synalizomenos*," 247-59. See also E. Donckel, "Sale Sumpto," *Ephem. Liturg.*
47 (1933) 101-12; Strecker, *Judenchristentum*, 109-213.

[26]In addition to Hom. 14.1.4 and *Contestatio* of James 4.3(4)
mentioned above, the other ten references (only one of which is
considered to be from *KP*) are Hom. 4.6.1; 6.20.5; 11.34.1; 13.8.4;
13.11.4; 14.8.4-5; 15.11.2 (*KP*); 19.25.5; 20.16.5; and the epistle of
Clement to James 9.1. In every case, however, the Latin renderings
of Rufinus do not mention salt, and salt is also sometimes missing
from the epitomes.

[27]Hom. 13.11.4; 14.1.4; *Contestatio* of James 4.3(4); epistle of
Clement to James 9.1. In addition, Hom. 11.34.1 and 13.8.4 may well
be sacramental.

[28]According to Strecker (*Judenchristentum*, 234-35), this section is
part of another early source (*AJ*). For a general discussion of the
messianic prophet, see Schoeps, *Theologie und Geschichte*, 87-98;
Cullmann, *Roman pseudo-clémentin*, 227-34.

[29]This point has long been recognized. See F. C. Baur, "Die
Christus partei in der korinthischen Gemeinde, der Gegensatz des
petrinischen und paulinischen Christenthums in der ältesten Kirche,
der Apostel Paulus in Rom," *Tübinger Zeitschrift für Theol.* 5 (1831)
61-206.

[30]See O. Linton, "The Third Aspect, a Neglected Point of View: A
Study in Gal. i-ii and Acts ix and xv," *ST* 3 (1949) 79-95.

[31]See Schoeps, *Theologie und Geschichte*, 115; see also Strecker,
Judenchristentum, 196-209.

[32]Compare the cautious attitude of Paul toward baptism in 1 Cor
1:14-17; 10:1ff.

[33]That the speeches probably represent Lucan thought is suggested
not only by ancient writing customs but also by the fact that the
various speeches in Acts are interdependent, so that one speech builds
upon a previous one. Among the speeches so linked are both the
Stephen speech of Acts 7 and the Areopagus speech of Acts 17. See
my study, "The Speeches in Acts," *ATR* 42 (1960) 150-59.

[34]Schoeps, (*Theologie und Geschichte*, 440-47) believes that the
similarities are so close that the Stephen speech must come from a
Jewish-Christian James source; see also R. F. Zehnle, *Peter's Pentecost Discourse: Tradition and Lukan Reinterpretation in Peter's
Speeches of Acts 2 and 3* (SBLMS 15; Nashville: Abingdon, 1971) 86-
88.

[35]According to a recent study by R. Kimelman ("*Birkat Ha-Minim*

and the Lack of Evidence for an Anti-Christian Jewish Prayer in Late Antiquity," *Jewish and Christian Self-Definition* [ed. E. P. Sanders et al.; Philadelphia: Fortress, 1981] 2. 227-44, 391-403), both *minîm* and *natsrim* (= *nôṣrîm*) here denote a sect of Jewish Christians, not Christians in general.

[36] The version in the Jerusalem Talmud has more concerns. In addition to *minîm* (changed to "Sadducees" in censored texts), the passage is concerned about those who would deny the resurrection (Sadducees) and about those who would not pray for the rebuilding of Jerusalem (Samaritans according to *Tanḥuma, Wayyiqra,* 3, in both the traditional and Buber recensions). In the Babylonian version there is concern only for *minîm.* Sadducees and Samaritans were no longer a threat. For a discussion of this prayer from a slightly different point of view, see my chapter "The Gospel of John and the Jews" in *Antisemitism and the Foundations of Christianity* (ed. A. T. Davies; New York: Paulist, 1979) 84-87.

[37] See Kimelman ("*Birkat Ha-Minim,*" 239-240) for additional evidence.

[38] For a full study of Justin and the *Birkat haMinim* (dated in the first century), see W. Horbury, "The Benediction of the *Minim* and Early Jewish-Christian Controversy," *JTS* 33 (1982) 19-61.

[39] In each case the Greek word for "curse" is a form of *kataraomai,* except in 47:4 (where it is *katanathematizontas*) and 137:2 (where it is *episkōpsēte* or "mock").

[40] Another aim would be to show that the followers of Jesus were politically harmless.

[41] The title by which the Muratorian Canon refers to Acts is "Acta . . . Omnium Apostolorum."

[42] Although in time the church received Pauline epistles as canonical, it did so only together with the Pastoral epistles, which insured the apostle's orthodoxy.

[43] Although Justin must have known about Paul through the debate with Marcion (*Apol.* 1.26.5; 58.1-3), he never even mentions Paul by name. For a convenient listing of passages that some have argued reflect the Pauline epistles, see B. F. Westcott, *A General Survey of the History of the Canon of the New Testament* (7th ed.; London: Macmillan, 1896) 171-74.

[44] Talbert, *Luke,* 109.

[45] The homogeneity of the Western text is seriously questioned. See O'Neill, *Theology of Acts,* 44-47, against R. P. C. Hanson, "The Ideology of Codex Bezae in Acts," *NTS* 14 (1967/68) 282-86 (a review article on Epp, *Theological Tendency).*

[46] Talbert, *Luke,* 109.

[47] *Pentecost Discourse,* 44-60.

[48] See ibid. for references to second-century usage of the first three titles. The fourth ("Holy One") occurs in Justin *Dial.* 116.1.

David L. Barr and Judith L. Wentling

THE CONVENTIONS OF CLASSICAL BIOGRAPHY AND THE GENRE OF LUKE-ACTS: A PRELIMINARY STUDY

The problem of how to classify the gospels as literary works has become a point of increasing interest in the course of the past two decades. Answering the question of what kind of literature the gospels[1] were understood to be by those who wrote them and those who first heard them read in the early Christian churches has sparked the production of a growing body of literature that inquires after the genre of the gospels.[2] No consensus has yet been reached on the answer to this important question.

It is possible to trace the history of the problem back to the time of Justin Martyr, who, within a century after the composition of the gospels, referred to them as the "memoirs" (apomnēmoneumata) of the apostles who "handed down what Jesus had ordered them to do" (1 Apology 66).[3] After Justin, these writings are simply called gospels, and we are aware of no attempt until the nineteenth century to relate them to other literary forms. In the mid-nineteenth century, E. Renan assumed that the gospels were biographies because they were similar to Greco-Roman biographies.[4] Early in this century, C. W. Votaw argued in favor of the biographical nature of the gospels and compared them with several classical biographies.[5] However, with the development of form criticism, it became highly problematical to view the gospels as biography; they were seen as collections of material created out of common traditions by a believing community. Bultmann concluded: "So it is hardly possible to speak of the Gospels as a literary genus; the Gospel belongs to the history of dogma and worship."[6]

In the late 1960s interest in the gospels as literary works once again raised the question of their genre, and this led to the formation of a seminar within the Society of Biblical Literature. Several publications have grown out of the work of this seminar, including a recent monograph by Charles Talbert. Once more a scholar argues directly and forcefully that "the gospels *are* biographies, albeit ancient ones."[7] While we cannot agree that Talbert has established such a conclusion, his work does demand that the issue be reconsidered. He has successfully shown that the criteria Bultmann used to separate the gospels from biographies do not in fact do so. This achievement is a most important one, and it demands that we ask once more about the relationship of the gospels to the ancient genre of biography.

An inquiry of this kind should be a relatively simple undertaking, but there are several complicating factors, including a basic one: the whole concept of genre is somewhat vague. Whether one examines genre in biblical studies or in general literary criticism, one soon discovers that there is no consensus on the meaning of the term. Criticism by genres seems to have been initiated by Aristotle in his *Poetics* and has been so little developed that one modern critic can lament that genre theory remains "precisely where Aristotle left it."[8] That is not true, but it is true that no compelling theory of genres has emerged.

There is general agreement that generic analysis is an attempt to organize literature according to kinds or types. Genre theory represents an extension of our overwhelming impulse to organize our environment. Somewhat like the naturalist who surveys an infinite array of specific flowers or birds and then organizes them by kinds and kinships, the literary critic surveys an infinite variety of discrete works of literature and arranges them into genres by seeing the similarities, differences, and kinships that exist between works.[9] As two of the leading literary theorists of our time have suggested, "the theory of genres is a principle of order: it classifies literature and literary history not by time or place (period or national language) but by specifically literary types of organization or structure."[10] Just what these "specifically literary" criteria of organization are remains unclear. Even more unclear is the scope of a genre or how one knows one has passed from one genre to another. There are no generally accepted answers to either problem.

While such ambiguities make progress with our problem difficult, some clarity is emerging. We can, for example, fairly conclusively reject the view held by many scholars that the gospels are *sui generis* —forming a unique literary genre disassociated from their literary milieu. We have learned enough about genre to understand that such absolute uniqueness is not possible. Although each work of literature is unique and the four gospels have no exact literary parallels, no work of literature can be read in isolation. From a historical perspective, every piece of literature must grow out of some generic conception even if it finally overflows the boundaries of the genre. A wholly unique literary invention would be, as Wellek and Warren assert, "unintelligible"—"indeed unthinkable."[11]

This same point can be made if we ask what we hope to gain by establishing the generic affiliations of the gospels. Quite simply, the interpreter would then hold the key to the code[12] by which the evangelist shared his meanings with his audience. The audience's ability to see this meaning depended on its capacity to view this gospel against the background of other works of literature. Thus, a totally new genre could not have been understood by its hearers. To know the genre of the gospels is to understand the code used by the evangelist and understood by the community; this understanding may provide new insights into the meaning of the gospels for the modern interpreter.

We must conclude, then, that even if the gospels were sufficiently distinctive to cause us to regard them as a unique group of documents, they must still be related to some kinds of literature and not to others. At this point, relevant questions distinguish the kinds of relationships involved and the kinds of literature to which the gospels are related. In this way Talbert has successfully refuted Bultmann's endeavor to build a great wall between the gospels and Greco-Roman biographies. Bultmann attempted to build this wall on "three foundation pillars: (1) the gospels are mythical, the Greco-Roman biographies are not; (2) the gospels are cultic, the Greco-Roman biographies are not; and (3) while the gospels emerge from a community with a world-negating outlook, the literary biographies are produced by and for a world-affirming people."[13] It has been assumed too easily that Bultmann's three criteria were adequate and necessary for the purpose of establishing literary genre.

As we have mentioned above in our discussion of genre, the "specifically literary" criteria determinative of genre remain unclear. Even if we translate Bultmann's categories into their literary counterparts as Talbert does (so that myth is related to structure, cultic use to purpose, and world view to attitude [p. 6]), it seems arbitrary to say that these criteria and no others are necessary and sufficient for determining genre. Certainly the examination of structure is essential in extrinsic criticism, but is that the only criterion that is important? While purpose and attitude are a necessary part of intrinsic criticism, are they the only criteria or even the most important ones? It seems more appropriate to begin with the literature and to try to elicit all those criteria that might bear on genre rather than consider just the three arbitrary criteria that Bultmann suggested. While they may be necessary, they are not sufficient to determine generic identification.

However, another problem remains with Bultmann's three "genre-determining" criteria. Bultmann has attempted to determine the literary genre of the gospels by determining the nature of early Christian communities.[14] He has tried to demonstrate that because primitive Christianity was eschatological, therefore world-negating, this "attitude" can be used as a literary criterion to determine the genre of the literary document (e.g., the gospels). We doubt that applying literary criticism to a *community* will determine anything about a literary work. If we are to ascertain the literary genre of the gospels, we must confine our attention to the literary works themselves. Only a minimum of interest in the specific beliefs of the communities for which the individual authors wrote can be maintained.

Therefore, it is our intention in this paper to examine selected Greco-Roman biographies (those usually seen as most closely resembling the gospels) and one gospel (Luke-Acts) by the same methods of literary genre criticism and, after carefully exploring our results, draw some tentative conclusions about whether or not this gospel belongs to the genre biography.

We will approach the issue pragmatically and inductively. Our approach is inductive in that it begins with the reading of specific literary works commonly assumed, and usually self-consciously claimed, to belong to the same genre: biography (in Greek *bios* and in Latin *vita*).[15] Taking Wellek and Warren's advice seriously, we have sought the "specifically literary" connections between these works by examining both their external forms and their internal intentions.[16] Though generalization is necessary, we have always sought to test generalizatons between works by a specific reading of both works.[17] This discrepancy between generalization and specific texts ultimately brings us squarely to the genre question: when may two separate works be said to belong to the same genre? What degree of affinity is required? Our answer is pragmatic: If a well-informed reader who reads both works may be imagined to expect the same sorts of things from each, the works may be said to belong to the same genre. Genre theory is useful only insofar as it reveals the expectations of the reader. The question becomes, what did the earliest hearers[18] of Luke-Acts think they were hearing when it was read to them: history? biography? memoir? cult? legend? romance? apology? a collected miscellany?

We will set forth below some of the "specifically literary" aspects of ancient biographies drawn from a comparative reading of several works. We will then determine how these literary traits relate to Luke-Acts and, in conclusion, summarize our results.

The Conventions of Classical Biography

It should be clear, purely on the basis of the titles of the biographies we examined, that there is great diversity in the kinds of biography written in the Greco-Roman world. Both internal and external criteria are useful for classifying the biographies.[19] An external classification of biography can be based on the type of hero depicted in the biography. We have examined biographies written about military leaders (Nepos, Tacitus), political leaders (Suetonius, Plutarch), philosophers and teachers (Plato, Xenophon, Lucian, Philostratus, Diogenes Laertius), and religious leaders (Philo). Biographies in the ancient world were written about "special people"; there are no common, ordinary, "little" people in this group (neither are there any women). Those who have their biographies written are those who have achieved a certain measure of distinction within and usually beyond their society or group, either as leaders of the state or of the spirit. The type of hero characterized in a biography has a determining effect on other aspects of the work, such as the type of language used and the kinds of incidents reported. For the most part, the heroes and their deeds are portrayed in terms suitable to their types.

Biography can also be classified by internal criteria, for example, according to the purpose for which the biography was written or according to the manner in which it is presented (aesthetic mode). Talbert has worked out a systematic classification based upon purpose.[20] His five categories of biography could be classified as (1) exemplary (Lucian, Nepos, Plato, Plutarch), (2) apologetic (Xenophon, Philostratus, Tacitus), (3) exposé (Lucian), (4) successions (Diogenes Laertius), and (5) validation of a hermeneutical key (Philo). We can generalize by saying that a biography was almost always written out of a high regard for the hero and commonly set him forth as an example. In addition, the biography might seek to defend the hero against slander (apologetic) or to tell who his true followers were (succession) or what his true teaching was (hermeneutical). Another way of conceptualizing the writer's purpose is to say that it may be primarily apologetic (to defend the subject), exemplary (to present a model), laudatory (to praise the subject), philosophical (to present the subject's teaching, or provide a hermeneutical key), or legitimating of a succession (to present the subject's true disciples).[21]

Classifying biographies in this manner focuses on one aspect, the author's intended purpose. A related aspect, the literary manner by which the purpose is achieved, results in another sort of classification. Some biographers were encyclopedists (Diogenes Laertius); they simply compiled the "facts" about their heroes. Some biographers were objective without being totally pedagogical (Plutarch, Nepos). Other biographers were more subjective and sought to involve their readers with the hero (Tacitus, Philostratus).

It should be clear already that biography was not a static or homogeneous kind of literature in antiquity. There were numerous kinds of biographies and several ways of presenting them approximating a continuum. No one kind was a clear favorite. However, only the "great" man could ever expect to have his biography recorded and generally not until after his death. He would usually be presented as either an exemplary statesman or a spiritual master.

The variety of organizational techniques evident in ancient biography also illustrates the diversity and fluidity of the genre. In general, biographies are found in one of three external patterns: an individual biography (*Apollonius, Demonax, Agricola, Memorabilia*), as one of a pair of biographies of similar men (Plutarch, Nepos), or as one of a series of biographies or a line of succession of great men (Diogenes Laertius, Suetonius). Paired and successive schemes are combined in both Nepos and Plutarch, and Philo wrote several individual biographies (of Abraham, Joseph, and Moses). Plato's exercise of writing a series of biographical works on one man is an anomaly. It should be noted that parallel and serial biographies exhibit strict formal similarities; they are written according to a common formula or pattern. Plutarch even goes so far as to add a separate section in which he compares his two parallel subjects.

Internally, biographies follow one of two distinct patterns: most are organized chronologically (typified by Tacitus), but some are organized thematically with collections of anecdotes designed to illustrate a particular aspect of the subject (typified by Suetonius, a contemporary of Tacitus).[22] These divisions are not absolute, since most ancient biography is anecdotal. Even Suetonius includes a rough chronological framework from birth to death. Lucian's *Demonax*, which is almost entirely anecdotal, still begins with a reference to his birth and ends describing how he died. Philo is unusual in that his *Life of Moses* consists of two books, the first of which is chronological, following the order of the biblical sources, and the second of which is thematic, exploring the meaning of Moses as king, lawgiver, priest, and prophet.

The combination of chronological and thematic approaches is typical of most ancient biographies. They focus on the character of the subject in his mature years and do not attempt a complete telling of his life. Only rarely is the story of the birth recounted (Apollonius and Moses) although some general comments on ancestry (Nepos, Philo, Plutarch, Tacitus, Suetonius, Diogenes Laertius) and a reference or so to his youth in a way that signifies his future greatness are often given (Philo, Plutarch, Tacitus, Suetonius, Philostratus, sometimes Diogenes Laertius and Nepos; even Lucian speaks of several tendencies evident in Demonax's youth).

Aside from such brief references (usually no more than one or two pages) the rest of the biography normally focuses on the public career of the subject. This material may be organized in brief, unified presentations (as in Diogenes Laertius, 54–1,600 lines each), in lengthy unified accounts (as in Philo, ca. 4,500 lines), in a unified account with many digressions and anecdotes (as in Philostratus, ca. 12,000 lines),[23] or in loosely knit thematic accounts (as in Lucian, ca. 600 lines, or Suetonius, ca. 2,100 lines).

Most typically, this material is presented in the third person, from the point of view of a reporter, with some introduction of person narration (Tacitus, Xenophon). If there is a preface it is regularly in the first person (Nepos, Philo, Plutarch). Direct dialogue (Plato, Xenophon, Diogenes Laertius) and direct speech of characters within a story (Lucian, Philostratus) are also regularly found.

In summary, while general tendencies in the organization of biographies can be discerned, the great variety of techniques indicates the vitality and range of the genre. Yet in each case there is little doubt that one is reading "the same sort of literature."

While interrelated, a writer's purpose (e.g., apologetic, exemplary, laudatory, philosophical, legitimating) and aesthetic intent (dramatic, pedagogic, entertaining) can be separated for analytical purposes. To speak metaphorically, the former refers to the content of the purpose, the latter to its form. The aesthetic intent represents the use of a certain literary mode to accomplish a certain purpose. The interaction of purpose and aesthetic intent can be traced to the origins of classical biography. Biography probably grew out of the encomium, a speech praising a famous person, as well as out of collected letters and sayings.[24] Though the evidence available is short of proof, there is no denying the laudatory nature of the early biographies, and of many of the later ones as well.

The early Socratics developed the potentials of the biography, although the origins of the genre are probably older. Neither Plato nor Xenophon wrote a "Biography of Socrates," but both Plato's first tetralogy (the *Euthyphro*, the *Apology*, the *Crito*, and the *Phaedo*; see Diogenes Laertius 3.57) and Xenophon's *Memorabilia* (better: memoirs) are biographical and stand recognizably at the source of the genre. Both works sprang from a similar purpose: to rescue the memory of their teacher from the slander of their contemporaries (as Xenophon begins, "I have often wondered by what arguments those who drew up the indictment against Socrates could persuade the

Athenians that his life was forfeit to the state" [*Memorabilia* 1.1]). Further, both strive for a similar literary intent: they engage the reader in their story so that not only the mind but also the emotions are challenged. They chose a dramatic form, a subtle blend of fact and fiction (though Plato is a far better dramatist than Xenophon, who occasionally stoops to lecturing the reader). This combination of the author's involvement with the subject on the one hand and with the reader on the other makes for lively and entertaining reading. It is characteristic of much, probably the majority of ancient biography, although in varying degrees. In addition to Plato and Xenophon, such dramatic presentation is found in Philo, Tacitus, Philostratus and—to a lesser degree—in Plutarch and Lucian. It may be contrasted with the sterile, encyclopedic approach of Diogenes Laertius, whose purpose seems almost wholly pedagogic (in the worst connotations of that word). This variation in aesthetic mode seems to correlate with variation in purpose. The most dramatic presentations intend to praise and defend the subject, the less dramatic intend to present a subject worthy of imitation, the least dramatic intend only to explore the subject, with little or no concern for moral examples. These should be thought of as a continuum rather than as isolated categories. Suetonius, for example, is somewhere between Diogenes Laertius and Philostratus, somewhat entertaining, somewhat scientific.[25]

Once again, we observe wide variation within the genre, but in this case, it was so wide that we sometimes found ourselves asking as we read if this is really the same sort of literature as that. This was especially so in reading Diogenes Laertius, whose biographies lack the living dynamic of the other works.

Authors of biography in antiquity incorporated a wide range of intellectual and aesthetic intents; they were not necessarily averse to infringing on the territory of some of the generic neighbors of biography. We have already noted the way Philostratus, in *Life of Apollonius*, drew upon some of the themes and techniques of the romance. On the other side, so to speak, biographers at times had to usurp the prerogatives of historians (as in *Agricola*). Several biographers felt enough compunction for this transgression to explain to the reader both the theoretical distinction between history and biography and their practical need to blur the distinction.

Plutarch, in his pair *Alexander* and *Caesar*, apologizes for not telling all of their deeds. This is not possible, he says, because he is writing lives, not histories. He asserts that some deeds manifest nothing at all about the character of a person. His analogy is self-explanatory: "Accordingly just as painters get the likenesses in their portraits from the face and the expression of the eyes, wherein the character shows itself, so must I be permitted to devote myself rather to the signs of the soul in men, and by means of these to portray the life of each, leaving to others the descriptions of their great contests" (*Alexander* 1.2, 3).

Nepos also differentiates between biography and history in his lives of the *Great Generals*. Speaking of a general who was apparently little known to the general public, he tells us, "I am in doubt how to give an account of his merits; for I fear that if I undertake to tell of his deeds, I shall seem to be writing a history rather than a biography; but if I merely touch upon the high points, I am afraid that to those unfamiliar with Grecian literature it will not be perfectly clear how great a man he was" (*Pelopidas* 16.1.1). Accordingly, history would seem to imply a somewhat complete account of a man's deeds, while biography uses only the deeds that demonstrate the character of the man—as Plutarch said, the face and eyes rather than the whole body. While this distinction is valid and useful, the very fact that these writers had to assert it indicates the tendency of biography and history to converge. Cicero, for example, urged a writer of some ability to write a history of his consulship, because "I am seized with the hope of immortality in the praises of the age to come" (*Letter to Lucceius*). While there is a different focus, there is also much overlap between history and biography. A biography like Tacitus's *Agricola* contains a good deal of historical information about Britain (e.g., 10-17); however, the basic intent is still different. The basic intent of all biography is to reveal the sort of person the subject is—his character—as perceived by the biographer (see also Polybius 10.24).

This same point is made by Talbert in his attempt to differentiate biography, history, and romance. He concludes: "In antiquity, history was concerned with a man's place in the process of political and social events. Biography was interested in the individual's character, his involvement in a historical process being important only insofar as it reveals his essence."[26] This fundamental concern of biography to present the essence of the man leads us to the heart of the genre. Whether it is presented romantically or historically, dramatically or prosaically, to defend, praise, or reveal true teaching, the center of biography is the man—the great general, the superior statesman, the pious philosopher, or the religious leader. Their lives may be presented singly, in pairs, or in series; organized chronologically or topically; objectively evaluated or artfully embellished. Yet when we finish reading a biography, we should feel we have come to know the very essence of an outstanding person.

These considerations bring us to the matter of the gospels. How does Luke-Acts appear to be related to the genre of biography when analyzed in these same terms?

The Conventions of Luke-Acts

Luke-Acts is both like and unlike the kinds of biography written in the ancient world. Classified by type of hero, Luke-Acts is closest to Philo among the works surveyed, although there are some correlations with the biographies of the philosophers, especially when such philosophers are regarded as religious figures (e.g., *Apollonius of Tyana*). But even here there is a difference that is often commented upon: Luke's hero does not already have a status in the culture as a superior or noble person. By class, he is a commoner, and commoners were not thought worthy of literary attention. It may be answered, however, that Luke does not present him as a commoner, and the birth stories and genealogy imply a person of social standing. We would never guess from Luke's gospel that Jesus was a carpenter.

Another difference involves the extent to which these works focus on the hero. Philo begins by declaring that he intends to write a *bios* of Moses (1.1); Philostratus has a typically lengthy preface but then focuses exclusively on Apollonius (1.1–4). In contrast, Luke calls his work "a narrative (*diēgēsis*) of the things which have been accomplished among us" (Luke 1:1; but see Acts 1:1). He begins with the birth of John the Baptist and carries the story well beyond the death of Jesus. We will deal with the organization of the work below; here we note only the lack of focus on the hero, which places Luke in some tension with other biographies.

We noticed that various kinds of biography exhibited corresponding kinds of language; ancient biographers attempted to tell their stories in language appropriate to the subject. It has long been observed that Luke's speeches are examples of such use of language, but only recently has it been suggested that his whole work is built on a principle of appropriate language. In general, Luke's style corresponds to his geography and shifts from Semitic (Septuagintal) to classical in the course of his work.[27] Especially in his birth stories, Luke seems consciously to imitate Septuagintal style. This imitation suggests that Luke saw these stories as somehow parallel to the biblical stories and opens another avenue of exploration not pursued here: the genre affinity of Luke-Acts with prophetic biographies in the Hebrew scriptures.[28]

Viewed from the perspective of the hero, Luke has chosen a person whom he deemed suitable for biographical treatment and seems consciously to have adapted his language to his character in a biographical style. However, he does not seem to focus as exclusively on Jesus as would be typical in a biography. Still, we would conclude that Luke-Acts is enough like other biographies of religious figures to warrant further investigation in terms of its organization and purpose.

Luke-Acts does not fit neatly into any of the external organizational patterns we found in classical biographies. The existence of Acts prevents us from considering it a biography of one person. Nor do we have paired biographies in the manner of Plutarch. While some patterns of parallel action exist, there is nothing like the common formula that shapes the works of Plutarch and Nepos. More obviously, there is simply no biography of either Peter or Paul, the two protagonists of Acts. This fact also raises doubts about seeing Luke-Acts as a series of biographies in the manner of Diogenes Laertius. A series of biographies must be expected to treat each subject on his own, which simply does not happen in Acts.

Unlike the biographies we read, Luke introduces characters simultaneously. Thus he interweaves the birth stories of John and Jesus (Luke 1–2) and inserts Paul into the same time frame as Peter (Acts 8–9). Even so, there is something like a succession: John is put in prison before Jesus begins his ministry (3:20); Jesus ascends to heaven before Peter begins his ministry (Luke 24 and Acts 1); and Peter is removed from the story (somewhat awkwardly, at 12:17) before Paul's ministry is told (13:2). It is not uncommon for a disciple to appear in his master's biography, but in a series such as Diogenes Laertius writes he would receive his own separate biography.

Only Talbert has suggested that a parallel exists between Lucan organization and that of classical biographies. He notes that Diogenes Laertius sometimes expands his biographies to include brief notes on the true disciples *within* the biography of a philosopher.[29] Although this phenomenon does not occur in each of Diogenes Laertius's biographies, it is common enough to be regarded as a formal component. Furthermore, it seems likely that this organization, in which information about disciples is included in the life of the founder, existed already in some of Laertius's sources and in such works as Hermippus's *Life of Aristotle*.[30] Thus, there is evidence for a fairly long-lived convention of biographical organization that includes disciples in their master's biography. Further, Talbert sees the *Life of Pachomius* as an example of the survival of this pattern in Christian circles.[31] Luke-Acts then appears to fit in a trajectory of a certain type of biography in which stories about the true disciples appear within a biography of the founder.

These are important observations and need to be more fully explored. There is, however, a serious problem of scale. In all the surviving examples of this organizational pattern the material about the disciples is very brief—often no more than a list of successors with perhaps an anecdote or two. Thus, Luke would represent a greatly expanded version of the note on the true disciples—in fact, it would rival the length of the original body.[32] Such an explanation for the existence of Acts seems possible, but not likely. We think it a more likely hypothesis that, in terms of the standard conventions of biography, Luke has compromised between this pattern and the patterns of paired and serial biographies. We have far too much material about Peter and Paul to regard it as a note within a biography of Jesus, yet the material about them cannot be seen as independent biographies. If this were so, it would have important implications for interpreting the work. It would also be the only example we have encountered from antiquity of such a synthesis of formal biographical patterns. At the very least, Luke seems to have stretched the genre.

This expanded presence of the disciples calls attention to a curious aspect of Luke-Acts: it does not seem that the author has much interest in developing the character of either Peter or Paul.[33] They are interesting not for their own sake, but rather for the part they play in the story. Here we see the analysis moving in two possible directions (1) viewing Acts as a biography of the church or (2) viewing Luke-Acts as a species of history. Both are projects to be pursued in the future.

Neither the internal organization nor the point of view presents any problem in relation to classical biographies. Luke's work is organized like most classical biography as basically chronological, with some thematic development, although his remarkable organization by geography (Galilee—journey—Jerusalem—journeys—Rome) is unparalleled in the works we read.[34] His use of first-person preface followed by a third-person narrative is typical. Presenting the material in dramatic form with direct speech is also common, as is the use of speeches. All of these features are reminiscent of classical biography.

Thus, Luke's inner organization relates closely to that of classical biography, but the overall structure of the work is not clearly in line with biography. It is possible that Luke synthesizes two genres, presenting biographical material within an overall historical-geographical structure. As we have seen in the cases of *Apollonius* and *Agricola*, biographies could be enriched by elements of romance and history; such a mixing of elements is not unlikely.[35] This kind of expansion would raise the question of which genre is primary, and this leads to the necessity of focusing clearly on Luke's central concern and purpose.

We have already expressed our reservation about viewing Luke-Acts as having the purpose of presenting the "true successors" of Jesus by means of a serial biographical work. When we turn from the purposes of biography to the concrete work of Luke-Acts and ask what its purpose is, our reservations increase. None of the standard commentators suggests such a purpose. Hans Conzelmann, the most influential modern commentator on Luke, sees Luke's purpose as presenting a new view of history, namely, that "the period of Jesus and the period of the church are . . . two distinct but systematically interrelated epochs."[36] While there are other purposes advanced, they are usually seen as subordinate to the purpose of presenting a certain view of history.[37] It is always possible that this dominant conclusion has been formulated without a consideration of the biographical nature of Luke-Acts, but it raises serious questions about the generic affinity of the work.

Let us try another approach. We spoke above of general aims such as apologetic (defending the reputation of a departed subject), exemplary (presenting the subject as a moral example), and laudatory (praising a great man). In these terms Luke-Acts seems apologetic, and such an apologetic motive has long been recognized. It has even been suggested that Acts was the brief prepared for Paul's trial![38] While this is untenable, the notion that Luke intends to defend "Christianity" from various slanders seems true. In fact, there seems to be a dual apology: Luke attempts to make Christians appear acceptable to Rome and Rome appear acceptable to Christians.

There is much at stake, however, in how we see this apologetic operating. Is Luke defending the character of Christianity? (In this case, the idea of a biography of the church makes sense.) Is he defending the character of Jesus, Peter, and Paul? (Then, clearly, we are dealing with biography.) Is he vindicating the Christian movement by detailing the unfolding of a certain pattern of history? (Thus, he would be writing some sort of history.) It is not easy to make a clear-cut case for any alternative. We could perhaps focus the question by asking whether Luke is attempting to sketch the character of a great man (or men) or whether he is telling a relatively complete story of men in relation to social movements. The answer seems to be neither and both. His historical concerns are not pervasive enough to be classified unambiguously in the genre history, but neither is his concern with character so clear as to elicit an immediate identification with biography.[39] It is perhaps best to see Luke operating with aspects of both genres. If we consider Luke's nexus between two cultures, Greek and Hebrew, this may be what we should expect.

Hebrew historiography is almost wholly person-oriented, although it can rarely be called biography. The story of the exodus is the story of Moses; the emergence of the nation is the story of David; the great catastrophe of the exile is the story of wicked kings. Here too we encounter the stuff of both history and biography. It is not our intention to point to the Pentateuch, Samuel, or Kings as the generic context of Luke-Acts; we suggest only that his apparent mixing of biographical technique and historical concern is probably best understood as inspired by his regard for the Hebrew scriptures and his social location at the intersection of two cultures.[40]

Finally, Luke's aesthetic mode is among the most dramatic of the biographies read. Like Plato he seeks to engage the readers/hearers with his subject, perhaps even to transform them. Recapitulating the gospel story in Acts, he has Peter call for this response:

> Repent and be baptized every one of you in the name of Jesus Christ for the forgiveness of your sins. (2:38)

This is literature at its most engaging, although the response goes beyond the aesthetic response called for by most biography. That Jesus is the subject of this proclamation (see Acts 2:22-38) would make biography a natural vehicle for expressing the Christian message.

Let us try to summarize our results. Reading and comparing representative examples of classical biography revealed both the great diversity of this genre and also the points of correlation. We chose those literary aspects of biographies that seemed to be generically important and compared them with Luke-Acts. We assumed that any specific work would exhibit both congruence with and dissimilarity from such a composite, but we have sought to construct the composite in full recognition of this diversity. We have found that on several points (kind of hero, appropriate language, internal organization, point of view, and to some extent aesthetic mode) Luke can be successfully related to biography. On other points serious questions arise (external organization, purposes, and to some extent aesthetic mode). The question of the genre of history and especially the question of the genre of prophetic biographies emerge at these points. While it is too much to conclude that the ancient readers/hearers of Luke-Acts would have understood it as biography, we believe the conclusion is warranted that they would have heard it with some of the same expectations with which they heard biographies.[41]

Thus, we think that Bultmann, in claiming that the gospels are not biographies, failed to take seriously the real similarities that the gospels share with classical biographies. This failure resulted largely from his use of nonliterary and limited means of comparison. While we are not ready to follow Talbert, especially in regard to Luke-Acts, we hope that we have shown that the systematic use of literary data raises the right questions. In raising these questions, we believe we have moved closer to an understanding of the gospels in their original setting.

NOTES

[1] We will speak explicitly about this problem only in relation to the four canonical gospels. The distinction between various kinds of literature titled "gospels" was most fully explored in a working paper presented to the SBL Seminar on the Genre of the Gospels by Norman Petersen: "The So-called Gnostic Type Gospels and the Question of the Genre 'Gospel'," 1970. For the particular purposes of this study, we will focus on Luke-Acts. We begin by presupposing that the work known as "Luke-Acts" is one literary work written in two books. While their unity is still debated in some quarters, the judgment of H. J. Cadbury holds: "They are not merely two independent writings from the same pen; they are a single continuous work" (*The Making of Luke-Acts* [1927; reprint, Naperville, IL: Allenson, 1958] 8-9).

[2] For the literature through 1970 see C. W. Votaw, *The Gospels and Contemporary Biographies in the Greco-Roman World* (1915; reprint, Philadelphia: Fortress, 1970). More recent literature is cited in R. H. Gundry, "Recent Investigations into the Literary Genre 'Gospel'," in *New Dimensions in New Testament Studies* (Grand Rapids: Zondervan, 1974); Howard Clark Kee, *Jesus in History: An Approach to the Study of the Gospels* (New York: Harcourt Brace Jovanovich, 1977); and David Aune, "The Problem of the Genre of the Gospels: A Critique of C. H. Talbert's *What Is a Gospel?*" in *Gospel Perspectives: Studies of History and Tradition in the Four Gospels*, Vol. 2 (ed. R. T. France and D. Wenham; Sheffield: JSOT, 1981).

[3] Kee is correct in recognizing an apologetic motive in this designation (*Jesus in History*, 136-38); however, he fails to see the importance of Justin's designation. Here is a well-educated Gentile, familiar with the first-century literary milieu in a way we will never be, who tells us the kind of literature he sensed was most like the gospels. The question is not Is Mark a memoir of Peter? but Is it *like* a memoir? It is a literary rather than a historical inquiry.

[4] *Life of Jesus* (1863; reprint, New York: Modern Library, 1955) esp. xxxiii-xli.

[5] *The Gospels and Contemporary Biographies.*

[6] *History of the Synoptic Tradition* (1931; Eng. trans., Oxford: Blackwell, 1963) 374.

[7] Charles Talbert, *What Is a Gospel?* (Philadelphia: Fortress, 1977) 135.

[8] Northrop Frye, *Anatomy of Criticism: Four Essays* (New York: Atheneum, 1957) 13, and 246. The irony is captured in the opening lines of a recent book, *Theories of Literary Genre* (ed. J. P. Strelka; University Park: Pennsylvania State University Press, 1978): "Theories of genre are not only one of the oldest, but also one of the most genuinely literary principles of order in literary studies. There seems, however, to be little agreement on how to use the concept of genre to create such order" (vii).

[9] Genre is not actually a "species" concept, as E. D. Hirsch pointed

out (*Validity in Interpretation* [New Haven: Yale University Press, 1967] 110), because it does not equate its members. It is rather a mental construct that relates similar objects on the basis of perceived similarities.

[10] Rene Wellek and Austin Warren, *Theory of Literature* (New York: Harcourt, Brace and World, 1956) 226.

[11] *Theory of Literature*, 235.

[12] See Roman Jakobson's communications model suggested by Norman Petersen in *Literary Criticism for New Testament Critics* (Philadelphia: Fortress, 1978) 38-48. Also see D. Patte's discussion concerning meaning as being imposed both by the author and by the cultural codes within which the author must operate (*What is Structural Exegesis?* [Philadelphia: Fortress, 1976] 21-25.

[13] Talbert, *What Is a Gospel?*, 2.

[14] Bultmann's vision of the gospels as the collections of believing communities seems to have influenced his ideas about literary genre. Talbert points to part of this problem, namely, community versus individual authors (*What Is a Gospel?*, 3).

[15] While Plato's early dialogues and Xenophon's *Memorabilia* predate the *bios* genre, they represent its beginnings and have had significant influence on the genre. See Arnoldo Momigliano, *The Development of Greek Biography: Four Lectures* (Cambridge: Harvard University Press, 1971).

[16] *Theory of Literature*, 231.

[17] A basic error of much genre criticism is to work at such a level of abstraction that two works sound alike even though they do not read alike. Some critics are able to convince themselves that Matthew belongs to the same genre as the *Manual of Discipline* (1QS) and the *Didache* because it is a "collection of community rules" (e.g., N. Petersen, "The So-called Gnostic Type Gospels and the Question of the Genre 'Gospel'," [unpublished working paper of the Society of Biblical Literature Seminar on the Genre of the Gospels, 1970] 27).

[18] On the oral mode of presentation see n. 2 above and Thomas Boomershine, "Mark the Storyteller: A Rhetorical-Critical Investigation of Mark's Passion and Resurrection Narrative," (Ph.D. diss., Union Theological Seminary, 1974) 7-9; idem, "Oral Tradition and Mark," (paper read at the Society of Biblical Literature annual meeting, 1979).

[19] By external criteria we mean those that result from comparing a work with something outside itself, even another work of the same sort. Internal criteria can be deduced solely from an analysis of the individual work.

[20] *What Is a Gospel?*, 94-96.

[21] These purposes may be correlated with Talbert's: philosophical includes what he calls "providing the hermeneutical key for the Teacher's doctrine" (*What Is a Gospel?*, 96) but also other attempts to present the reader with an idea to be accepted; apologetic includes both positive and negative endeavors (exposé); exemplary is the same; laudatory is an additional category for those works which intend to

praise without being either apologetic or exemplary.

[22]Duane Reed Stuart, *Epochs of Greek and Roman Biography* (Berkeley: University of California Press, 1928) 185-86.

[23]The great length of the *Life of Apollonius* and its many digressive tales and high adventures show kinship to another genre, the romance (or ancient novel). In fact Grant refers to it as a "religious romance" and Renan regarded it "as purely a romance," a view recently advocated by E. L. Bowie, "Apollonius of Tyana: Tradition and Reality," *Aufstieg und Niedergang der römischen Welt*, part II, 16/2 (Berlin and New York: de Gruyter, 1978) 1664. See also the recent dissertation of Thomas G. Knoles, "Literary Technique and Theme in Philostratus' *Life of Apollonius of Tyana*," (Rutgers University, 1981). Knoles calls it "semibiographical."

[24]See Momigliano, *Greek Biography*, 33-42; and Stuart, *Greek and Roman Biography*, 196-230.

[25]See, for example, *Augustus* 79.

[26]*What Is a Gospel?*, 16.

[27]Cadbury, *The Making of Luke-Acts*, 223-25; E. Haenchen, *The Acts of the Apostles: A Commentary* (Philadelphia: Westminster, 1971) 75.

[28]See R. E. Brown, "Jesus and Elijah," *Perspective* 12 (1971) 85-104; Eric Franklin, *Christ the Lord: A Study in the Purpose and Theology of Luke-Acts* (Philadelphia: Westminster, 1975) 177. M. G. Kline, "The Old Testament Origins of the Gospel Genre," *WTJ* 38 (1975) 1-27.

[29]*What Is a Gospel?*, 107-8; and more clearly in *Literary Patterns, Theological Themes, and the Genre of Luke-Acts* (SBLMS 20; Missoula: Scholars Press, 1974) 125-40.

[30]*Literary Patterns*, 130-31.

[31]Personal letter of 24 November 1982.

[32]As Talbert recognized (*Literary Patterns*, 131); his point seems to be that the formal pattern exists regardless of the scale.

[33]Indeed, Luke has only a modest interest in the character of Jesus. To say that Luke has little interest in Jesus would be an overstatement, but it would raise the issue of whether Luke intends to present us with Jesus-as-person or with Jesus-as-doer, that is, whether he intends to write biography or history.

[34]Cynthia King, of the Classics Department of Wright State University, has pointed out to us a parallel in Plutarch's Lives of *Alcibiades* and *Demetrius*, which are organized geographically.

[35]E. I. McQueen discusses mixed genres in Latin biographies in his essay "Quintus Curtis Rufus," in *Latin Biography* (ed. T. A. Dorey; London: Routledge and Kegan Paul).

[36]*The Theology of St. Luke* (New York: Harper & Row, 1961) 14.

[37]For example, Nils A. Dahl, "The Purpose of Luke-Acts" in *Jesus in the Memory of the Early Church* (Minneapolis: Augsburg, 1976) 87-98; H. H. Oliver, "The Lucan Birth Stories and the Purpose of Luke-Acts," *NTS* 10 (1963) 202-6; for a dissenting view see Franklin, *Christ the Lord*, 173ff.

[38]Johannes Munck, *The Acts of the Apostles* (AB 31; Garden City: Doubleday, 1967) LV-LVI.

[39]Vernon Robbins has done extensive comparisons of Luke's preface with those of histories and those of biographies and has concluded: "The oratorical and epistolary features in the Lucan prefaces are more common to biography than to historiography" ("Preface in Greco-Roman Biography and Luke-Acts," *Society of Biblical Literature 1978 Seminar Papers* [ed. P. J. Achtemeier; Missoula: Scholars Press, 1978] 2.207).

[40]H. A. Fischel's excellent study, "Martyr and Prophet": A Study in Jewish Literature (*JQR* 37 [1946-47] 265-80, 363-86) shows just this creative intermingling of themes between Greek and Jewish literature; see also Dieter Georgi's study *The Records of Jesus in the Light of Ancient Accounts of Revered Men* (Berkeley: Center for Hermeneutical Studies in Hellenistic and Modern Culture, University of California, 1973).

[41]Philip L. Shuler's new book, *A Genre for the Gospels: The Biographical Character of Matthew* (Philadelphia: Fortress, 1982), appeared too late to be considered in this essay. He shows some of the specific concerns, techniques, and expectations that relate Matthew to biography.

AUTHOR DATES	PLATO 429-347	XENOPHON 428-354	CORN. NEPOS 99-24
TITLE	1. *Apology* 2. *Crito* 3. *Phaedo*	*Memorabilia*	*Great Generals*
LANGUAGE	Greek	Greek	Latin
DATE	390	385	35
LENGTH	1. 1200 lns. 2. 600 lns. 3. 300 lns.	5700 lns.	4000 lns.
SOURCES	Phaedo claims to have been an eyewitness	Some personal recollection; no others mentioned	None recounted but does give variant versions of an incident
POINT OF VIEW	1. 1st person & dialogue 2. Dialogue 3. 3rd person & speech by characters	1st person with dialogue	Preface in 1st Account in 3rd
TYPE OF HERO	Wise man	Wise man	Military leaders of Greece and Rome
CHARACTER-IZATION	Superior man, teacher and philosopher	Superior man, teacher of practical ethics	Superior men of action
DIVINE TRAITS	None	None	None

AUTHOR DATES	PHILO 30-A.D. 45	"LUKE" 50-100?	PLUTARCH 50-120

TITLE	*Life of Moses*	Luke-Acts	*Lives:*
			    Demosthenes
			    Cicero

LANGUAGE	Greek	Greek	Latin
DATE	25 B. C.	90	100
LENGTH	4500 lns.	5400 lns.	3000 lns.
SOURCES	The sacred books which are "monuments of his wisdom" and the "sayings of the elders"	"Many other" narratives plus "eye witnesses & ministers of the word"	Some named; some used indirectly; "Stories are told," Some contradictions noted

POINT OF VIEW	Preface: 1st Account:
	    Book I-3rd
	    Book II-1st & 3rd
		Preface: 1st Account: 3rd
		    with speech
		    by characters
		    in the story
			Preface: 1st Account: 3rd

TYPE OF HERO	Wise and Godly man	Wise and Godly Man	Political leaders
CHARACTER- IZATION	Presented as king, priest, Lawgiver, prophet (not as teacher)	Son of God, teacher, agent of divine plan	Superior Orator, Counselor & patriot
DIVINE TRAITS	Marvelous birth, unusual death, miracles & foreknowledge	Virgin Birth, Resurrection, and Ascension, Miracles	Unusual birth

AUTHOR DATES	TACITUS 57-117	SUETONIUS 69-130	LUCIAN 125-180
TITLE	*Agricola*	*Lives of the Caesars: Augustus*	*Demonax*
LANGUAGE	Latin	Latin	Greek
DATE	100	120	165
LENGTH	1000 lns.	2100 lns.	600 lns.
SOURCES	Claims the authority of an eyewitness, "I remember"	Names sources and presents direct citations from their works	No sources mentioned; gives the impression of personal recollection
POINT OF VIEW	Largely 3rd but with some in 1st	3rd person	3rd per. with speech by characters in the story
TYPE OF HERO	Wise general	Ruler	Philosopher/ Wise man
CHARACTER-IZATION	Man of action & a statesman	Man of action, statesman, able administrator	Witty and clever
DIVINE TRAITS	None (death is told but is not narrated)	Minor: normal birth & death but with "report" of an apparition	None

AUTHOR DATES	LUCIAN 125-180	PHILOSTRATUS 175-245	D. LAERTIUS 250-300
TITLE	*Alexander the False Prophet*	*Apollonius of Tyana*	*Lives of Eminent Philosophers*
LANGUAGE	Greek	Greek	Greek
DATE	180	216	275
LENGTH	1000 lns.	1200 lns.	50-1600 lns. avg. = 200 lns. Total = 1600 lns.
SOURCES	Personal experience and the impression of personal recollection	Another biog. by Damis, a disciple of Apollonius. Plus his own research in places where A. traveled.	Many sources; some named, others alluded to. Some indirectly quoted
POINT OF VIEW	Preface: 1st per 3rd per. with speech by characters in the story	3rd per. with speech by characters in the story	3rd person with dialogue
TYPE OF HERO	False Prophet/ Villain	Philosopher/ Wise man	Philosophers
CHARACTER-IZATION	" . . . the most perfect rascal of all . . ." master of deception	A divine man of superior wisdom & power	Superior heads of schools
DIVINE TRAITS	Alexander claims divine relatives and miracles; author claims fraud.	Divine vision at birth; son of Proteus; precocious childhood; post-death appearances	None

AUTHOR DATES	PLATO 429-347	XENOPHON 428-354	CORN. NEPOS 99-24
TECHNIQUE	Detailed, fictionalized presentation of specific incidents Irony	Generalizations & illustrative incidents in dialogue— loosely organized by themes	"Historical" presentations of incidents from careers & surrounding political events; no dialogue
PATTERN	Development of a story	Interspersed narration & dialogue in 4 books; composed at different times	16 books in pairs: Foreign Greek/Roman
PURPOSE	To present the true Socrates; to clarify Socratic ideas	To present the true Socrates; to disprove disparaging reports	To present exemplary models from corresponding cultures
AESTHETIC INTENT	To capture the reader in a highly dramatic presentation	To convince the reader both intellectually & emotionally; used dramatic incidents	To involve the reader in an experience which is educational

AUTHOR DATES	PHILO 30–A.D. 45	"LUKE" 50–100?	PLUTARCH 50–120
TECHNIQUE	Book I: Chrono- logical. Book II: Thema- tic—Moses as King, Priest, Lawgiver & Prophet	"Historical" pre- sentation of 3 careers, only one developed from birth to death	Unified pre- sentations of person via incidents from birth to death
PATTERN	Two books	Two books con- taining inter- connected & somewhat parallel actions	Parallel presen- tations of the public careers of each with separate section comparing the two
PURPOSE	To make Moses known to worthy Greeks (apolo- getic)	To present a sympathetic & apologetic picture of Jesus & of early Christianity	To present exemplary models
AESTHETIC INTENT	To involve the reader in a dramatic and imaginative account	To maintain a certain view of history; to involve & move the reader in a very dramatic account	To involve the reader in a good story while remaining some- what objective & pedagogic

AUTHOR DATES	TACITUS 57-117	SUETONIUS 69-130	LUCIAN 125-180
TECHNIQUE	Unified account of his life & public career in basically chronologic manner	Collections of anecdotes illustrating some aspect of his life & character	Almost entirely anecdotal without much connection
PATTERN	Individual biography	One of a series of biographies only generally related to historical events and chronology	Individual biography
PURPOSE	To praise and defend the reputation of the subject	To praise & present an exemplary leader	To praise a leading philosopher & show his ironic/sarcastic world-view
AESTHETIC INTENT	To present the reader with the facts	To present the reader with a true, entertaining story (and a little gossip)	To entertain the reader with a clever account of a clever person

AUTHOR DATES	LUCIAN 125-180	PHILOSTRATUS 175-245	D. LAERTIUS 250-300
TECHNIQUE	Almost entirely anecdotal with some evidence of chronological arrangement	Basically chronological presentation of his life with many digressions, anecdotes, and travel narratives	Short chronological presentations with appended lists of publications and letters
PATTERN	Individual biography	Individual biography	Series of individual biographies of two lines of philosophers: Ionian & Italian in 10 Books
PURPOSE	To expose Alexander as a fraud and to show him as a deceitful character	To praise a favorite philosopher & please his patroness	To write a "history" of philosophy
AESTHETIC INTENT	To convince the reader by means of an educational and entertaining account	To present the reader with a charming, educational and entertaining account	To present the reader with a factual and educational account

PART II
THEMATIC STUDIES

Charles H. Talbert

PROMISE AND FULFILLMENT
IN LUCAN THEOLOGY

Since World War II the focus of Lucan research has shifted from the sources of Luke the historian to the point of view of Luke the theologian. Given the inadequacies of the Bultmann school's interpretation of Luke-Acts as the substitution of a history of salvation in three stages for an imminent End—a substitution that resulted from the pressures of a delayed Parousia—it is not surprising to find subsequent attempts to draw alternate descriptions of the Lucan achievement. One such alternative goes under the slogan "proof-from-prophecy" or "promise-fulfillment."[1] The purpose of this paper is twofold: first, briefly to describe this paradigm for viewing Luke-Acts; and, second, to raise three questions about it in an attempt to clarify issues and advance the discussion.

A Brief Description of the
Proof-from-Prophecy Perspective

One of the most forceful advocates of the fulfillment of prophecy paradigm for viewing Luke-Acts in recent years has been Robert Karris. Although he shows his awareness that the promise-fulfillment schema for Luke-Acts has advocates far and wide,[2] when he defines his own stance Karris says: "My position stands in line with the Yale professors—Paul Schubert, Paul Minear, Nils Dahl, and Luke Johnson —who view Luke-Acts from the perspective of promise and fulfillment."[3] He could very well have added to the list William Kurz, a recent graduate of Yale whose doctoral dissertation reflects this point of view.[4] The brief description that I will give of this position, therefore, will be based on three of Karris's Yale circle and on Karris himself.

Paul Schubert's article "The Structure and Significance of Luke 24," in the Bultmann Festschrift (1957), constitutes the origin of Karris's paradigm.[5] In this essay Schubert made two points: (1) Luke

24 is held together by the proof-from-prophecy motif, and (2) this motif is Luke's central theological idea throughout his two-volume work. Two observations about these theses need to be made. On the one hand, Schubert cannot understand the proof-from-prophecy theme to refer solely to the fulfillment of the Old Testament in the events of Jesus and his disciples. In Luke 24, although prophecy refers to the Old Testament in vv. 25-27, 32 and in vv. 44-47, in vv. 5-9 and in v. 44 prophecy refers to Jesus' own words uttered prior to his passion. On the other hand, the proof-from-prophecy theme is not the unifying element in *all* of Luke 24. Luke 24:50-53 has no promise-fulfillment component. This raises a question about its being *the* central theme of all of Luke-Acts.

Nils A. Dahl's contributions are located in two articles: "The Story of Abraham in Luke-Acts," in the Schubert Festschrift (1966),[6] and "The Purpose of Luke-Acts," in Dahl's collection of essays entitled *Jesus in the Memory of the Early Church* (1976).[7] Dahl's position, which explicitly acknowledges his agreement with Schubert, may be summarized in four points: (1) proof-from-prophecy is understood in terms of the fulfillment of the Old Testment only (a significant reduction); (2) it is deemed *a*, not *the*, main device of Luke (an instance of exemplary caution); (3) it is used in imitation of biblical historiography, where, for example, in the Pentateuch God's promise to the fathers and the fulfillment of it is *a*, or *the*, main theme (Dahl is cautious enough to point out that such a schema is not exclusively biblical but he does not explain why, if this is a general cultural device, he insists solely on Jewish roots for Luke); and (4) the motif functions in several ways—to establish historical continuity between the church and Israel so that the Gentile church is seen as the legitimate continuation of the Israel of old, to guarantee that all the promises as yet unfulfilled will be, to give certainty that what has happened has occurred according to the will of God, and to marshal the argument from antiquity on the Christian's side. One may note Dahl's commendable awareness of a multiplicity of functions of the passages in which there is a fulfillment of Old Testament promises, including one which takes into account the Lucan milieu—the argument from antiquity.

Luke Johnson's *The Literary Function of Possessions in Luke-Acts* (1977)[8] recognizes that the proof-from-prophecy literary pattern includes prophetic words both from the Old Testament and from Jesus, though his emphasis is on the former. Further, fulfillment of the Old Testament functions, he thinks, in the interests of giving certainty that the Gentile church was in continuity with ancient Israel. One must note here the constriction of functions over against Dahl's contribution.

Robert Karris's contributions may be found in two places: the popular *What Are They Saying About Luke and Acts* (1979)[9] and "Missionary Communities: A New Paradigm for the Study of Luke-Acts," *CBQ* 41 (1979) 80-97. Three points summarize Karris's contribution: (1) proof-from-prophecy means the theme of the fulfillment of the Old Testament; (2) promise-fulfillment is Luke's basic theology, but he, like a pastoral theologian, does not solve all problems of faith in a consistent way from this perspective (for example, in Luke 9:51-19:44 one must use a magnifying glass to find this theology); (3) it functions both in a debate with Jews to guarantee continuity in the church's relation with Israel of old and in an attempt to instill hope for the fulfillment of yet unrealized promises in persecuted missionary communities. Like Dahl and Johnson before him, Karris understands proof-from-prophecy to mean essentially fulfillment of the Old Testament promises. Like them, he views the schema as functioning to establish historical continuity between the church and Israel and, like Dahl, as a guarantee of future fulfillment of as yet unrealized promises.

These brief comments may suffice as a sketch of the promise-fulfillment model for understanding Luke-Acts. It is now necessary to turn to three questions that may be addressed to the representatives of this position.

Questions for Discussion

1. Most of the discussion about proof-from-prophecy theology in Luke-Acts has, in my opinion, suffered from a lack of precision with reference to the data about which one is talking. The first question, therefore, is: What data is one talking about when one speaks of proof-from-prophecy theology in Luke-Acts?

a. On the one hand, not all references and allusions to the Old Testament in Luke-Acts fall into the promise-fulfillment schema, a point made against Schubert convincingly by Martin Rese in 1969.[10] Luke does not use the Jewish scriptures only in a promise-fulfillment pattern. (1) John Kilgallen speaks of the same thing that Rese calls Luke's "hermeneutical use of scripture" when he shows how in Acts 7 the event of Jewish opposition to Christ is put against past history to show it is *like* that of Jewish ancestors through the generations.[11] Although the Old Testament is the light by which one is enabled to read the event, this is not a promise-fulfillment schema. Behavior in the present is *like* this or that scriptural behavior in the past. (2) Luke 7:11-17 tells the story of Jesus' raising the widow's son at Nain so as to echo the experience of Elijah in 1 Kings 17 and of Elisha in 2 Kings 4. This is what Rese calls a "typological use of the Old Testament." In Luke 9:52-56 the story of Jesus' rejection by a Samaritan village is told in language that makes it an antitype of 2 Kings 1. Again, although the Old Testament sheds light on the gospel story, this is not a promise-fulfillment pattern. (3) In Luke 2:23-24 the parents of Jesus obey the legal demands of the Old Testament law. Here, although the Old Testament is fulfilled, it is a legal demand and not a promise that is actualized. In this connection it is important to see that the divine *dei* in Luke-Acts, which expresses the will of God, refers not only to the course of holy history (Luke 4:43; 9:22; 13:33; 17:25; 19:5; 22:37; 24:7, 26, 44; Acts 1:16; 1:21-22; 3:21; 19:21; 23:11; 27:24) but also to God's expectations for human behavior (Luke 2:49; 11:42; 18:1; 22:7; Acts 4:12; 5:29; 9:6, 16; 14:22; 15:5; 16:30; 20:35).[12] If Luke pictures Jesus as knowledgeable about the course of holy history, he also depicts him as aware of the divine will in matters of conduct, even at points where it differs from the understanding of Jewish officialdom (Luke 13:14, 16).[13] The important thing to remember, for our purposes, is that fulfillment of the divine *dei* in Luke-Acts means fulfillment both of the prophetic promise and of the ethical demand. The latter, however, is not a promise-fulfillment schema. (4) Now it is certainly true that in passages like Luke 4:16-21; 22:37; Acts 13:23, 27-29, 33 we do find a clear-cut promise-fulfillment pattern. For the sake of clarity, however, one must recognize that Luke's use of the Jewish scriptures does not always fit into the promise-fulfillment category.

b. On the other hand, the proof-from-prophecy pattern in Luke-Acts cannot be reduced to the theme of the fulfillment of the Old Testament promise. It includes not only (1) the fulfillment of a specific Old Testament prophecy (e.g., Luke 4:16-21; Acts 13:23, 27-29, 33) but also (2) the fulfillment of a prophecy given by a heavenly being, whether an *angel* (Luke 1:13-17 fulfilled in 1:57-66; 1:26-37 fulfilled in 1:39-44 and 2:1ff.; 2:8-12 fulfilled in 2:15-20; Acts 27:23-24 fulfilled in 27:44b and 28:14b) or the *risen Christ* (Luke 24:48-49 and Acts 1:8 fulfilled in the rest of Acts), and in addition (3) the fulfillment of an oracle uttered by a living prophet, whether *Jewish* (Luke 1:67-79 fulfilled in 3:1-20 and 7:24-27) or *Jesus* (Luke 9:22, 44 and 18:31-33 fulfilled in chapters 22-24; 11:13 fulfilled in Acts 2; 12:11-12 fulfilled in Acts 5:29; 13:35b fulfilled in 19:38; 22:10-12 fulfilled in 22:13; 22:34 fulfilled in 22:61) or a *Christian* (Acts 11:27-28a fulfilled in 11:28b; 20:23 and 21:10-11 fulfilled in 21:27ff.). This says at the very least that the function of a proof-from-prophecy motif is broader than showing continuity between the church and Israel, though it may be that as well. If Jesus, for example, both prior to Easter and afterwards told of things to come and if some of these are shown in the Lucan narrative to be fulfilled, then surely there is confidence that the as yet unfulfilled ones will also be realized. Further, if Jesus knows the divine will as it relates to the unfolding of holy history—as is demonstrated by the fulfillment of his promises—then it seems reasonable to believe that he also knows the divine will about what God expects in the area of human conduct. The fulfillment of prophecies made by the Lucan Jesus, then, would in part be legitimation for his parenetic discussions (e.g., Luke 9:51-19:44, with which Karris has difficulty).

To sum up the import of the first question: one needs to be clear about the data designated by a proof-from-prophecy label. The data are broader than the fulfillment of the Old Testament and not all Lucan uses of the Jewish scriptures fit into a promise-fulfillment pattern.

2. The second question for the proof-from-prophecy school is: Can the inference from *what* Luke says to *why* he said it be made as facilely as is apparently assumed? Specifically, can the proof-from-prophecy motif in Luke-Acts be used to infer that the Lucan community was troubled exclusively by a Gentile Christian preoccupation about establishing links with ancient Israel and its promises?

a. In the first place, not all examples of the promise-fulfillment schema are concerned with continuity in holy history. Without trying to be exhaustive, consider several examples. (1) Acts 18:9-10 tells of a vision of Paul in which the risen Lord appears to him and tells him: "Do not be afraid, but speak and do not be silent; for I am with you, and no man shall attack you to harm you; for I have many people in this city." The promise is fulfilled in 18:12-17 when Gallio refuses to be a party to the Jews' attack on Paul. This emphasizes the divine protection of the Christian missionary.[14] It does not point to continuity between the church and Israel in holy history but rather to the confidence the Christian may have when Jesus promises him protection. (2) In Acts 27:23-25 an angel of God appears to Paul to promise him that he will not perish in the storm at sea nor will those with him. This is fulfilled in the verses that follow. Again this promise-fulfillment schema serves to reassure the Christian that what God says to his children in hard times he will do. (3) In Acts 20:23 and 21:11 there are prophecies about Paul's coming imprisonment in Jerusalem, which happens in Acts 21ff. These prophecies do not demonstrate the continuity in salvation history but rather serve as concrete reinforcements of the specific *didachē* given in Acts 14:22 about the nature of the Christian life ("through many tribulations we must enter the Kingdom of God"). The Christian life will include suffering. Here the promise-fulfillment schema functions parenetically to instruct about Christian life in the world. (4) It is in the same way that one should read Acts 11:27-30 and 12:25. The prophecy about the famine allows the Christians in Antioch to act as

Jesus says they should in Acts 20:35: "It is more blessed to give than to receive." While, therefore, certain passages in Acts (e.g., Acts 13:16-41) clearly function to demonstrate the continuity of Jesus and his cause with Israel's history, there are others with a prophecy-fulfillment schema that do not have this function at all. Restraint is needed in inferring an occasion.

b. In the second place, it seems futile to try to determine the Lucan intent in his use of a promise-fulfillment pattern apart from a knowledge of the Lucan cultural context, which will allow one to hear what is said the way the original hearers would have heard it. A literary critic works with three entities: the text and what it says, the author and the author's intention, and the readers/hearers of the text and how they would have perceived what it said. The critic uses as many of these as possible to uncover the original meaning of the text. The New Testament scholar can uncover the theme of promise-fulfillment in Luke-Acts. There is, however, no direct way into the intent of the author. Indirectly the scholar may approach the matter of why Luke wrote in terms of a prophecy-fulfillment theme by concentrating on how the readers would have understood what was being said to them. This, of course, requires some knowledge of the Mediterranean world in antiquity.

It is now necessary to take the major components of Luke's motif and ask how a Mediterranean person would likely have heard the Lucan presentation. The motif may be divided into three components for the sake of analysis: (1) the divine necessity that controls the course of history; (2) the idea that history's course fulfills oracles, both written and oral, either through human beings' understanding or misunderstanding of them; and (3) the functions of a prophecy-fulfillment schema.

(1) The notion that a divine necessity controls human history, shaping the course of its events, was a widespread belief in Mediterranean antiquity. (a) Polybius (b. 208 B.C.) saw early in his career that Roman power was irresistible. A Stoic, he believed that the Roman order of things was part of a divine providence that ruled the world. This belief he expounded in his *Histories*.[15] In 1.4.1-2 he says: "Fortune (*hē tychē*) having guided almost all the affairs of the world in one direction and having forced them to incline towards one and the same end, a historian should bring before his readers under one synoptical view the operations by which she has accomplished her general purpose." (b) Josephus shared in this cultural belief, but as a Jew he viewed the divine necessity as deriving from the personal will of God who is a living person and not a neutral necessity. So in *Antiquities* 10.8.2-3 §142 he tells of Jeremiah's prophecy of the fall

of Jerusalem being fulfilled and says that these events manifest the nature of God, "which foretells all which must (*dei*) take place, duly at the appointed hour." Pagan and Hellenistic Jew alike thought of history's unfolding according to a divine necessity or compulsion that could be expressed in terms of *dei* or *deon esti*. A Jew would have heard it in terms of his belief in a personal deity, but the cultural context was agreed that history unfolded according to a divine necessity. It was in these terms that Luke's language about the *dei* of events would have been heard.[16]

(2) The idea that history's course fulfills oracles, whether oral or written, was also a cultural commonplace. Three examples from the pagan world will give one a feel for that segment of the culture. (a) Lucian's *Alexander the False Prophet* tells of one Alexander who wanted to start a new religion. As a first step to this end, he and a companion went to Chalcedon and buried bronze tablets which stated that in the near future Asclepios and his father, Apollo, would migrate to Pontus. These tablets were found, and as a result the people set about building a temple. Alexander, dressed like Perseus, then went to Abonutichus, declaiming an oracle which said he was a scion of Perseus. A sibylline prophecy of his activity was then produced. As a result of two written prophecies and one oral prophecy the stage was set. A new religion could emerge. (b) Suetonius's *Life of Vespasian* contains a section of omens that prophesy his ascendancy to emperor. Among these references are not only Josephus's declaration that he would soon be released by the same man who would then be emperor but also mention of antique vases dug up by soothsayers which had on them an image of Vespasian. (c) Apuleius's *Golden Ass* moves to its climax with Lucius trapped in the form of a donkey as a result of his experimentation with magic. Despairing over his plight, he cries out to Isis to save him. The goddess appears to him by night and gives an oracle (11.7). The next day Lucius does exactly as Isis has said. He eats the roses that are a part of the procession in Isis's honor and is miraculously changed back into a human being. Having been saved from his fate, Lucius is initiated into the Isis cult. He says, "I was not deceived by the promise made to me" (11.13). In all three of these pagan examples the fulfillment of the oracle legitimates the religious or political authority of the person referred to by the prophecy or the god who gave it. In the strict sense, this is proof-from-prophecy. What happened was in line with what the divine realm had revealed before the fact.

Three examples from the Jewish milieu should also suffice. (a) The Deuteronomic history (Deuteronomy through 2 Kings) uses the device of prophecy and fulfillment. For example, in Deuteronomy 28 Moses says that if Israel does not keep the covenant and obey the commandments, then she will go away into exile (vv. 25, 36-37). In 2 Kings 17 the northern kingdom falls to the Assyrians and the Israelites are taken into bondage. Verse 7 says the exile was because of Israel's sins; v. 23 says what was done was "as the Lord spoke by all his servants the prophets." In 2 Kings 25 the southern kingdom is taken away into Babylonian exile. Moses' prophecy in Deuteronomy 28 about what would happen if Israel proved disobedient is shown to have been fulfilled in the subsequent narrative of 2 Kings. This in effect legitimates the other things Moses said in Deuteronomy about how Israel should live. (b) At Qumran one finds a religious community that believed its own history was the fulfillment of the prophecies of the Jewish scriptures. In the commentaries on Isaiah, Micah, Psalm 37, and especially Habakkuk, there are statements of their position. When they interpret the prophets and the Psalms as prophecies that are fulfilled in the wickedness of Qumran's enemies and in the righteousness of Qumran's covenanters, they are saying not only that the time of fulfillment has come but also that they are the heirs of the promises of Israel, the true people of God. This is in effect an argument for the continuity of their community with Israel of old. (c) In his *Antiquities* Josephus uses the motif of prophecy and its fulfillment as evidence for the providence of God (2.16.5 §333).[17] In 8.4.2 §§109-10 the fact that the prophecy of David was fulfilled makes clear the providence of God. In 10.11.7 §§278-81 the fulfillment of Daniel's prophecies of the destruction of Jerusalem by Antiochus IV Epiphanes and the Romans is said to demonstrate God's providence (against the Epicureans). The pattern of prophecy-fulfillment in the history of Israel constitutes evidence for belief in a providential God. The providence of God, moreover, consists primarily in his rewarding of virtue and punishing of vice.

It was also a part of the Mediterranean mind-set that viewed history as the fulfillment of oracles to hold that an oracle could be misunderstood as well as understood. The very act of misunderstanding could be the means by which the prophecy was fulfilled. Herodotus's *History* is a storehouse of examples.[18] The classic example is his story of Croesus, who, after acknowledging the Delphic oracle to be the only true place of divination, asked it if he should send an army against the Persians. The oracle replied that if he should send an army, he would destroy a great empire. Mistaking the meaning of the oracle, Croesus went to war against the Persians and lost. Sending his chains to Delphi, Croesus asked if it were the manner of the Greek gods to be thankless. The priestess replied that the oracle was right. Croesus should have sent to ask whether the god spoke of Croesus's or Cyrus's empire. "But he understood not that which was spoken, nor made further inquiry: wherefore now let him blame himself" (1.91). When Croesus received the answer, he confessed that the sin was not the god's but his own. The similarity of this way of thinking to Acts 13:27 would not be lost on Luke's original hearers: "those who live in Jerusalem and their rulers, because they did not understand the utterances of the prophets which are read every sabbath, fulfilled these by condemning him." Whether Luke's community was composed of former Jews or pagans—or both—his original hearers would have found no surprises in the theme of history's course being determined by the fulfillment of prophecies.

(3) The functions of a prophecy-fulfillment theme in the Mediterranean world match up remarkably well with what one finds in Luke-Acts. (a) As the pagan evidence showed, prophecy made by a person or about a person, when fulfilled, legitimated the individual's religious or political status. It could evoke conversion to the one whose promise was kept. This is the function for which the expression "proof-from-prophecy" should be used. It is in this way that some prophetic utterances are used in Luke-Acts (for example, prophecy made *by* Jesus, when fulfilled, legitimates his authority—Luke 9:22 fulfilled in chapters 22-24; Luke 11:13 fulfilled in Acts 2; Luke 12:11-12 fulfilled in Acts 5:29, etc.; prophecy made *about* Jesus, when fulfilled, legitimates him—Luke 1:31 fulfilled in 1:42 and 2:7, 21, etc.).

(b) As the evidence from the Deuteronomic history showed, a prophetic promise, when fulfilled, can serve to legitimate the other things that the prophet has said. Just so, when Jesus predicts the destruction of the temple (Luke 13:35a; 21:6) and the capture of Jerusalem by the Gentiles (19:43-44; 21:20-24; 23:28-31) and Luke's readers know of the events of A.D. 70, or when the risen Lord predicts the Gentile mission (Luke 24:47; Acts 1:8) and Luke's readers are told of the progress of the gospel to Rome, these fulfilled words function to give authority to the other things Jesus says, like his parenetic sayings of 9:51-19:44.

(c) As the evidence from Qumran shows, the claim that one's particular history and that of one's founder fulfilled the prophecies of the Jewish scriptures argues not only for the arrival of the eschaton but also for one's continuity with the history of ancient Israel. As the heirs of the promises, Christians, Luke thinks, are the true descendants of Israel of old. The speech in Acts 13:16-41 seems especially emphatic in this regard. After a survey of Israel's history up through David, Paul is made to say: "Of this man's posterity God has brought to Israel a Savior, Jesus, as he promised" (v. 23). The events of Jesus' death (vv. 27-29) and resurrection (vv. 30-37) are then told as fulfillments of promises. The argument emphasizes the continuity between

Jesus and the history of ancient Israel as well as shows that his death and resurrection were in accord with the divine will. What has not been made clear to this point, however, is exactly how such an argument on behalf of continuity would have been heard by Greek-speaking people, whether Jews or pagans.

It was a cultural commonplace in the Hellenistic age for a people to try to trace its own origins back to the remotest antiquity (see Josephus, *Against Apion* 2.152; Diodorus 1.44.4; 1.96.2).[19] This was in large measure due to the Greek belief that what was most ancient was most valuable.[20] The Jews picked up the practice (note the parallels between Josephus's *Antiquities of the Jews* and the *Roman Antiquities* of Dionysius of Halicarnassus) and claimed that their writings were the oldest that existed. It was in terms of such a belief that the early Christian apologists built their arguments. Tertullian can say: "that is evidently more true which is earlier" (*Against Marcion* 4.5), or "I am accustomed, in my prescription against all heresies, to fix my compendious criterion of truth in the testimony of time; claiming priority therein as our rule, and alleging lateness to be the characteristic of every heresy" (*Against Marcion* 5.19), or "Our religion is supported by the writings of the Jews, the oldest which exist" (*Apology* 21). The line of continuity between Christians and Israel and between the events of Jesus' career and the Old Testament prophecies was important because it allowed the Christians to appeal to the argument from antiquity. This being the case, an emphasis on continuity between the Gentile church and Israel in Luke-Acts need not be regarded as an argument against Jews who had problems with Paul. It may very well have been an effort at consciousness-raising for Gentile Christians who needed to feel not the least bit inferior to pagans with their cultural and religious claims rooted in antiquity.

(d) The evidence from Josephus shows that the motif of prophecy-fulfillment in the history of Israel was used to provide evidence for the providence of God in human affairs, that is, that a personal God acts to reward virtue and punish vice. It seems, first of all, that the promises that no harm would come to Paul in Acts 18:9-10 and 27:23-24 and their fulfillment fit into this function. God cares for his own who work as missionaries. It seems, second, that this is how one should understand the perplexing focus on the resurrection in Acts 24:14-21. Paul said he believed everything written in the scriptures, among which was the belief in the resurrection. Since he believed what the scriptures taught about a future resurrection, he took pains to have a clear conscience toward God and humanity. This sounds as though the resurrection was understood as it was in intertestamental Judaism, namely, as a time of recompense for deeds done in the flesh, a time of settling accounts that have not been settled in this life. Since there would be such a time of accounting, Paul tried to keep his conscience clear. Since this was his aim, he brought alms, a virtuous act, to his nation and went purified into the temple, which was admirable. Paul acted virtuously because scripture promised a resurrection. To believe in the promise of the resurrection is, therefore, to believe in a providential God who punishes evil and rewards righteousness.

To sum up: It seems that in Luke-Acts the prophecy-fulfillment schema functions very much as it does in its Mediterranean milieu. Hearers of Luke-Acts would encounter no surprises as far as this motif is concerned, when they heard it in church. The complexity of the functions of the theme in both the Mediterranean milieu and in Luke-Acts, however, warns against too facile a move from what Luke says to some alleged occasion that prompts him to speak. For example, there is no justification for the claim that the prophecy-fulfillment motif in Luke-Acts functions to assist Gentile followers of Paul in their struggle with Jews.

3. The third question to be put to the proof-from-prophecy school is prompted by an assertion of Paul Minear: "We show our respect for an author only by recognizing both the coherence of his thought world as a whole and the significance within that world of each specific idea."[21] Is it possible, however, to explain Luke-Acts as a whole by the explication of one theme in it?

The usual procedure for redaction criticism has been to trace a theological theme through Luke-Acts and then, on the basis of the results, to infer an occasion for it. Problems arise (a) when one has to arbitrate among the many competing themes in the two-volume work and assign positions of relative importance to them, and (b) when one has to do an analogous thing for the proposed occasions. Redaction criticism has enabled us to see the author as a creative theologian with a perspective of his own and to discern parts of that point of view. It has not enabled us to discern the unity of the author's thought.

Though there can be no doubt that the theme of prophecy-fulfillment is a major one in Luke-Acts, it is certainly not the only one. It is doubtful, moreover, that it is *the* major one under which all else can be subsumed.[22] That this reservation has substance is reinforced by Robert Karris's admission that Luke does not solve all problems of faith in a consistent way from this perspective.[23] To say that Luke is a pastoral theologian and therefore may be inconsistent seems to beg the question. When all is said and done, this is but a euphemism for the old stance that the author is muddle-headed.

Thus, after a comprehensive delineation of the theme of prophecy and its fulfillment in the Lucan writings, one is left with the challenge of how to arbitrate among the various themes in Luke-Acts and decide which is central and which are derivative. Current redaction-critical methodology does not allow us to answer that question.

NOTES

[1] The emphasis is found in such sources as Jacques Dupont, "L'utilisation apologetique de l'ancien Testament dans les discours des Actes," *ETL* 29 (1953) 289-327; E. Lohse, "Lukas als Theologe der Heilsgeschichte," *EvT* 14 (1954) 256-75; S. Schulz, "Gottes Vorsehung bei Lukas," *ZNW* 54 (1963) 104-16; Christoph Burchard, *Der dreizehnte Zeuge* (Göttingen: Vandenhoeck & Ruprecht, 1970) 185; Karl Löning, *Die Saulustradition in der Apostelgeschichte* (Münster: Aschendorff, 1973); G. Schneider, "Zur Bedeutung von *kathexēs* im lukanischen Doppelwerk," *ZNW* 68 (1977) 128-31; D. L. Tiede, *Prophecy and History in Luke-Acts* (Philadelphia: Fortress, 1980); O. C. Edwards, *Luke's Story of Jesus* (Philadelphia: Fortress, 1981).

[2] Karris mentions F. Danker, *Luke* (Philadelphia: Fortress, 1976); and W. C. Robinson, Jr., "Acts," *IDB Supplementary Volume* (ed. K. Crim; Nashville: Abingdon, 1976) 9.

[3] Robert J. Karris, *What Are They Saying About Luke and Acts?* (New York: Paulist, 1979) 118-19.

[4] William S. Kurz, "The Function of Christological Proof from Prophecy for Luke and Justin" (Ph.D. diss., Yale, 1976).

[5] Paul Schubert, "The Structure and Significance of Luke 24," in *Neutestamentliche Studien für Rudolf Bultmann* (ed. W. Eltester; Berlin: Töpelmann, 1957) 165-86.

[6] N. A. Dahl, "The Story of Abraham in Luke-Acts," in *Studies in Luke-Acts: Essays presented in honor of Paul Schubert* (ed. L. E. Keck and J. L. Martyn; Nashville: Abingdon, 1966) 139-59.

[7] (Minneapolis: Augsburg, 1976) 87-98.

[8] (Missoula: Scholars Press, 1977).

[9] See n. 3.

[10] Martin Rese, *Alttestamentliche Motive in der Christologie des Lukas* (Gütersloh: Mohn, 1969) 134, 209.

[11] John Kilgallen, *The Stephen Speech* (Rome: Biblical Institute Press, 1976).

[12] *Dei* is found eight times in Matthew, six times in Mark, eighteen times in Luke, twenty-two times in Acts, and ten times in John. So Robert Morgenthaler, *Statistik des Neutestamentlichen Wortschatzes* (Frankfurt am Main: Gotthelf-Verlag, 1958) 86. On the importance of this term for Luke, see Schulz, "Gottes Vorsehung bei Lukas."

[13] W. Grundmann, "*dei*," *TDNT* 2. 21-25.

[14] That this is a point with which Luke is concerned is shown by

S. H. Kanda in his discussion of miracles of liberation in Acts ("The Form and Function of the Petrine and Pauline Miracle Stories in the Acts of the Apostles" [Ph.D. diss., Claremont, 1973]).

[15] H. J. Edwards, "Introduction to Polybius," in *Polybius: The Histories* (LCL; New York: Putnam, 1922) 1. vii-xvi.

[16] E. Haenchen (*The Acts of the Apostles: A Commentary* [Philadelphia: Westminster, 1971] 113) says Luke's tendency "smacks of that ineluctable destiny known to pagan belief."

[17] I am indebted here and later in my discussion of Josephus to H. W. Attridge, *The Interpretation of Biblical History in the Antiquitates Judaicae of Flavius Josephus* (Missoula: Scholars Press, 1976).

[18] E.g., Herodotus *History* 4.164, where, after giving the contents of the Delphic oracle to Arcesilaus, Herodotus tells how he acted wrongly and concludes: "So Arcesilaus whether with or without intent missed the meaning of the oracle and fulfilled his destiny" (i.e., his death). Jewish polemic against the pagan oracles emphasized the clarity of the Jewish prophecies. For example, *Midrash Rabbah* on Esther 3:14 says: "The prophecy of the nations of the world is ambiguous. . . . But the prophecy of Israel is clear" (see Saul Liebermann, *Hellenism in Jewish Palestine* [New York: Jewish Theological Seminary of America, 1950] 198-99). The Lucan evangelist apparently disagreed. After all, some of the rulers and the people misunderstood the Old Testament prophecies (Acts 13:27).

[19] E. J. Bickermann, "The Jewish Historian Demetrios," in *Christianity, Judaism and Other Greco-Roman Cults: Studies for Morton Smith at Sixty.* Part 3: *Judaism before 70* (ed. J. Neusner; Leiden: Brill, 1975) 72-84.

[20] B. A. van Groningen, *In the Grip of the Past* (Leiden: Brill, 1953); see also Plato, *Epinomis* 987e; Polybius 5.32.1-2.

[21] *To Heal and To Reveal: The Prophetic Vocation according to Luke* (New York: Seabury, 1976) 7.

[22] J. A. Fitzmyer (review of *Das Evangelium nach Lukas*, by Josef Ernst, *TS* 40 [1979] 349-51) says that promise-fulfillment is not an adequate category for grasping Lucan salvation history (p. 350).

[23] Karris, "Missionary Communities: A New Paradigm for the Study of Luke-Acts," *CBQ* 41 (1979) 83.

Jack T. Sanders

THE SALVATION OF THE
JEWS IN LUKE ACTS

What is the theological position of the author of Luke-Acts regarding the salvation of the Jews? Can Jews be saved or not? The question is of course most acute regarding the author's opinion of the possibilities that exist at the conclusion of the book of Acts. Can Jews be saved after Paul's quotation of the Isaiah passage to his Roman Jewish hearers and his interpretation of that passage, as described in Acts 28:23-28? But the question must also be posed for the period covered by Luke-Acts. To what degree does the author intend to describe a "mission to Israel" in his two volumes? The standard view in modern scholarship on the subject is that (in the theology of the author of Luke-Acts), after the end of Acts, Jews no longer have the opportunity to accept the gospel, because they have so completely rejected it during the period covered by Luke-Acts. Thus Jacob Jervell refers to "the common opinion that Luke described the Jews as a whole as rejecting the gospel."[1] In support of Jervell's assessment, one may refer to the two most important commentaries on Acts, those of A. Loisy and of E. Haenchen, as well as to the important monographic study by H. Conzelmann, *Die Mitte der Zeit*, although the views of these authors on the subject, as we shall see, are not entirely uniform.

In his study of the theology of Luke-Acts, Conzelmann explained, regarding the "hope of Israel" (Acts 1:6; 28:20), that "the emphatic passage, 28:28 . . . , shows who now shares in this hope: salvation is passing to the Gentiles." Thus one "can see quite clearly how Luke thinks of the Christians, according to plan, taking over the privileges of the Jews as one epoch is succeeded by the next."[2] It is the change of epochs that is significant; the Jews have had their *last* chance; the gospel now goes *from* the Jews *to* the Gentiles. Conzelmann distinguished, however, between "the Jews" and the individual Jew. Thus, while "the Jews" oppose Christianity, "for the individual the way of salvation is open, now as always. The polemic is at the same time a call to repentance."[3] Loisy, of course, had already noted the shift of the gospel from the Jews to the Gentiles at the end of Acts, and he explained that Christianity was, for the author (that is to say, for the "redactor" in Loisy's understanding) of Acts, "if one dare say it, the true Jewish religion. It is only that the Jews, by an inconceivable blindness [fully attested elsewhere in Acts], have repulsed God's gift." But the gospel had *first* to be offered to them: It is a part of the function of the concluding part of Acts for the "redactor" to "render the position believable that the proposal of the gospel had not been made to the pagans before having been made to the Jews."[4] Haenchen, then, takes essentially the same position as Conzelmann. Thus, he refers to "the transfer of the saving proclamation from the Jews to the Gentiles,"[5] and he tenders the explanation of the conclusion of Acts that the author was bringing two purposes together, one to show that the gospel was convincing (thus some of the Jewish audience were "persuaded" or "convinced" but not converted, just as the Pharisees in Acts 23:7-10 spoke in Paul's behalf but did not become Christians) and the other to show that the period of Jewish salvation was past and that salvation henceforth would be offered only to Gentiles (thus Paul's citation and interpretation of the Isaiah passage).[6] Loisy and Haenchen do not, however, think of the continued possibility of the salvation of individual Jews.[7]

If Jervell could cite the views thus far sketched, however, as a "common opinion," it was his own persuasion that such common opinion was in large part mistaken and that, in fact, "Luke does not describe a Jewish people who, as a whole, reject the early Christian message, and in which the believing Jews are exceptions." Acts contains, indeed, "numerous references to mass conversions of Jews."[8] On the other side of the coin, Gentiles do not begin to be saved only after a Jewish rejection of the gospel; rather, "from the beginning of the mission it is certain that, according to Scripture and in agreement with the missionary command, the Gentiles have a share in salvation."[9] It is thus clear that Jervell rejects the notion that, in the development of the early church, salvation is offered first to the Jews and then to the Gentiles. There exists no first period during which the gospel is offered to the Jews alone, which is then followed by a second period of turning to the Gentiles; rather, from first until last, some Jews accept the gospel and others reject it. Thus, in the early part of Acts, the Sadducees reject the gospel, and, in the period of the Gentile mission, some diaspora Jews convert while others do not, just as in the closing scene of Acts.[10] Rather than seeing a division in Acts between Jew and Gentile, therefore, Jervell finds a division between "obdurate" Israel and "repentant (i.e., Christian)"

Israel.[11]   This renewed Israel is then composed of both Jews and Gentiles—that is, those who accept the gospel.   "The addition of Gentiles is part of the restoration of Israel."[12]   This understanding of Acts leads Jervell to conclude that the author of Luke-Acts gives a theological explanation for the fact that the church of his own day is Gentile while a non-Christian Judaism still exists.   That theological solution is that the apostles have already offered the gospel to all the Jews who would accept.   "How can the church," he asks, attempting to state Luke's problem, "justify its neglect of the Jewish mission while it preaches the Messiah of Israel?"   Luke's answer, according to Jervell, it that the apostles "have gathered the repentant Israel and have given to Gentiles a share in the salvation that comes from the repentant people of God."[13]   It is this theological position, according to Jervell, that explains the role of the Jews in Luke-Acts, and not the epochal scheme proposed by Loisy, Conzelmann, and others.[14] *After the conclusion of Acts*, however, there is no need for any further attempt to convert Jews, since "there can be no talk about a renewed mission to Jews without . . . calling into question the right of Gentiles to the promises."[15]

A second recent work, Eric Franklin's *Christ the Lord*,[16] has also sought to show the incorrectness of the epochal explanation of Jewish salvation and rejection in Luke-Acts and to support the explanation that salvation of Jews continues throughout, with only those Jews who reject the gospel being rejected.   While Franklin is more willing than Jervell to agree that the Jews as a whole reject the gospel,[17] nevertheless he goes beyond Jervell in proposing that, even after the conclusion of Acts, Jews may still be saved.   "The final episode at Rome," he argues, "is to be understood as a justification of Christianity in spite of its refusal by the Jews rather than as a turning aside from them"; and he adds, "Paul's work among the Jews at Rome is not a total failure ([Acts] 28:24)."[18]   On the issue of whether the author of Luke-Acts intends to describe an epoch of the offering of the gospel to the Jews, after which they no longer have an opportunity to accept it, Franklin is quite clear.   "Christianity" at the end of Acts "is still put forward as the 'hope of Israel' (28:20)"; and he understands Paul's statement in 28:28 that the gospel will henceforth go to the Gentiles as "less a programme for the future than a justification of what has happened" in the course of the Gentile mission described in Acts.[19]

It is thus clear that an answer to the question regarding the salvation of the Jews in Luke-Acts hangs on the interpretation of the closing verses of Acts and also on the acceptance or rejection of Loisy's and Conzelmann's epochal understandings of the work.   Can any further clarity on these points be achieved?   We begin with the former issue, the concluding scene of the book of Acts.

What is the point of Paul's citation of Isa 6:9-10 LXX to his Roman Jewish hearers in Acts 28:26-27 and of his interpretation thereof in v. 28: "This salvation of God has been sent to the Gentiles; they will listen"? In order to understand this concluding statement of Paul in Acts, it is necessary first of all to recall that it is not an isolated statement but the third in a chain of similar statements. In Acts 13:46, after a mixed reaction to his preaching of the gospel to the Jews in Antioch of Pisidia, Paul announces to them, "Since you thrust it from you and judge yourselves unworthy of eternal life, behold, we turn to the Gentiles"; and, in Acts 18:6, after opposition to the gospel develops in the synagogue in Corinth, Paul declares, "From now on I will go to the Gentiles," and he moves next door. In all these cases Paul has been "persuading" Jews,[20] but it is not entirely clear of what; and it is not certain that he has been converting them. If the "standard" position regarding Luke's attitude toward the salvation of the Jews is correct, then the "persuasion" of these three accounts does not necessarily refer to conversion, but, even if this "persuasion" does refer to conversion, we have in any case a reiteration or an ascending emphasis on Jewish rejection of the gospel and on the exclusion of the Jews from salvation. If Jervell and Franklin are correct, however, then the persuasion certainly does refer to conversion, and the three occurrences of the announcement of turning to the Gentiles do not refer to the exclusion of the Jews but rather show that, in spite of the perceived general opposition of Jews to the gospel, still, where it is preached, some Jews convert.

Haenchen remarks regarding Acts 28:28, "The transfer of the saving proclamation from the Jews to the Gentiles is thereby established here (as in 13:48; 18:6)."[21] Jervell, however, finds that Acts shows throughout how the preaching of the gospel divides the Jews into two groups, those who believe and those who reject, and this is how he understands the closing scene in Acts. "Once more we find the familiar picture of some believing, other unbelieving";[22] and he supports his observation with this reasoning: "If it is really Luke's intention to describe the complete rejection of the gospel on the part of the Jews, then it is very strange that he seems to emphasize clearly the division among the Jews and appears to speak about the unbelief of only a portion of the Roman Jewish community."[23] Franklin's position is less a direct opposition to the "standard" opinion about Jewish rejection in Acts than is Jervell's—he does, as noted above, agree that the Jewish rejection of the gospel in Acts is total— nevertheless he affirms that "Paul's work among the Jews at Rome is not a total failure (28:24). . . . Christianity is still put forward as the 'hope of Israel' (28:20), a designation that suggests that even now the

Jews are unlikely to be abandoned. . . . Paul's final statement is not a rejection of the Jews."[24] Obviously it cannot be both ways. We turn therefore to a further examination of the "persuasion" of the Jews.

Of the numerous places in Acts where the word πείθω occurs,[25] only in the three accounts of Paul's turning to the Gentiles (13:43; 18:4; and 28:23-24) and in 17:4 and 19:26 may this "persuasion" be understood as referring to conversion to Christianity. The occurrence in 17:4 sheds little light on the precise meaning of the three accounts that include announcements of turning to the Gentiles, since the usage in 17:4 is exactly the same as in the three other passages. It is Jews who are persuaded, but this persuasion is followed immediately by a Jewish attack on Paul. The instance that most likely involved the meaning "conversion" for "persuasion" is 19:26, where Demetrius charges that Paul has "persuaded and turned away a considerable company of people," so that they are no longer willing to consider idols gods. Even here, however, the meaning of "conversion" for "persuasion" is not crystal clear, since the author of Luke-Acts may mean only to have Demetrius say that Paul has persuaded people not to believe in idols, not that he has converted them to Christianity.

Luke's normal word for "conversion" is "belief," often connected with an account or mention of baptism.[26] Thus, the first conversions in Acts, after Peter's first sermon, are characterized by baptism (2:41), after which it is said that "all who believed were together"; or Acts 14:1 refers to Jews and Greeks in Iconium who "believed"; and the reference to Jewish Christians in 21:20 (to which we must return below) is to "those who have believed." It is thus striking and surely not accidental that immediately following both 13:46 and 18:6 we find accounts of such belief/conversion. In 13:48 we read that "as many [of the Gentiles] as were ordained to eternal life believed," and 18:8 relates how "Crispus . . . believed in the Lord . . . ; and many of the Corinthians . . . believed and were baptized." In Acts 13:44-49, therefore, and in 18:4-8 we have this pattern: *persuasion* of Jewish hearers, opposition on the part of Jews to the gospel, announcement of turning to Gentiles, belief (Gentile and, in chap. 18, Jewish), and baptism.[27] The fact that, in both cases, belief/conversion is mentioned later, after the announcement of turning to the Gentiles, supports the contention that the earlier "persuasion" is not conversion. Acts 28:23-28 then begins the pattern and follows it through exactly up to the point at which the turning to the Gentiles is announced. This announcement is more elaborate here than in the two previous occurrences of the pattern, but the pattern breaks off at this point. The final turning has been announced; no belief is mentioned. When one adds to these observations Dibelius's notice that the three announcements of the turning to the Gentiles occur, respectively, in

Asia Minor, on the Greek mainland, and in Rome[28]—thus in all the major geographical areas of Paul's missionary activity—then one should see that the author of Luke-Acts has not set up a pattern that implies continued missionary activity among the Jews after the conclusion of Acts. Rather, he has emphasized the thoroughness of the mission to the Jews and the thoroughness of their rejection of the gospel. J. Gnilka correctly observes that "Luke . . . gains the possibility, by this presentational means, of keeping the Jewish obduracy all the more impressively before the eyes of the reader; and thus the consequences that follow therefrom become weightier."[29] Acts 28:25-28 is Luke's final judgment on the Jews, after which it would be foolish, in Luke's opinion, to waste any further missionary effort on them.[30] The correctness of this assessment will be borne out further in the following observations.

It is usually not noticed that, aside from the questionable references to Jewish "persuasion" under Paul's preaching, there is precious little Jewish conversion to Christianity in the diaspora, according to Acts. In 14:1 "a great crowd of Jews and also of Greeks [in Iconium] believed"; in 17:11-12 the Jews in Beroea "received the word with all eagerness. . . . Many of them therefore believed"; and, as mentioned previously, Crispus and his household believed in Corinth (18:8). There are no other clear references to Jewish conversion to Christianity in the context of the Gentile mission in Acts! Even if one were to add the four cases of persuasion, still these seven accounts of Jewish conversion would be meager. Surely the author of Acts intended to show that the conversion of Jews to Christianity as a result of Paul's mission was an oddity and that their normal response was one of open hostility![31] This very disappointing failure of the Gentile mission to gain Jewish converts to Christianity, as sketched by the author of Luke-Acts, would certainly justify Paul's final speech, the meaning of which is that *it is inherent in being Jewish to be incapable of understanding* (especially the gospel) and that God therefore sends his missionaries to the Gentiles, who *are* capable of understanding.[32]

Franklin recognizes this Lucan theme, even though Jervell does not, and therefore gives over a considerable amount of space to the discussion of it, especially in terms of Stephen's speech at his martyrdom.[33] Franklin sees that "the main point of the speech is to show that the hostility of the Jews to the Christian proclamation is of one piece with the hostility to the purposes of God which is characteristic of their history."[34] The climax of this long harangue—which the author, of course, places on the lips of Stephen[35]—is reached in 7:51: "You always resist the Holy Spirit. As your fathers did, so do you." It is inherent, endemic in the Jewish people to behave so, and it was therefore no surprise that they killed the "Righteous One," since they had always persecuted and killed all the prophets (v. 52—hardly a historically accurate description of the fate of prophets in ancient Israel).[36]

This hostility of the Jewish people to the purposes of God, so vehemently denounced here and portrayed ad nauseam throughout the rest of Acts right up to the concluding scene, can occasionally be called ignorance. Peter, in his second sermon, tells his hearers that he knows that they acted "according to ignorance" in killing Christ, wherefore they now have the opportunity to repent (Acts 3:17, 19);[37] and Paul, in his first missionary sermon, explains that the Jerusalem-ites were "ignorant of [Christ] and of the voices of the prophets which are read every Sabbath" (Acts 13:27). There can be little doubt that the author of Luke-Acts intended these formulations to be similar.[38] Both mention the people generally (in Peter's speech "you," in Paul's "those dwelling in Jerusalem") and also *archontes*, and these are the only places in Acts where ignorance is mentioned, except for Paul's sermon in Athens, where he first (Acts 17:23) picks up on the dedication *Agnōstō Theō* and then (v. 30) explains that God has "overlooked the times of ignorance" in offering salvation on the occasion of Paul's visit to the city. It appears, therefore, that, according to the author of Luke-Acts, God is willing to overlook ignorance regarding himself and his plan of salvation, even when that ignorance leads to the murder of Christ himself, *until the gospel is preached.*[39] The preaching of the gospel should remove all ignorance, and ignorance cannot be an excuse for rejecting God's will after the preaching of the gospel. Thus Peter's sermon excuses the former ignorance of the Jews, just as Paul's sermon in Athens excuses the former ignorance of the Gentiles (who show their intellectual honesty, one may note, by recognizing their ignorance and by erecting a statue to it). But Paul's sermon in Antioch does not mention Jewish ignorance as an excuse; it rather *accuses* the Jews of ignorance![40] The Jerusalemites could not even understand the Bible, although they heard it read every Saturday. They could find Jesus guilty of no crime deserving capital punishment (Acts 13:28), but they still urged his death.[41] As Stephen charged at the conclusion of the Gentile mission, the Jews "always resist the Holy Spirit"; they "hear but never understand." We may, of course, inquire whether the preaching of the gospel in the face of Athenian ignorance was more successful than the preaching of the gospel in Pisidian Antioch or in Jerusalem, but the author of Luke-Acts never entertained such a question. For him, the details of the narrative he lays before us should not obscure the overriding truth that Jews reject the gospel whereas Gentiles accept it. "They will hear" (Acts 28:28). Theology does not like to be confused by facts.

Jervell, however, views the facts themselves differently. "Mass conversions of Jews," he writes, "are again and again reported," and he cites "2:41 (47); 4:4; 5:14; 6:1, 7; 9:42; 12:24; 13:43; 14:1; 17:10ff.; (19:20); 21:20."[42] Franklin gives a somewhat different set of passages in Acts (4:4; 5:12-16; 9:26-28; 11:2, 29-30; 12:25; 15:22; 21:20), and his position regarding them is again rather more cautious than that of Jervell: It is not that conversions are "reported" in these passages; rather, one sees in them that "Luke points out that many in Jerusalem did accept the Christian proclamation."[43] Only those references to Jewish conversion that follow Acts 9 are of concern to us here, since such conversion in the first nine chapters of Acts is not at issue.[44]

Whether Acts 12:24, "The word of God grew and multiplied," refers to new conversions is not entirely clear. While it is possible that the note—entirely disconnected as it is from its context—refers to new conversions, it is markedly different from the previous summary statements that explicitly mention conversions. Even if we were to allow that conversions were implied, it would still not be clear who has been converted, since the gospel has already expanded into Samaritan and Gentile regions. Verse 25, of course, does not refer to conversions. Acts 19:20, however, like 12:24, reports that "the word of the Lord grew and prevailed mightily." Not only can this not be used to show that there were Jewish conversions, since it falls within the Gentile mission, but also its context weighs heavily on the side of considering neither it nor the similar 12:24 as summaries of conversions, since its reference is to the gospel's destruction of magic in Ephesus! The point is just what the note maintains—the *power* of the gospel increased. This "power" is not limited to winning converts to Christianity, and references to such power should not necessarily be so taken. Three of the references in Acts mentioned by Jervell—13:43; 14:1; and 17:10-12—have already been discussed (Jervell has overlooked Acts 18:8). Acts 15:22 does not refer to any new conversions.

We are brought, therefore, to Acts 21:20: "You see, . . . how many thousands there are among the Jews of those who have believed." Does this attestation mean, as Jervell takes it, that the number of Jewish converts in Jerusalem has increased since the events narrated in chap. 10?[45] It does not. In the first place, the statement is not a "report" of a "mass conversion of Jews," since it is not a "report" in the sense of a narrative at all. It is a summary of what has already happened. If Acts 21:20, however, is a summary, then it summarizes earlier conversions of Jews in Jerusalem, either reported or not reported. Jervell has to assume that the summary of Acts 21:20 refers to unreported conversions of Jerusalem Jews that have taken place since chap. 10. This assumption is not necessary, however, since the three thousand of Acts 2:41, the unspecified additional number of 2:47, the five thousand men (plus additional women?) of 4:4, the multitude of 5:14, the multiplying disciples of 6:1, and the greatly multiplying disciples of 6:7 will surely produce the "so many myriads" of 21:20. We are therefore able to arrive at the sum given in 21:20 without the assumption of a single Jewish convert in Jerusalem after 6:7.[46] It is therefore not proper to assume, as Jervell does, that Acts 21:20 refers to such additional converts *when that is the very point that needs to be proved*.

But if Acts shows us "many myriads" of Jews who are converted before chap. 10 and only a few who are converted in the context of the Gentile mission, it is also true that the myriads of Jewish conversions in the first part of the book are not matched by myriads of Gentile conversions in the latter part. Consequently, while there are rather more Gentile conversions than Jewish conversions in the Gentile mission, the latter part of Acts is hardly an account of mass Gentile conversion to Christianity. The author of Luke-Acts seems more concerned with showing, in Acts 12-28, the universal and pervasive hostility of the Jews to the gospel and how this hostility repeatedly forces the preaching of the gospel to Gentiles.[47] Thus, it is the purpose of the characterization of the Gentile mission in Acts 12-28 to show not that myriads of Gentiles were converted but that consistent and pervasive Jewish hostility to the gospel drove the Christian preachers from this place to that, saturating the several regions of the Gentile world with their preaching, finally even Rome itself.[48] It was this contrast that led Johannes Weiss to note, "The victory of Gentile Christianity and the repression of Jewish Christianity have their literary reflection in the Book of Acts."[49]

One more aspect of the pervasive Jewish hostility toward the purposes of God, especially toward the gospel (as it is represented in Acts), deserves to be mentioned, and that is that the hostility of the Jews to the gospel is part of God's plan, it being his will to offer salvation to the Gentiles and to accomplish that by the means of Jewish rejection of the gospel.[50] This theme is seen most clearly in Acts 13:42-49, the account of the conclusion of Paul's first missionary activity, in Pisidian Antioch. Here Paul "urges" (ἔπειθον, i.e., "persuades") the Jews to continue in grace (v. 43), then they turn on him (v. 45), in response to which Paul pronounces the divine necessity and, by implication, foreknowledge of the chain of events: "It was necessary (ἀναγκαῖον) that the word of God should be spoken first to you. Since you thrust it from you, . . . we turn to the Gentiles" (v. 46). While Paul does not here give a reason for the necessity of preaching first to the Jews, that reason will have been obvious to the author of Luke-Acts: to the Jews were given the prophecies in the first place.[51] But the Jewish rejection of the gospel must be just as much a necessity as the preaching to them in the first place—that is, God must have known in advance of their rejection, since the rejection is followed by the prophecy of the Gentile mission, Isa 49:6 (Acts 13:47). Thus the pattern of proclamation to the Jews, rejection by them, proclamation to the Gentiles is the divine plan. Had the Jews accepted the gospel and had they thereby not forced the Gentile mission, they would have thwarted the purposes of God! This theological construction then also underlies the exchange between Paul and the Roman Jews in the concluding scene of Acts, and it lies equally behind Acts 7:51-53. Especially in the conclusion of Stephen's speech we see that this divine necessity provides no more excuse for the Jews than does their ignorance. They still fall under the accusation of rejection; and, for the author of Luke-Acts, there is no longer, after the time of Acts 28:28, any salvation for any Jews.[52] They have consistently, in keeping both with God's plan and with their natural disposition, rejected the gospel and have thereby judged themselves "unworthy of eternal life" (Acts 13:46). If this, however, is the position of the author of Luke-Acts found in Acts after chap. 10, then how can it be explained that myriads of Jews are converted to Christianity before chap. 10? The answer lies in the recognition of Luke's periodization of history.

The contrast between the earlier and the later periods in Acts is so marked—and so obviously schematized—that it is impossible to overlook it. In the opening chapters, when the Christian preaching is confined to Jerusalem, myriads of Jews convert to Christianity, as has just been noted, and the former opposition of the Jews to God's plan is excused as ignorance, as was explained above.[53] In chaps. 6 and 7, then, comes the martyrdom of Stephen, in whose final words the Jews are denounced as incorrigible and whose death leads to the expansion of the gospel outside Jerusalem.[54] The author of Luke-Acts has a little difficulty making the transition from the Jewish mission to the Gentile mission,[55] but it is begun by Peter in chap. 10 and gets underway in chap. 11 or in chap. 13. From chap. 13 on the Jews take the place in Acts that has already been described.

For Conzelmann, who has discussed the successive periods in Luke-Acts in great detail, all of Acts, of course, belongs to Luke's "epoch of the church," but "the initial period comes to be thought of as a unique kind of period; . . . it stands apart as the unique period of the witnesses" and is characterized both by the persecution of the church and by peace in the church.[56] Loisy also notes that "from this point [the martyrdom of Stephen] this conclusion [pronounced by Paul in

Acts 28:25-28] is prepared by showing that Israel was never worthy of the promises made to it";[57] and Haenchen observes that "the expulsion of the primitive congregation by this unbelieving Israel brought about and justified the Gentile mission."[58] Even Jervell is forced to recognize the transition and observes that "Stephen's sermon, which marks the conclusion of missionary activity in Jerusalem, signifies the end of the apostles' direct missionary activity to Israel."[59]

This "initial" and "unique" (Conzelmann) period of the church described in Acts 1-6, during which time myriads of Jews convert, is partially to be explained by the viewpoint of the author of Luke-Acts, which is elucidated by Haenchen in his discussion of the conclusion of Acts. There, he observed, Luke was attempting to bring together two viewpoints: (1) that the gospel was "in essential agreement with Judaism" and (2) that the Jewish rejection of the gospel brought about the Gentile mission.[60] To this "essential agreement" of the gospel with Judaism one will want to add both Luke's conviction that the gospel was always "persuasive" or "powerful"[61] and his geographical plan as laid down in Acts 1:8. Then one will have Luke's rationale for the salvation of the Jews in Acts 1-6. Luke makes this theology effective with the theme of excusable ignorance. The preaching of the gospel offers a second chance to the Jews after their initial rejection; but, after appropriate success, the gospel is rejected in the same way in which Jesus was rejected. This second rejection (Acts 6:9, which includes—N.B.! a rejection by diaspora Jews as well) is shown to be a sequel to the first rejection by the parallelism between the martyrdom of Jesus and that of Stephen. The Stephen episode, therefore, is properly viewed as containing in microcosm Luke's entire theology about the Jews.[62]

We noted at the outset that the position of Jervell and that of Franklin stand or fall on the answer to two questions, whether Acts 28:25-28 represents a final rejection of the Jews and whether the epochal understanding of Acts put forward by Loisy, Conzelmann, and others was correct. The analysis here presented has shown the incorrectness of both Jervell's position and Franklin's position. The theology of the author of Luke-Acts regarding the salvation of the Jews, if we may now summarize it briefly, is that the Jews are by nature stubborn and both unable and unwilling to recognize the will of God, even though God had for centuries attempted to explain his will to them alone. This racial characteristic—which then also happens to coincide with the divine plan—led them to kill the prophets and to kill the Messiah. And, when God was even willing to excuse those earlier murders on the basis of ignorance and to offer them still one other chance at salvation in the preaching of the gospel, *the truth of which is attested by the conversion of myriads of them,* still they rejected

God's salvation and murdered Stephen just as they had murdered Jesus, thus forcing the gospel to go to the Gentiles (which movement was, after all, God's plan). In the context of the Gentile mission, then, the Christian preachers still attempted to convert Jews, but the success of the early days of the church was no longer there, and the Jewish response to the gospel was primarily one of hostility. The Gentile mission therefore served to attest the truth displayed in the martyrdom of Stephen, which Paul finally and for the last time announces at the end of Acts. A final solution of the Jewish problem has been indicated.[63]

This once-only chance for salvation given to the Jews by the author of Luke-Acts is expressed not only in the Acts, but in the Gospel of Luke as well. As a matter of fact, when one views Luke and Acts together, one is able to see that their central theme is the two-sided Jewish rejection (the Jews' rejection of the gospel and God's rejection of them) and the carrying of the gospel to the Gentiles.[64]

Following the two preliminary chapters of Luke, the author presents the ministry of the Baptist, Jesus' baptism, and the temptation. Those accounts are preliminary to the activity of Jesus, which is the subject of the Gospel; and *that activity begins with Jesus' denunciation of the Jews and his announcement that salvation is sent to the Gentiles.*[65] It is widely recognized, of course, that Luke has pulled the scene of Jesus' preaching in Nazareth forward from its earlier setting in his sources to make it the opening scene of the public ministry (Luke 4:16-30). What is thereby accomplished? The answer to that question can be found by looking at the differences between Luke, on the one hand, and Matthew and Mark, on the other. Only Luke includes here a prophecy of the mockery thrown at Jesus in Luke 23:35 and parallels, "Physician, heal yourself." Only Luke includes the examples of the Gentiles in Elijah's and Elisha's time— the Sidonian widow and Naaman the Syrian—and throws it into the teeth of the Jewish hearers that there were Israelite widows and lepers in those days. And only Luke tells of the attempt by the Jewish hearers to stone Jesus. Thus the statement of Jesus to his Jewish audience that God favors Gentiles over Jews—and what other inference could be drawn from his examples?[66]—leads to Jewish hostility, just as in Acts the proclamation of the gospel leads to hostility; and the Jews take Jesus out of the city to stone him, just as in Acts the Jews take Stephen out of the city to stone him.[67] Naturally, Jesus escapes, since this is only the beginning of the public ministry and he cannot be killed by the Jews until the end, but the author of Luke-Acts has here set the course of the entire two-volume work straight toward the conclusion in Acts 28:25-28.[68] Another way of emphasizing the point is to observe that, just as Luke's entire theology about the Jews may be seen in the Stephen episode, so Luke's theology about the plan of God's salvation is contained in microcosm in the first scene of the public ministry.[69] God's salvation is coming to the Gentiles and not to the Jews; the Jews react to that "gospel" message in a hostile manner; their final rejection at the end of Acts is therefore a foregone conclusion at the outset of Jesus' public ministry. The salvation of the Jews was never at any time of any concern to the author of Luke-Acts. For him, theirs is the role of those who seek to thwart the purposes of God.

We have seen that the theme of two-sided Jewish rejection is dominant in the Acts and is also prepared in the Gospel of Luke. Is there, however, some difference between the two works in this regard? Is the Gospel of Luke less strongly disposed to reject the possibility of Jewish salvation than is the Acts? Is the Gospel "more subtly" anti-Semitic than the Acts?[70] Once one begins to look for the standard theme of Jewish rejection, it soon becomes clear that it is hardly less prominent in the Gospel than in the Acts.

We may begin again with the opening scene of the public ministry, the preaching and rejection in Nazareth. After his miraculous escape from stoning, Jesus does a few deeds and says a few sayings, and then (9:51) he starts the journey toward Jerusalem. Immediately when he gets underway he is rejected by some Samaritans (9:51-56), but this rejection is different in two ways from the standard Jewish rejection. On the one hand, a reason is given for the Samaritans' rejecting Jesus (he is journeying toward Jerusalem), and, on the other hand, when the opportunity is given to destroy the Samaritans (v. 54), Jesus rejects such a possibility.[71] This scene at the outset of the travel narrative provides an interesting contrast to and comparison with the rejection scene (in parable) at the conclusion of the travel narrative.[72] Here (19:11-27), Jesus tells of a throne pretender who journeys to another country in order to receive authority over his realm, who is followed by some of his subjects who oppose his rule, and who then slays his opponents after having received his kingdom and having returned to it—all a thinly veiled allegory of Jesus, who departs to heaven to come again in power, whose rule is opposed by the Jews, and who will destroy them when he returns. This framework for the travel narrative—excusable and excused Samaritan rejection versus unforgivable Jewish rejection; rejection of destruction versus promise of destruction—determines its tone throughout and allows the careful reader to observe throughout the travel narrative the standard pattern of Jewish rejection, already indicated at the beginning of the public ministry.[73] Thus we can recognize the parable of the Good Samaritan (10:29-37) as being directed against the (religious) Jews and as showing the Samaritans to be superior in their response to the will of God; and the parable of the Great Supper (14:15-24), with its two invitations to the uninvited, as again rejecting the (religious) Jews while seeking out either Jewish religious outcasts or Samaritans, and Gentiles.[74]

When we once recognize the pervasive character of the theme of Jewish rejection in the Gospel, then we are not surprised when the Jews carry out the most infamous act of rejection possible by murdering Jesus, an act Luke accomplishes, as is well known, by omitting the scene in which the Roman soldiers mock Jesus (Mark 15:16-20a and parallels) and moving directly from "he delivered Jesus to their will" (Luke 23:25; cf. Mark 15:15) to "and as they led him away" (Luke 23:26; cf. Mark 15:20b).[75] Finally, the Lucan version of the Great Commission (24:44-49) simply takes as given the theme of Jewish rejection and of the consequent sending of salvation to the Gentiles. The "forgiveness of sins" is to go to "πάντα τὰ ἔθνη," and it is to begin "from Jerusalem."[76] The apostles, however, are to remain in Jerusalem (only) until they receive the heavenly power. The Jewish mission of Acts 1-6 seems hardly to be envisioned here and is, indeed, inconsequential in view of the overall soteriological plan of Luke-Acts.[77]

NOTES

[1]J. Jervell, *Luke and the People of God* (Minneapolis: Augsburg, 1972) 44.

[2]H. Conzelmann, *The Theology of St. Luke* (New York: Harper & Row, 1960) 163; see also pp. 145, 160, 212, and also Conzelmann's statement in his commentary on Acts that, after the conclusion of Acts, "Luke no longer considers that there is any success of the Christian mission among 'the Jews'" (*Apostelgeschichte* [HNT 7; Tübingen: Mohr (Siebeck), 1963] 149). A somewhat similar interpretation is given by J. Gnilka (*Die Verstockung Israels. Isaias 6, 9-10 in der Theologie der Synoptiker* [SANT 3; Munich: Kösel, 1961] 132), who views Jesus' earthly ministry in Luke as a "last grace period" for the Jews.

[3]Conzelmann, *Theology*, 145; also Gnilka, *Verstockung*, 146.

[4]A. Loisy, *Les Actes des Apôtres* (Paris: Nourry, 1920) 939.

[5]E. Haenchen, *Die Apostelgeschichte* (MeyerK 3; 7th ed.; Göttingen: Vandenhoeck & Ruprecht, 1977) 691-92. See also Haenchen, "The Book of Acts as Source Material for the History of Early Christianity," *Studies in Luke-Acts* (ed. L. E. Keck and J. L. Martyn; Philadelphia: Fortress, 1980) 259-65.

[6]Haenchen, *Apostelgeschichte*, 697.

[7] See Haenchen, "Source Material," 278: "Luke has written the Jews off."

[8] Jervell, *People of God,* 42.

[9] Ibid., 43.

[10] Ibid., 48

[11] Ibid., 49. This position is not so different from that of Conzelmann, who refers to "penitent" and "impenitent." This division among the Jews allows Luke a "sharpness of polemic" against them "but at the same time [avoids] a summary Christian anti-Semitism" (Conzelmann, *Theology,* 146). This division could be seen as early as the distinguishing of "two distinct groups" in the response to John's baptism (*Theology,* 21; see also p. 190: "the true or the false Israel"). The position was shared also by A. Harnack (*The Acts of the Apostles* [New Testament Studies 3; New York: Putnam, 1909] 286-87) and G. W. H. Lampe (*St Luke and the Church of Jerusalem* [London: Athlone, 1969] 9-10), both of whom saw the later apologists as taking the position that Jervell now describes as the "common" one, and both of whom saw Luke as halfway between Paul and that position. Thus Lampe (*St Luke,* 9) refers to "two 'successions' in Israel." Gnilka (*Verstockung,* 143) also sees the Jewish rejection of the gospel as an opting out of Israel. He endorses Conzelmann's position and sees Luke as attempting to distinguish church from Israel without hurting the Jews: It is the leaders and those who follow them who are at fault (p. 151). With Conzelmann, however, he also emphasizes the epochal plan of Luke-Acts and thus sees the final position of Luke-Acts as being that the Jews have rejected their own proper salvation (p. 153).

[12] Jervell, *People of God,* 60. F. Menezes ("The Mission of Jesus According to Lk 4:16-30," *Biblehashyam* 6 [1980] 258) comes to the same conclusion, as does J. Dupont ("La conclusion des Actes et son rapport a l'ensemble de l'ouvrage de Luc," *Les Actes des Apôtres* [ed. J. Kremer; BETL 48; Gembloux: Duculot; Louvain: University Press, 1979] 359-404, except that Dupont sees that Jewish rejection pushes the gospel toward the Gentiles.

[13] Jervell, *People of God,* 68. A similar position is maintained by C. Burchard (*Der dreizehnte Zeuge. Traditions- und kompositionsgeschichtliche Untersuchungen zu Lukas' Darstellung der Frühzeit des Paulus* [FRLANT 103; Göttingen: Vandenhoeck & Ruprecht, 1970] 113-77), who holds that, "in Luke's sense [the Gentile church] is an ecumenical church without Jews" (p. 176).

[14] See also F. Mussner, "Wohnung Gottes und Menschensohn nach der Stephanusperikope (Apg 6,8-8,2)," *Jesus und der Menschensohn. Für Anton Vogtle* (ed. R. Pesch et al.; Freiburg: Herder, 1975) 291-92. Jervell's position is supported by D. L. Tiede, *Prophecy and History in Luke-Acts* (Philadelphia: Fortress, 1980) 10: "It is the 'unpersuaded' or 'unbelieving' Jews (14:4; 28:24) . . . who generate a division among the 'Jews' which is displayed before the Gentiles (cf. 14:4; 23:7)." Tiede goes even farther than Jervell in seeking to

counteract the notion that the author of Luke-Acts himself harbored some kind of hostility toward Jews by proposing that the author was, in fact, some kind of Jew ("at home in the synagogue," p. 8), although Tiede leaves open the possibility that the author may have been in some manner a Gentile adherent of Judaism (p. 10).

[15] Jervell, *People of God*, 69.

[16] E. Franklin, *Christ the Lord. A Study in the Purpose and Theology of Luke-Acts* (Philadelphia: Westminster, 1975).

[17] Ibid., 99-108.

[18] Ibid., 114. S. Sandmel (*Anti-Semitism in the New Testament?* [Philadelphia: Fortress, 1978] 73) also refers to "a residual concern in Luke to win Jews to Christianity." But he bases this judgment on Luke's "pity" for the Jews, which turns out to be rather short-lived; see further below.

[19] Franklin, *Christ the Lord*, 115.

[20] Acts 13:43: [Παῦλος καὶ Βαρναβᾶς] ἔπειθον [τοὺς Ἰουδαίους] προσμένειν τῇ χάριτι τοῦ θεοῦ; Acts 18:4: [Παῦλος] ἔπειθέν τε Ἰουδαίους καὶ Ἕλληνας; Acts 28:24: οἱ μὲν [τῶν Ἰουδαίων] ἐπείθοντο τοῖς λεγομένοις [ὑπὸ Παύλου].

[21] Haenchen, *Apostelgeschichte*, 691-92. R. B. Rackham (*The Acts of the Apostles: An Exposition* [London: Methuen, 1901] 220) emphasizes that the apostles turn to the Gentiles only when the Jews push them to it. L. Cerfaux and J. Dupont (*Les Actes des Apôtres* [La Sainte Bible; Paris: Editions du Cerf, 1964] 128) refer in this regard to "*un fil conducteur.*" See also Dupont, "Le salut des gentils et la signification theologique du Livre des Actes," *NTS* 6 (1959-60) 135, 141; and similarly Harnack, Acts, 128-29. See further Conzelmann, *Apostelgeschichte*, 149, and E. Preuschen, *Die Apostelgeschichte* (HNT 4/1; Tübingen: Mohr [Siebeck], 1912) 86.

[22] Jervell, *People of God*, 63; see his entire chapter, "The Divided People of God," pp. 41-74. A. George ("Israël dans l'oeuvre de Luc," *RB* 75 [1968] 514-15) also considers the instances of persuasion to be accounts of conversion.

[23] Jervell, *People of God*, 63.

[24] Franklin, *Christ the Lord*, 114-15. P.-G. Müller ("Die jüdische Entscheidung gegen Jesus nach der Apostelgeschichte," *Les Acts des Apôtres* [see n. 12] 523-31) goes even further than Jervell and Franklin and attributes Paul's view on the salvation of the Jews (their salvation remains God's goal) to Acts. See also Dupont, "Conclusion," 377-80.

[25] On πείθω and πιστεύω see H. J. Hauser, *Strukturen der Abschlusserzählung der Apostelgeschichte (Apg 28,16-31)* (AnBib 86; Rome: Pontifical Biblical Institute, 1979) 62-66.

[26] See the similar statement given by U. Wilckens, *Die Missionsreden der Apostelgeschichte* (WMANT 5; 3d ed.; Neukirchen-Vluyn: Neukirchener Verlag, 1974) 182-83. See also Conzelmann, *Theology*, 229; S. Brown, *Apostasy and Perseverance in the Theology of Luke* (AnBib 36; Rome: Pontifical Biblical Institute, 1969) 46-47; and B.

Sauvagnat, "Se repentir, être baptisé, recevoir l'Esprit: Actes 2,37 ss.," *Foi et Vie* 80 (1981) 77–86, where the instances of persuasion are not mentioned.

[27] Loisy (*Actes,* 937) and Haenchen (*Apostelgeschichte,* 691) have seen this point correctly.   Even E. Jacquier (*Les Actes des Apôtres* [EBib; 2d ed.; Paris: Gabalda, 1926]), whose commentary was intended to present a properly Catholic interpretation of Acts after that of the heretic Loisy, admits that "it does not seem that their conviction was sufficient to lead them to faith" (p. 758).   It is thus mistaken for S. G. Wilson, Conzelmann, and others to think that Acts 28:24 refers to conversion of some of the Jews; see the discussion in S. G. Wilson, *The Gentiles and the Gentile Mission in Luke-Acts* (SNTSMS 23; Cambridge: University Press, 1973) 226 n. 1.   See further Loisy, *Actes,* 523.   F. Stagg (*The Book of Acts: The Early Struggle for an Unhindered Gospel* [Nashville: Broadman, 1955] 265) also thinks that the persuasion of these accounts is conversion.

[28] M. Dibelius, *Aufsätze zur Apostelgeschichte* (FRLANT nf 42; 4th ed.; ed. H. Greeven; Göttingen: Vandenhoeck & Ruprecht, 1961) 129.   See also Haenchen, *Apostelgeschichte,* 691–92; Gnilka, *Verstockung,* 146; Wilson, *Gentiles,* 226.   Dupont ("Conclusion," 379, 384, 386) incorrectly takes the examples of persuasion to refer to conversion.

[29] Gnilka, *Verstockung,* 147.

[30] That this is Luke's intention has also been correctly seen by F. Overbeck (W. M. L. DeWette, *Kurze Erklärung der Apostelgeschichte* [4th ed. revised by F. Overbeck; Leipzig: Hirzel, 1870] 480–81) and by Loisy (*Actes,* 938–39).   See further R. P. C. Hanson (*The Acts in the Revised Standard Version with Introduction and Commentary* [Oxford: Clarendon Press, 1967] 255), who states that Acts 28:28 is "a fine summary, in a sentence, of the main message of Acts."

[31] So also Sandmel, *Anti-Semitism,* 98–99; J. Weiss, *Earliest Christianity* (New York: Harper, 1937) 665.   The statement of Tiede (*Prophecy and History,* 10) that "Luke was eager to document the success of Christian preaching among the Jews in the face of great opposition" is true only of Acts 1–6, not of the successive phase(s) of the Christian mission.

[32] See also Weiss, *Earliest Christianity,* 666.   It is not that—as Hauser (*Apostelgeschichte,* 69) thinks—it is the nature of Jews to disagree, but it is that their nature is to oppose the gospel.   It is Hauser's lack of clarity regarding the use of πείθω in Acts (see above, n. 25) that clouds his vision here.

[33] Franklin, *Christ the Lord,* 98–108.   Jervell does not discuss Stephen's speech except to characterize it as marking the end of the missionary effort of the twelve to Jerusalem (*People of God,* 77).

[34] Franklin, *Christ the Lord,* 103.   So also N. A. Dahl ("The Story of Abraham in Luke-Acts," *Studies in Luke-Acts,* 148): "Stephen's own history is the continuation of that history which began by God's revelation to Abraham; it leads to the preaching in Samaria and

beyond." Thus, Dahl correctly sees the Stephen episode as the main turning point in Acts.

[35]The literature on the speeches in Acts and on the Stephen episode is enormous and cannot all be surveyed here. One should note particularly Wilckens, *Missionsreden;* Haenchen, *Apostelgeschichte,* 265-81; J. Bihler, "Der Stephanusbericht (Apg 6,8-15 und 7,54-8,2)," *BZ* nf 3 (1959) 252-70; J. Zmijewski, *Die Eschatologiereden des Lukas-Evangeliums* (BBB 40; Bonn: Hanstein, 1972); C. H. Talbert, *Literary Patterns, Theological Themes, and the Genre of Luke-Acts* (SBLMS 20; Missoula: SBL, and Scholars Press, 1974) 96-97; and esp. R. Pesch, *Die Vision des Stephanus: Apg 7,55-56 im Rahmen der Apostelgeschichte* (SBS 12; Stuttgart: Katholisches Bibelwerk, n.d.) 32, 38-39. Wilckens (*Missionsreden,* 222-23) considers Stephen's speech to be a pre-Lucan piece of Hellenistic Jewish Christian missionary preaching to Jews, which Luke has not only appropriated but also used as a model for the other speeches in Acts.

[36]The theme is so pronounced that nearly all commentators have seen it; see esp. Overbeck (DeWette), *Apostelgeschichte,* 110; and Loisy, *Actes,* 345-47; E. Kränkl (*Jesus der Knecht Gottes* [Regensburg: Pustet, 1972] 112) refers to Jewish guilt as a *"roter Faden"* running through the speech. See Bihler, "Stephanusbericht," 266, 270; Overbeck (DeWette), *Apostelgeschichte,* 94. Gnilka (*Verstockung,* 144-45) also sees that it is here the Jews' own fault that salvation goes over from them to the Gentiles. Haenchen ("Judentum und Christentum in der Apostelgeschichte," *ZNW* 54 [1963] 168) notes that here "the Jews had not ever even been the people of God." See also W. Schmithals, *Das Evangelium nach Lukas* (Zürcher Bibelkommentare; Zurich: Theologischer Verlag, 1980) 12.

[37]Wilckens (*Missionsreden,* 98) observes that the early speeches in Acts must combine the "Jesus Kerygma," dealing with Jesus' death, with "the call to repentance," but he is also keenly aware of the anti-Jewish polemic in Acts: "Whereas the passion tradition simply *established* . . . human dealing with the Son of man, the statements of the sermons [in Acts] have throughout a sharply *accusatory* note" (p. 119, emphasis his). Gnilka (*Verstockung,* 141) observes that Jewish ignorance *excuses* the Jews but does not *acquit* them.

[38]See further Wilckens, *Missionsreden,* 134.

[39]Conzelmann (*Theology,* 90) observes that "after the Resurrection . . . unbelief becomes inexcusable"; see also p. 93. While that is not incorrect, it is also clear that it is not the resurrection itself but the preaching about it that provides the κρίσις. Conzelmann also thinks that the accusation against the Jews and the excuse of ignorance stem from the interplay between Luke and his source (p. 92) and that "for the individual the way of salvation is open, now as always" (p. 145); but the themes are rather related to Luke's epochs. See further p. 162 n. 1. Gnilka (*Verstockung,* 141) has seen the point exactly; see also Kränkl, *Knecht,* 106.

[40] This point is widely recognized; see Loisy, *Actes,* 233;

Haenchen, *Apostelgeschichte*, 206 n. 3, 210; Hanson, *Acts*, 143; Conzelmann, *Apostelgeschichte*, 76; A. Wikenhauser, *Die Apostelgeschichte* (RNT; 3d ed.; Regensburg: Pustet, 1956) 155; Kränkl, *Knecht*, 103. Even Jacquier (*Actes*, 400) see that 13:27 is an accusation. It is this difference that Sandmel (*Anti-Semitism*, 73) has overlooked in finding "a residual concern in Luke to win Jews to Christianity"; see above, n. 18. Sandmel, however, correctly observes that "the theme of Jewish guilt for the death of Jesus is ascribed not to whatever Jews were present but to all the Jews in Jerusalem" (*Anti-Semitism*, 98).

[41] See Wilckens, *Missionsreden*, 134.

[42] Jervell, *People of God*, 44. A critique of Jervell's position on this point is also given by Wilson, *Gentiles*, 222-24.

[43] Franklin, *Christ the Lord*, 103.

[44] I do not intend by this statement to take a position regarding the much debated issue as to whether the Samaritans are Jews or Gentiles.

[45] While Franklin is more cautious at this point, I take his implication to be at least similar to Jervell's opinion about Acts 21:20. There is a variety of opinions among commentators on this issue. G. Stählin (*Die Apostelgeschichte* [NTD 5; Göttingen: Vandenhoeck & Ruprecht, 1962] 277) agrees that the reference is to new converts; but Overbeck ([DeWette], *Apostelgeschichte*, 381) and Loisy, (*Actes*, 794) think of all Jewish Christians, including those in the diaspora. Haenchen (*Apostelgeschichte*, 582) sees a hyperbole, and Jacquier (*Actes*, 632) votes both for all Jewish Christians and for a hyperbole. H. J. Holtzmann (*Die Apostelgeschichte* [HKNT 1/2; 3d ed.; Tübingen and Leipzig: Mohr (Siebeck), 1901] 131) thinks that the myriads are in Jerusalem.

[46] G. Lohfink (*Die Sammlung Israels: Eine Untersuchung zur lukanischen Ekklesiologie* [SANT 39; Munich: Kösel, 1975] 51-55) also describes massive Jewish conversions in the first section of Acts but resistance in the rest of the book. The "reversal . . . in 6:8-8:1 occurs abruptly and suddenly" (p. 54). The "true Israel" responds to the gospel immediately; the Israel that rejected the gospel in that first period of opportunity is incorrigible and "became Judaism" (p. 55).

[47] Jervell (*People of God*, 44) also notes the small number of Gentile conversions in Acts but reaches, as may be imagined, a conclusion different from the one presented here. Wilson (*Gentiles*, 227-33) presents a refutation of Jervell on this point but does not emphasize the role of Jewish rejection of the gospel portrayed by Luke for the Gentile mission. M. Tolbert ("Leading Ideas of the Gospel of Luke," *RevExp* 64 [1967] 445-46) sees that it is the Jews, not the gospel, who are to blame for their not being saved. Thus E. Trocmé (*Le "Livre des Actes" et l'histoire* [Etudes d'histoire et de philosophie religieuses 45; Paris: Presses universitaires de France, 1957] 118) considers Acts 13-28 "the trial of Israel, particularly of its *diaspora*." See further Haenchen ("Judentum und Christentum," 175-76) who observes that

"the entire *course of the Christian missionary Paul's life* is determined by the argument with the Jews."

[48]Since the Gentile mission, the hostility of the Jews, and the
salvation of the Gentiles are not the topic of this paper, they will not
be discussed further here, but it seemed necessary to refer at least
briefly to the major themes of the latter part of Acts in order better
to clarify the issue of Jewish salvation in Acts 12-28. For the conflicting viewpoints, see, on the one hand, Loisy, *Actes*, 541; and
Conzelmann, *Apostelgeschichte*, 77-78; and *Theology*, 212; and, on
the other hand, Jervell, *People of God*, 64-67; and Franklin, *Christ
the Lord*, 119-24 and 139-44. Haenchen (*Apostelgeschichte*, 398)
takes a middle position. The study of Dupont, "Le salut des gentils,"
while showing clearly the importance of the Gentile mission in Luke-
Acts, is somewhat ambiguous regarding the Jews. On the one hand,
Dupont observed (correctly) that the author of Luke-Acts emphasized
that the gospel should be preached first to the Jews and then to the
Gentiles (Dupont, "Le salut des gentils," 141, 146) and that it was
Jewish rejection of the gospel that impelled it toward the Gentiles
(p. 144). Yet he also emphasized the universal character of the gospel
in Luke-Acts (p. 154) and stated, "Whether one be Jew or Greek, to be
saved it is necessary to believe in Christ" (p. 149). His later essay
("Conclusion") was written to remove this ambiguity.

[49]Weiss, *Earliest Christianity*, 672. Wilckens (*Missionsreden*, 119)
observes that the mission to the Jews "is, as a whole, determined by
this polemical tendency."

[50]Conzelmann (*Apostelgeschichte*, 77) refers to the "*heilsgeschichtliche Prinzip*"; Loisy (*Actes*, 541) refers to the "*disposition
providentielle*." See also E. Lohse, "Lukas als Theologe der Heilsgeschichte," *Das Lukas-Evangelium. Die redaktions- und kompositionsgeschichtliche Forschung* (Wege der Forschung 280; ed. G. Braumann;
Darmstadt: Wissenschaftliche Buchgesellschaft, 1974) 79-80. Hauser
(*Apostelgeschichte*, 76-79) confirms the temporal distinction (a time
of salvation for the Jews is followed by a time of salvation for the
Gentiles) and the element of divine economy but denies that Jewish
rejection propels the gospel toward the Gentiles. He has, I believe,
overlooked the nuances observed above.

[51]Also Wilckens, *Missionsreden*, 134; see further J. Munck (*Paul
and the Salvation of Mankind* [Atlanta: John Knox, 1977] 245), who
also describes the transfer of salvation from the Jews to the Gentiles
as due, according to the author of Luke-Acts, both to God's plan and
to the Jews' disobedience.

[52]This is also, in general, the view of J. C. O'Neill, *The Theology
of Acts in Its Historical Setting* (2d ed.; London: SPCK, 1970) 87-95.
O'Neill does, however, hold out the possibility of an eventual conversion of Israel" (p. 87 n. 1). Similarly Rackham (*Acts*, 505): "So
through the fall of the Jews came the salvation of the Gentiles"; yet
he adds that those who believe were not rejected. Gnilka (*Verstockung*, 149) states that "a new Israel has come into existence, but

the old Israel . . . in its entirety is not included therein"; see further p. 150.

[53]With keen insight, Wilckens (*Missionsreden*, 182) has seen that the mission to the Jews in "the first Jewish Christian phase of church history" is, in Acts, a reformulation of "the general pattern of Hellenistic Christian conversion." This "*ordo salutis* for the guilty Jews" then appears as a "generally inclusive and normative image of conversion."

[54]See Bihler ("Stephanusbericht," 266): "*Das Judentum kann nicht mehr Gottesvolk sein*"; see further p. 270. Haenchen ("Source Material," 262) observes that, in the first part of Acts, the author "has constantly steered the plot toward a climax. . . . This conflict reaches its climax in the stoning of Stephen and the flight of the entire congregation (8:1)."

[55]Haenchen (*Apostelgeschichte*, 113, 289-90) offers an explanation of chaps. 8-11 that may suffice for now. It seems superfluous to discuss further here the transition from chap. 7 to chap. 12, since it is clear that Luke gets us, in the intervening chapters, from the Jewish to the Gentile mission. See also Dibelius, *Apostelgeschichte*, 146; Gnilka, *Verstockung*, 150 n. 105.

[56]Conzelmann, *Theology*, 210; see also idem, *Apostelgeschichte*, 50 (the martyrdom of Stephen "prepares theoretically the transition to the Gentile mission"); further, Conzelmann, *History of Primitive Christianity* (Nashville and New York: Abingdon, 1973) 35. The pronounced parallelism between the martyrdoms of Jesus and of Stephen (see below, n. 62) convince me of the superiority of Conzelmann's analysis to later attempts to improve on his position. In the theology of the author of Luke-Acts, an early and never-to-be-repeated phase of the time of the church, which was inaugurated by the martyrdom of Jesus, was brought to a close by the martyrdom of Stephen, which in turn inaugurated the time of the Gentile mission, which continues (theoretically) down to this day. Different dividing points for the history of the church have been proposed by Talbert (*Patterns*, 106) and by H. C. Kee (*Jesus in History* [New York: Harcourt Brace Jovanovich, 1977] 189-90).

[57]Loisy, *Actes*, 320. Dahl ("Abraham," 151) also sees that the salvation of the Jews is of no concern to Luke after the Stephen episode.

[58]Haenchen, *Apostelgeschichte*, 289.

[59]Jervell, *People of God*, 77. Hauser (*Apostelgeschichte*, 238) argues that the offering of salvation to the Jews is not over until the end of Acts. While we must keep clear the distinction between *offering* of salvation and *acceptance* of it, we need to note that Hauser has given an adequate and satisfactory explanation of the continued preaching of the gospel to the Jews in Acts right up until the end. Rome symbolizes "the end of the earth" for Jews as well as for Gentiles; when the Jews have finally rejected the gospel in Rome, they have rejected it in all the world. Hauser, himself, then confuses the issue when he adopts the view of Jervell, Conzelmann, and others

that individual Jews still have the opportunity to be saved. One cannot have it both ways. Either the Jews have rejected the gospel everywhere, since Stephen's death, or they have not. Conzelmann's epochal explanation is also supported by Wilckens (*Missionsreden*, 96-100, esp. p. 97). He also notes that it is in keeping with this epochal understanding that Jesus' ministry was among the Jews, concluding in Jerusalem (p. 97). G. Bornkamm ("The Missionary Stance of Paul in I Corinthians 9 and in Acts," *Studies in Luke-Acts* [see n. 5] 201), clarifies the Lucan perspective by a contrast with Paul: "While Paul views the Jewish and Gentile missions as simultaneous enterprises, Luke sees them as forming a *succession*." See also M. Hengel (*Acts and the History of Earliest Christianity* [Philadelphia: Fortress, 1979] 87), who refers to "Luke's pattern of a mission to the Jews, rejection by the Jews, mission to the Gentiles, which runs like a scarlet thread right through his work." See further Hanson (*Acts*, 102), who states that Stephen's "speech does not so much prepare us for the movement of the Church's mission towards the Gentiles as for its movement away from the Jews"; and E. Richard ("The Polemical Character of the Joseph Episode in Acts 7," *JBL* 98 [1979] 265): "The Stephen speech . . . is . . . a farewell speech to Judaism."

[60] Haenchen, *Apostelgeschichte*, 697. The need to bring together these two conflicting views is also noted by J. A. Fitzmyer ("Jewish Christianity in Acts in Light of the Qumran Scrolls," *Studies in Luke-Acts* [see n. 5] 235), who observes that "during all this growth the Christian group is marked off from the Jewish people as such"; see further pp. 234-39.

[61] See again the discussion above.

[62] Again, an analysis of the Stephen episode would take us beyond the scope of this paper. The parallelism between Jesus' martyrdom and Stephen's is well explained by Talbert, *Luke and the Gnostics. An Examination of the Lucan Purpose* (Nashville and New York: Abingdon, 1966) 76; Talbert, *Patterns*, 97; and W. Radl, *Paulus und Jesus im lukanischen Doppelwerk* (Europäische Hochschulschriften 23/49; Bern: Herbert Lang; Frankfurt: Peter Lang, 1975) 237; and one may also note that his speech is the longest of all the speeches in Acts (see Dibelius, *Apostelgeschichte*, 143-46).

[63] On the position sketched here, see also in general K. Löning, "Lukas—Theologe der von Gott geführten Heilsgeschichte (Lk, Apg), " *Gestalt und Anspruch des Neuen Testaments* (ed. J. Schreiner; Würzburg: Echter-Verlag, 1969) 222. Haenchen ("Source Material," 278) says that "Luke has written the Jews off." In light of this understanding, it is shocking to read a statement like that of Hengel (*Acts and History*, 64): "There is not a trace in his work of the ancient anti-semitism which was similarly not unknown to him." Hengel's reference to Luke's awareness of Gentile anti-Semitism, as is found in Acts 16:20-21, does not reduce Luke's own consignment of the Jews to ruin (p. 64). G. Braumann ("Das Mittel der Zeit. Erwägungen zur Theologie des Lukasevangeliums," *ZNW* 54 [1963] 135-40) argues that Luke presents no opposition between Judaism and church and that

Judaism and paganism are both secular political entities that stand over against the church as both mission field and opponent. Consequently, the only opposition in Luke-Acts is that between saved and unsaved, but this argument is so obviously contrary to the evidence that it will have to be labeled a tour de force. Braumann seems not to have read Acts 28:28.

[64]Thus W. C. Robinson, Jr. (*Der Weg des Herrn: Studien zur Geschichte und Eschatologie im Lukas-Evangelium: Ein Gespräch mit Hans Conzelmann* [TF 36; Hamburg-Bergstedt: H. Reich, 1964] 39, 43, 67) understands the Lord's "way" in Luke-Acts to be a way to the Gentiles. This is also the view of Zmijewski (*Eschatologiereden*) maintained at length in an analysis of Luke 20:5-36. See esp. p. 316: "The radical hardening of Judaism leads to its radical rejection. . . . At the same time, however, this hardening provides the means with which the help of which God can realize his universal plan of salvation. Salvation goes finally over to the Gentiles by the rejection of Israel." See in general pp. 43-325. So also R. Morgenthaler (*Die lukanische Geschichtsschreibung als Zeugnis* [Zurich: Zwingli, 1949] 1. 188): "If anything is clear, then it is this [overall conception]; it says that salvation is going over from the Jews to the Gentiles. . . . This and only this is the key to the riddle of the construction of the Lucan work."

[65]C. G. Montefiore (*The Synoptic Gospels* [2d ed.; London: Macmillan, 1927] 2. 395) has seen the role of this pericope exactly, as has also Loisy (*Les Evangiles synoptiques* [Ceffonds, près Montier-en-Der (Haute Marne): published by the author, 1907-8] 1. 839). See also W. Grundmann, *Das Evangelium nach Lukas* (THKNT 3; 7th ed.; Berlin: Evangelische Verlagsanstalt, 1974) 119; E. Klostermann, *Das Lukasevangelium* (HNT 5; 2d ed.; Tübingen: Mohr [Siebeck], 1929) 62; F. Hauck, *Das Evangelium des Lukas* (THKNT 3; Leipzig: Deichert, 1934) 63. W. J. Harrington (*The Gospel According to St. Luke* [New York: Newman, 1967] 87) calls the pericope a "synopsis" of Luke-Acts. See J. Wellhausen, *Das Evangelium Lucae* (Berlin: Reimer, 1904) 10; Holtzmann, *Apostelgeschichte*, 20; J. A. Fitzmyer, *The Gospel According to Luke (I-IX): Introduction, Translation, and Notes* (AB 28; Garden City: Doubleday, 1981) 529; I. H. Marshall, *The Gospel of Luke. A Commentary on the Greek Text* (NIGTC; Grand Rapids, MI: Eerdmans, 1978) 178. So also Sandmel, *Anti-Semitism*, 76-77. Tolbert ("Leading Ideas," 442-43) has correctly emphasized the importance of Jewish rejection in the framework of the narrative of Luke-Acts, namely, Luke 4:16-30 and the closing scene of Acts. Radl (*Paulus und Jesus*) compares Luke 4:16-30 with Acts 13:14-52, seeing both as "*Eröffnungsperikopen*" (p. 97) and as presenting "the opposition of Jews and Gentiles" (p. 98).

[66]H. Schürmann (*Das Lukasevangelium, erster Teil: Kommentar zu Kap. 1,1-9,50* [HTKNT 3; Freiburg: Herder, 1969] 236-39) makes this meaning abundantly clear. "πατρίς" (v. 24), he notes, "becomes ambiguous in the context," meaning both "father city" and, from v. 25 on, "fatherland" (pp. 237-38). See also Haenchen, "Historie und

Verkündigung bei Markus und Lukas," *Das Lukas-Evangelium* (see n. 50) 300; Kee, *Jesus in History*, 195; E. E. Ellis, *The Gospel of Luke* (NCB; Greenwood, SC: Attic Press, 1966) 96-98; Harrington, *St. Luke*, 88-89; E. J. Tinsley, *The Gospel According to Luke* (The Cambridge Bible Commentary, NEB; Cambridge: University Press, 1965) 53-54; Löning, "Theologie," 218-20; Dupont, "Le salut des gentils," 144. The way in which a few modern commentators endorse Luke's anti-Semitism is disheartening. The worst I have encountered is A. Plummer (*A Critical and Exegetical Commentary on the Gospel According to S. Luke* [ICC; 4th ed.; Edinburgh: T. & T. Clark, 1910] 128-29: "To this day the position remains the same; and Gentiles enjoy the Divine privileges of which the Jews have deprived themselves." J. M. Creed (*The Gospel According to St. Luke* [London: Macmillan, 1969] 66) takes the reference to Elijah and Elisha to be justifications of the absence of miracles in Nazareth. This is to overlook the references to Israel in vv. 25, 27.

[67]Similarly H. Gollwitzer, *Die Freude Gottes. Einführung in das Lukasevangelium* (5th ed.; Berlin-Dahlem; Gelnhausen/Hessen: Burck-hardthaus, n.d.) 54; Schmithals, *Lukas*, 63.

[68]Conzelmann's understanding of this important pericope (*Theology*, 33, 38) is inadequate; see Tolbert, "Leading Ideas," 442-43; and Radl, *Paulus und Jesus*, 97-98.

[69]So also Schürmann, *Lukasevangelium*, 1. 225; Menezes, "Lk 4:16-30," 250; further, Marshall, *Gospel of Luke*, 178 ("many of the main themes of Lk.-Acts in nuce"). Fitzmyer (*Luke*, 529) has come close to seeing this when he states that the story is an "encapsulation" of "the entire ministry of Jesus and the reaction to it." See J. W. Packer (*Acts of the Apostles* [The Cambridge Bible Commentary; Cambridge: University Press, 1966] 222, on Acts 28:28): "Since the Jews refused to listen, *this salvation of God has been sent to the Gentiles*, who will. This is the whole burden of Luke's great work. The mission to the Gentiles has been foretold by Simeon (Luke 2:32). The gospel narrative led up to Israel's rejection of the Messiah, as Stephen reminded his hearers (7:52). Therefore, it is now the Gentiles' turn and they will accept the message." Schmithals (*Lukas*, 62) observes that "the people from Nazareth thus become the example of all Jews, the people of his hometown the example of all his countrymen, his native city the symbol of the fatherland."

[70]This is the opinion of Sandmel (*Anti-Semitism*, 73), who finds "in Luke a frequent subtle, genteel anti-Semitism," whereas in Acts the subtlety "recedes and the anti-Semitism becomes overt and direct."

[71]So also K. L. Schmidt, *Der Rahmen der Geschichte Jesu* (Berlin: Trowitzsch & Sohn, 1919) 267. Schmidt notes (p. 268) that one may learn from the following verses "that Jesus is not rejected by the Samaritans everywhere" (p. 268). He sees this characterization as part of Luke's "*Missionspolitik*," since "many Samaritans became Christians" (ibid.). Conzelmann (*Theology*, 65) sees the two rejections as parallel, inaugurating the main stages of Jesus' public ministry.

[72]For a fuller discussion of this point, see my article, "The Parable

of the Pounds and Lucan Anti-Semitism," *TS* 42 (1981) 660-68. Lohse ("Lukas als Theologe," 79) connects the three rejections in Luke 4:30; 9:51-56; and 19:37 to three periods in Jesus' ministry but does not note the theologically loaded differences among the three episodes.

[73] See M. D. Goulder (*Type and History in Acts* [London: SPCK, 1964] 59): "The theme of Luke 10-13 is the failure of Israel, its keyword is ὑποκριταί." Loisy (*Evangiles synoptiques*, 2. 102) also contrasts the attitude toward the Samaritans in Luke 9:51-56 to the attitude toward the Jews in 4:16-30. Fitzmyer (*Luke*, 827) thinks that Jesus' rejection of retribution in 9:54 is a rejection of identification with Elijah. What will he propose for 19:27?

[74] Sandmel (*Anti-Semitism*, 77-80) gives these and other instances of anti-Semitic constructions in the Gospel of Luke.

[75] So also Weiss, *Earliest Christianity*, 664; Creed, *St. Luke*, 283, 285, very mildly.

[76] So also Lohse, "Lukas als Theologe," 81; Dupont, "Le salut des gentils," 139-41. Weiss (*Earliest Christianity*, 661) takes this to mean that "the original destination of the Twelve to Israel [as in Matthew] is completely forgotten"; and he contrasts the Lucan program of Acts 1:8 ("to the ends of the earth") with the narrative of Acts, which confines the twelve to Jerusalem.

[77] The tone of these remarks on the opinion of the author of Luke-Acts about the salvation of the Jews has probably made my own attitude clear; but, for the record, I should like to state that, as far as I am concerned, Jews—and all other people—are entirely free and welcome to convert to Christianity—or to any other religion—if they so wish.

Robert L. Brawley

PAUL IN ACTS: LUCAN
APOLOGY AND CONCILIATION

The problem of the Lucan Paul in its briefest form is that the Paul of the Epistles is a different Paul.[1] What is one to make out of the fact that Luke accommodates Paul toward Judaism? Nineteenth-century *Tendenz* criticism offered answers ranging from views that Acts is an apology against Jewish detractors of Christianity to opinions that it is an irenic attempt to reconcile conflicts between Jewish and Gentile Christianity.[2] These solutions today are only slightly considered, because of the dominant opinion that Luke so definitively rejects the Jews that he could not have addressed them or their sympathizers. This essay is an avowed revisionist attempt to reclaim some of the seminal features of these dormant concepts. The thesis is that Luke textures his portrait of Paul to counter anti-Paulinism from both Jewish and Christian sectors. It hangs on the proposal that Luke focuses on the Pauline Gentile mission rather than on the general advance of Christianity in the Roman Empire, and it challenges notions that Luke makes no attempt to legitimate Paul. The approach to the problem that follows is to demonstrate that Luke does not repudiate the Jews but uses them to explain Paul's Gentile campaign (Section I), to cite Hellenistic literary parallels that show some of the ways Luke legitimates Paul (Section II), and to identify Luke's anti-Pauline opponents from traces he leaves in the text (Section III).

I. Luke and the Jews

Hans Conzelmann typifies the preponderant interpretation of Luke's view of the Jews. Conzelmann detects a design whereby Luke intentionally rejects Jews in Asia Minor (Acts 13:46), Greece (18:6), and Rome (28:28). When Luke repeats the rejection of the Jews for the third time, the divorce of Christianity and Judaism becomes final.[3] But the repudiation of the Jews is the reciprocal reaction of

129

their initial rejection of the gospel. When the Jews refuse to believe, the gospel passes to the Gentiles.

In contrast, Jacob Jervell argues strongly that Jewish acceptance of the gospel rather than rejection forms the presupposition for the Gentile mission.[4] The progressive growth of Jewish converts shows that to a considerable extent the Jewish mission is a success.[5] Jewish conversion to the gospel means that Israel's role is to mediate the gospel to Gentiles. For Jervell, therefore, Jewish unbelief has no causal relationship to the Gentile mission. Rather, the mission is the result of the plan of God alone.

Both the standard theory of reciprocal rejection and Jervell's theory of Israel as mediator for the Gentiles place far too much emphasis on the Gentile mission in its broader scope. Luke exhibits less interest in the extension of the gospel beyond Israel than do most of his commentators.[6] Rather, he concentrates on *Paul's* Gentile campaign.

To be sure, Luke has a stake in the larger Gentile mission. He validates the accession of Gentiles to the church in his accounts of the conversion of Cornelius and the Jerusalem Council. But he has no interest in following Peter or Philip beyond Caesarea. After Barnabas and Mark separate from Paul, Luke provides only the barest summary of their activities (Acts 15:39). Luke leaves Apollos as quickly as he finds him (18:24-19:1). Paul's associates Silas, Timothy, and Erastus play subsidiary roles for Luke. Luke focuses single-mindedly on Paul's Gentile mission.

Some particular features of those passages where Paul reorients his mission to Gentiles bring Luke's emphasis on the Pauline ministry into greater clarity. In Antioch of Pisidia the opposition of Jews to Paul and Barnabas leads to the resolution, "We turn to the Gentiles" (Acts 13:46). The explicit reference to Paul and Barnabas in the first person plural means that these two (and these alone) now turn to the Gentiles. On another occasion Jewish opposition to Paul produces Paul's personal declaration to go to the Gentiles: "I am innocent. From now on I will go to the Gentiles" (18:6). In Acts, Jewish antagonism is connected causally with the Gentile mission only when Paul is involved.[7]

The failure of Jews to accept the gospel has little to do with the overall fact that the gospel extends to Gentiles, but it has much to do with the fact that Paul himself moves beyond the Jews. Jewish unbelief forms half of a double-edged explanation for Paul's own Gentile mission. On the one hand, the course of Paul's ministry is controlled supernaturally. On the other hand, it has an empirical cause. From the time of Paul's conversion Acts testifies that his Gentile mission proceeds from God's plan. His experience on the road near Damascus destines him to be God's envoy to the Gentiles as well as to the Jews (Acts 9:15; 22:21; 26:17). His selection along with Barnabas for a mission beyond Antioch is made in response to the word of the Holy Spirit (13:2). Paul and Barnabas claim God's command as the basis for their turning toward the Gentiles (13:47). Thus, God clearly controls the direction of Paul's mission. But on an experiential level the opposition of unbelieving Jews coincides with the supernatural impetus for Paul's departure to the Gentiles. God's design for Paul's mission to the Gentiles moves toward its fulfillment because Jews refuse Paul's preaching.[8]

But at no place are the Jews definitively rejected. The excursion into the Jewish synagogue in Iconium is Paul's first reported activity after he declares his intention to go to the Gentiles (Acts 14:1). Similar scenes occur at 16:13; 17:1, 10, 17; 18:4. Likewise, after Paul's second announcement of his decision to go to the Gentiles (18:6), he continues to frequent the synagogue (18:19; 19:8). Furthermore, Paul's interest in reflecting a positive image to Jews leads to his purification in the temple (21:20-26). In his apologetic speeches he consistently claims solidarity with Judaism.[9] Three days after Paul's arrival in Rome he summons Jewish leaders to tell them that his imprisonment is the result of his commitment to the hope of Israel (28:17-20). His ministry in Rome indicates that in spite of his declarations to go to the Gentiles, the Jews continue to occupy a strategic place in his mission (28:3).

Although Paul meets Jewish obduracy with severe warnings, he never gives up on the Jews as such. In Acts 13:46 Paul holds impenitent Jews responsible for renouncing the word of God and thereby judging themselves unworthy of eternal life. His emphasis there is on the personal accountability of Jews who have heard the word of God rather than on some implicit resolve to forsake all Jews. The responsibility of the Jews who have heard Paul's testimony is once again the issue in Acts 18:6. Paul apparently alludes to Ezek 3:18, 20, where the destiny of the guilty is placed under the responsibility of God's representative. But here Paul reverses the agument. The representative disclaims his own liability and places the burden of responsibility on the unbelieving Jews.

The gestures of shaking dust from the feet (Acts 13:51) and shaking out clothing (18:6) further implicate the Jews and exonerate Paul. Shaking dust from the feet releases Paul from responsibility, and the dust remains as an inescapable testimony against the unbelieving Jews.[10] Words of Paul interpret the act of shaking out clothing: "Your blood be upon your heads! I am innocent" (18:6). Clearly, therefore, these symbolic actions warn the Jews of their responsibility and absolve Paul of his.

But neither gesture indicates that Paul repudiates the Jews. Immediately after Paul shakes out his clothing, he converts Crispus, the ruler of the synagogue, and his entire household (Acts 18:8). After Paul and Barnabas leave Antioch of Pisidia, they go to the synagogue in Iconium, where many Jews believe along with many Greeks (14:1). Moreover, shaking dust from the feet does not impede the return of Paul and Barnabas to Antioch.[11] Paul counters Jewish opposition with stringent warnings, but the alleged reciprocal rejection does not materialize in 13:46 or 18:6.

Acts 28:28 repeats the pattern of 13:46 and 18:6. The incredulity of some of Paul's Jewish visitors in Rome merits the insulting characterizations of Isa 6:9-10: "This people's heart has grown dull, and their ears are heavy of hearing and their eyes they have closed" (Acts 28:27). But once again the alleged reciprocal rejection does not develop. The unbelief of some of the Jews forces Paul to turn to the Gentiles. But there is no anathema against Jews as such. The unbelief of some Jews in Rome is a confirmation of the harsh prophecy from Isaiah 6. But Isaiah 6 applies to the hardening of Jews who have already been addressed instead of Jews to be addressed in the future.[12] Moreover, prophetic reproofs are so common in Jewish tradition that Acts 28:28 would hardly convey final rejection.[13] The sense of Acts 28:28 is that the behavior of the Jews explains Paul's mission to the Gentiles.

In his admirable study on the use of Isa 6:9-10 in Acts 28, Joachim Gnilka falls prey to the fallacy of considering Acts an account of the expansion of the gospel to Gentiles in general. He quite correctly concludes that, at the end of Acts, Isa 6:9-10 shows that the hardening of unbelieving Jews was foreseen by God and predicted by Isaiah. But he incorrectly infers that the hardening results in the transition of the gospel from Jews to Gentiles and, therefore, that Luke rejects the Judaism of his own time.[14] In Acts 28:29 Gentiles claim no exclusive proprietorship of the gospel. In fact, 28:30 makes it clear that even Paul's mission is still open to "all" (pantes).[15] The second half of Acts, rather than describing in general the accession of the Gentiles to the gospel and their assumption of a place of preference over the Jews, chronicles the development of Paul's mission to Gentiles and demonstrates why he turns to them without reservation.

The way Isa 6:9-10 functions elsewhere supports the conclusion that Acts 28 does not write off the Jews. In the original setting in the concrete circumstances of the Syro-Ephraimite war, Isaiah proclaimed what he had heard as an observer of a heavenly council, namely, that God's judgment upon Judah had been predestined. So strongly had Judah's destruction been determined that it was the task of the prophet to keep the people unaware of the inevitable judgment: "Make the heart of this people fat, and their ears heavy, and shut their eyes" (Isa 6:9).[16] Nevertheless, Isaiah pursued the salvation of the people of Judah rather than their rejection.[17]

New Testament allusions to Isa 6:9-10, following the Septuagint, give up the idea that the hardening of the people is a part of the prophet's task. Rather, the failure to understand has become characteristic of the people from the start. In the synoptic gospels, Isa 6:9-10 explains the failure of the crowds to understand the parables of Jesus. In John 12:40 it explains the unbelief of the Jews in the face of Jesus' entire ministry.

A similar tendency to explain a refusal to believe appears in Justin Martyr's use of Isa 6:10. Although there is only slight literal correspondence between Justin's vocabulary and that of the Septuagint and although in one instance Justin claims to refer to Jeremiah, he likely has Isa 6:10 in mind in at least three places in the *Dialogue with Trypho*. In chaps. 12 and 33 he chides Jews for their refusal to repent. In chap. 69 he speaks of Gentiles who did not believe before their access to the gospel. Thus, although Justin polemicizes against Jews, he uses Isa 6:9-10 to explain unbelief rather than to express rejection.[18]

Just as little does Acts 28:26-27 refer to the rejection of the Jews. Acts 28:28, therefore, is no more a final abandonment of the Jews than was 13:46 or 18:6. Its location at the conclusion of Acts and its rounding off of the threefold schema of announcing the reorientation of Paul's mission are not designed to depict the ultimate renunciation of the Jews. Rather, on the basis of the patterns established after 13:46 and 18:6, there is every reason to interpret the reference to Paul's welcome to "all" (*pantes*) in 28:30 as indicating that he is still engaged in a mission to Jews after 28:28.

Luke does not leave us in the dark about why he wishes to account for the course of Paul's ministry. In Acts 21 the mob in Jerusalem tolerates Paul's defense until he claims that the risen Christ commanded him to go to the Gentiles. At that point they cry out against him (vv. 21-22). According to Acts 26:21, 23 Jewish opponents protest when Paul extends the gospel to Gentiles. It is against such objections to Pauline universalism that Luke takes up the challenge of defending Paul's Gentile mission.

The threefold announcement of Paul's mission to the Gentiles, occurring strategically in Asia Minor, Greece, and Rome, is designed to serve as part of Luke's response to the question, Why does Paul go to the Gentiles? Luke provides two basic answers. First, God determines the direction of Paul's mission. Second, the unbelief of some

Jews causes Paul to turn to Gentiles. In a sense Luke also has a third answer. Paul does not simply ignore the Jews in order to embrace the Gentiles. Rather, he consistently proclaims the gospel to both.

II. Legitimating Techniques

That Luke thinks it necessary to explain Paul's Gentile mission implies that Luke attempts to legitimate Paul. Karl Löning resists such a conclusion. He argues that Luke does not validate Paul but simply allows him to speak. Löning claims that Luke makes use of Paul as an established figure in the Christian community rather than defending him.[19] But Luke's explanation of why Paul turns to the Gentiles proves Löning to be in error. Furthermore, Luke feels compelled to defend Paul as a faithful Jew (see Section III). And if the explanation of the reorientation of Paul's mission to the Gentiles and of his Jewishness were not enough, Luke's use of literary techniques of legitimation adds confirmation to his efforts to justify Paul.

Luke punctuates significant junctures in his narrative with prodigious events. Strange signs accompany the inauguration of the Christian mission on Pentecost (Acts 2). Peter extends the mission to a Gentile God-fearer because his own heavenly vision coincides with Cornelius's vision of an angel (Acts 10). Saul the persecutor stops devastating the saints and becomes a Christian missionary when a heavenly light and the voice of the risen Jesus confront him (Acts 9, 22, 26). In a larger context such signs provide divine sanction for the course of *Heilsgeschichte*. Legitimation is thus a key to the entire structure of Acts.[20] But in a more particular way portentous signs also explain Paul's motivations and legitimate his activities.

The conspicuous correspondence between Acts and a wide range of literature from antiquity makes it certain that Luke accommodates to Hellenistic literary devices and adapts them for his purposes.[21] Among those literary devices are conventional methods of legitimation, which Luke uses to project his portrait of Paul.

When Paul performs miracles, has visions, receives oracles from God, and survives mortal dangers, that is enough for many commentators to conclude that Luke attempts to depict Paul as a Hellenistic "divine man."[22] Although the concept of *theios anēr* may help to demonstrate parallels between Luke's Paul and other ancient heroes, it may also obscure the function of the miraculous in the Lucan portrait of Paul. It is not as if Luke is obligated to fit Paul to a stereotype of the divine man, but that he uses conventional techniques to enhance the status of Paul.[23]

David Tiede traces two distinct traditions in which ancient heroes are authenticated—the wise man and the miracle worker.[24] These two traditions tend to exclude each other. Cultured authors in the wise man tradition frequently reject the miraculous. Luke-Acts synthesizes the two traditions so that the miraculous stands in close proximity to appeals to the cultured.[25] But this means that Luke enlarges the range of legitimating factors. Luke takes such great pains to authenticate Paul that he even uses competing methods. So wide a range of methods forces us to expand the standard *theios anēr* category and even to move beyond it. No one category is sufficient to encompass Luke's efforts to authenticate Paul. Luke uses whatever means he considers appropriate.

The criteria of Luke's intended audience, however, apparently determine the appropriateness of the legitimating techniques. To the degree that there are literary parallels to Luke's methods of legitimation, the probability increases that Luke employs conventional devices to authenticate Paul. That is, Luke so paints the portrait of Paul that he fits a popular scale of values for judging authenticity.[26] Luke uses at least six major categories of legitimating techniques, all of which have strong counterparts in Hellenistic literature: (1) divine approval, (2) access to divine power, (3) high motivation, (4) benefiting others, (5) possessing a high level of culture, and (6) adhering to an ancient tradition.

The three accounts of Paul's conversion constitute an intricate system of techniques that convey the sense of divine approval and demonstrate high motivation. Complexity arises from Luke's use of secondary legitimating factors within the basic Christophany. Paul's blindness (Acts 9:8, 12, 18) substantiated the Christophany; Ananias's vision (9:10-16) provides its meaning. The divine message indicates overtly that Paul is chosen by God and his mission divinely ordained. But the Christophany and the vision of Ananias are themselves legitimating techniques that communicate divine sanction quite apart from the explicit message.

Euripides employs a strikingly similar technique. In the *Bacchanals* (469) Dionysus defends his mission to bring a new religion to Greece by claiming that it was based on a theophany of Zeus.[27] In the context Pentheus questions the status of Dionysus as well as the basis for spreading his mysteries in Hellas. Thus, the theophany, like Paul's Christophany, vindicates Dionysus and provides divine motivation for his mission.

Paul's survival of opposition and danger also clearly communicates God's approval. In Lystra hostile Jews foment a near-fatal attack on Paul. But miraculously Paul gets up, reenters Lystra, and continues his journey the very next day (Acts 14:19-20).[28]

A similar theme emerges in Paul's escape from a shipwreck (27:13-44) and his survival of a snakebite (28:3-6).[29] Both events reflect conventional ideas in antiquity that calamity metes out divine justice upon evildoers.[30] But Luke presents the opposite side of those ideas, so that survival reveals God's approbation. The unflappable Paul[31] prophesies disaster for the sea voyage in 27:10 and then by means of a message from an angel of God describes the outcome of the shipwreck ahead of time. When things turn out as predicted, his relation to God is vindicated. If that were not enough, all 276 passengers on board the ship escape with their lives because God wishes to save Paul (27:24; cf. 27:42-43). Moreover, Paul remains unscathed in spite of a viper's bite. To survive both shipwreck and snakebite reverses the expectations of the Maltese and so astounds them that they consider Paul divine (28:6).

The belief that shipwreck is divine punishment comes to light repeatedly in antiquity. The mariners on Jonah's ship presuppose that divine powers enrage the sea against an evildoer (Jonah 1:4-8). In b. B. Meṣ. 59b R. Gamaliel, the Nasi and principal leader in banning R. Eliezer b. Hyrcanus, is traveling in a ship. When a huge wave threatens him, he deduces that it is divine judgment on account of the excommunication, and he cries out, "Sovereign of the Universe! Thou knowest full well that I have acted not for my honour, nor for the honour of my paternal house, but for Thine, so that strife may not multiply in Israel!" Then the sea subsided.

In another example of the belief that maritime disaster represents divine retribution, Antiphon presents a defense at the trial of Helos, who has been implicated in the death of Herodes during a journey by ship. Helos declares that the murder took place on land while the ship was in harbor. He then argues that the fact that the voyage continued without difficulty proves that the malefactor was not on board. That is, Helos assumes that his jury shares his own belief that if he were guilty, divine retribution would have brought disaster upon the subsequent voyage.[32]

There is also wide circulation in antiquity of the view that serpents dispatch divine justice. When the Israelites grumble in the wilderness, God sends fiery serpents to bite them (Num 21:5-6). In t. Sanh. 7:3 Shimeon b. Shatah follows a man who chases another into a deserted building. Inside Shimeon discovers the pursuer with a bloody sword standing over the dead body of the other man. Since the law requires two witnesses, his testimony against the murderer is inadequate. "But he who knows the thoughts, he exacts vengeance from the guilty; for the murderer did not stir from that place before a serpent bit him so that he died."[33] In another case, a papyrus fragment tells about a son who has murdered his father. He attempts to escape into the desert, but a lion pursues him. When he climbs a tree to elude the lion, he encounters a snake.[34]

In a reversal of expectation, however, Paul's survival of the viper's bite reflects divine approval. This idea also surfaces elsewhere. In the longer ending of Mark, mastery over snakes and poison legitimates the gospel message and indirectly its proponents (16:18-20). Moreover, the tendency to embellish the status of heroes is so strong that in some instances it is the serpent that dies. *B. Ber.* 33a relates an incident about a poisonous reptile that has been injuring people. When R. Ḥanina b. Dosa hears, he puts his heel over the reptile's hole. The reptile bites him and it dies. Similarly, in *Acts of Thomas* 30-33 a jealous serpent kills the suitor of a beautiful woman it loves. Thomas commands the snake to suck the poison back out of the corpse. The man revives, and the serpent dies.

Evidence of divine sanction stands behind miraculous release from prison and fetters. After Paul and Silas are imprisoned in Philippi, an earthquake opens the prison doors and the fetters (Acts 16:19-26). The jailer exhibits a typical interpretation of such an incident. When he prostrates himself before Paul and Silas trembling with fear and pleads for his salvation, he testifies that God vindicates his messengers.[35]

Comparable marvels validate Dionysus. Pentheus commands his servants to fetter and imprison Dionysus. He yields willingly, but the fetters fall from his feet of their own accord, and the doors unbar themselves.[36] In another case, when Apollonius's companion Damis is distressed because his master is in prison, Apollonius takes his leg out of the fetters and inserts it once again. The narrator indicates the legitimating force of the incident by remarking that when Damis observed the marvel, he realized for the first time that Apollonius was divine and superhuman (Philostratus *Life of Apollonius* 7.38).

In addition to demonstrating God's approval, another way in which Luke attempts to authenticate Paul is to show that Paul has access to divine power. In Acts 28 healing miracles follow Paul's survival of the viper's bite. The healings result in the enhanced status of Paul among the Maltese so that they shower him with gifts (vv. 7-10). In Acts 20:7-12 Luke somewhat cryptically relates the raising of Eutychus from the dead. Admittedly, Luke makes no mention of the manifestation of the power of God in either case. But his programmatic summary in 19:11 sets the stage for inferring such a manifestation: "And God did extraordinary miracles by the hands of Paul."[37]

Parallels from a wide variety of sources show once again that Luke is using popular devices. In *Acts of Peter* 31.2 Peter heals the sick, in contrast to Simon the magician, who only appears to do so. Simon is discredited, but Peter's miracles reveal his faith in the true God. The raising of Eutychus carries overtones of similar actions of Elijah (1 Kgs 17:17-24) and Elisha (2 Kgs 4:32-37). Another miraculous raising of the dead occurs when Apollonius touches a young woman who died on her wedding day and whispers a secret spell to her (Philostratus *Life of Apollonius* 4.45). The restoration to life enhances the status of each miracle worker, but it is nowhere more clear than in the words of the widow of Zarephath to Elijah: "Now I know that you are a man of God, and that the word of the Lord in your mouth is truth" (1 Kgs 17:24).

Besides showing that Paul's mission is divinely motivated from the beginning, Luke presents Paul's subsequent behavior as based on high motives. Paul obeys the guidance of visions and of the Spirit (Acts 16:9; 18:9-10; 19:21; 22:18-21). Moreover, he explicitly declares that he risks his life to fulfill the commission from Jesus Christ (20:24; 21:13-14) and that he seeks no personal gain (20:33).

To attribute behavior to dreams and oracles is a prominent means of justifying motives in antiquity. Socrates feels commanded by God through oracles and dreams (Plato *Apology* 33C). Apollonius detours on a trip to Rome because he has a dream that compels him to go to Crete (Philostratus *Life of Apollonius* 4.34). Although Lucian views Alexander of Abonoteichus as a fraud, he reports that the impostor attempted to legitimate himself and to enhance the reputation of a new temple by oracles (*Alexander* 22-24).[38]

Disregard of hardship and death also legitimates heroes. Socrates willingly accepts hardship and faces death most nobly.[39] Demosthenes' suicide by poison to avoid capture by the Macedonians reveals his invincible soul and brave spirit (Lucian *Demosthenes* 43-50). Diogenes is a model for a young scout to emulate, because he disdained death and hardship (Epictetus *Discourses* 1.24.3-10).

A closely related authenticating characteristic is the willingness to disregard personal gain. Part of Socrates' defense is that he does not profit from his philosophy (Plato *Apology* 19D-E), and he denounces those who do (Xenophon *Memorabilia* 1.2.6-7). Philo notes that some people travel for pleasure or financial advantage, but he portrays Abraham as one who migrates in obedience to God and gives no thought to personal gain (*On Abraham* 62-67). Josephus charges that his colleagues accept bribes to allow John of Gischala access to imperial grain, but he defends himself as unswayed by monetary enticements (*Life* 13 §§70-73).

The other side of disregard for personal gain is concern for the benefit of others. Throughout his mission in Acts, Paul exemplifies the saying of Jesus "It is more blessed to give than to receive" (Acts 20:35). But the behavior of Paul and Silas when the Philippian jail is opened aptly illustrates the extent to which others receive benefit. After saving the jailer from suicide, Paul imparts to him and his household yet another salvation (16:25-34). Moreover, if the goodness of God has already been manifested prior to the advent of the gospel

(14:17), how much more the benefit now that Paul calls his hearers to God.[40]

Laudable action on behalf of others redounds to the honor of many of the ancients. Socrates claims that he merits no punishment, since he has been the benefactor of Athens (Plato *Apology* 36 A-D). Demosthenes defends himself as worthy of a golden crown awarded to him by Ctesiphon, because he has acted for the genuine benefit of the city (*De Corona*, passim). Josephus claims that the Galileans in Gabaroth rally to him and proclaim him benefactor and savior (*Life* 47 §244).

When Luke presents Paul as cultured and educated, he relies on a stock method of claiming authenticity. The clearest examples of Paul's social standing are his claims to Roman citizenship (Acts 16:37; 21:39; 22:25-28) and his account of his education under Gamaliel (22:3). But elsewhere in Acts, Paul more subtly exhibits his culture. In the Areopagus scene Luke uses motifs reminiscent of Socrates (17:16-31),[41] and a sophisticated Paul quotes poets who express Stoic themes.[42] Moreover, Luke spatters Paul's speech before Agrippa (26:2-23) with cultivated language[43] and has Paul claim a heavenly message that has literary antecedents: "It is hard for you to kick against the goads" (26:14).[44]

In antiquity education and culture appear repeatedly as important factors in establishing the recognition for heroes.[45] Demosthenes expresses the negative side of the value of culture by arguing that his opponent Aeschines was reared in poverty as a servant rather than as a freeborn son (*De Corona* 258). Josephus extolls his own illustrious genealogy and boasts of his education (*Life* 2 §§8-9). When Cicero wishes to place himself among the orators, he details his education and emphasizes that much of it took place among distinguished teachers in Greece and Asia Minor (*Brutus* 306-21).

Cicero prizes the location of his education, because many ancients were infatuated with long-standing traditions from the East.[46] Luke betrays his own distrust of novelty by describing the curiosity of the Athenians (Acts 17:21) and then having Paul allude to their disposition as the "times of ignorance" (v. 30). Although the Athenians label the resurrection a "new teaching" (v. 19), Paul traces God's activity back to creation (v. 24). Elsewhere Luke shows that Paul's proclamation of the resurrection represents ancient Jewish tradition attested by written prophecies (24:14; 26:6, 22). Thus, for all the novelty of the specific resurrection of Jesus, Paul's message is nothing other than the venerable Jewish tradition.

Parallels in other ancient literature verify the veneration of tradition. Demosthenes repeatedly defends his actions as being in accord with the forefathers (*De Corona* 199, 204, 210). Although Apollonius has supernatural knowledge, he still associates with the sages of the

East and claims that the Indians are the true fathers of philosophy (Philostratus *Life of Apollonius* 1.18; 3.13; 6.6-11). Josephus acknowledges a tendency of virtually every nation to trace its law back to early dates to create the impression that it set the example for its neighbors. Then Josephus asserts that Moses is the most ancient of all legislators (*Ag. Ap.* 1.20-21 §§151-56). Tertullian takes advantage of the common acceptance of the value of high antiquity to argue that Christianity is supported by Jewish scriptures, ". . . the oldest which exist" (*Apology* 19-21).

The upshot of this documentation of parallels in ancient literature is that Luke employs conventional literary techniques to project his image of Paul. Because those devices are so widespread, the evidence stops short of demonstrating direct literary borrowing. Rather, the techniques belong to the public domain. Moreover, the extensive distribution of the devices makes it unnecessary to trace genealogical relationships. The vast diffusion of similar methods testifies to their far-reaching effectiveness whether the authors predate or postdate Luke. What is noteworthy is that on a large number of counts Luke uses popular methods to explain Paul's motivation and to legitimate his activities. Luke's explanation of the reorientation of Paul's mission to the Gentiles, his concern with the defense of Paul, and his use of legitimating techniques make the conclusion unavoidable that Luke expends considerable energy to justify Paul as an emissary of the divine.

III. Luke's Opponents

In the light of the effort Luke devotes to the legitimation of Paul, the question now arises: For what purpose does the legitimation take place? For some time scholars have recognized a general propagandistic intent behind the use of legitimating devices.[47] They facilitate the acceptance of an author's program among curious Hellenistic audiences. Luke wants his work to find popular acceptance. But he also manifests a more precise purpose especially by the way he combats perspectives he wishes to discredit, that is, by the way he deals with opponents.

Paul's speech at Miletus (Acts 20:18-35) is an informative starting point to discover the identity of the opponents. Here Luke uses a farewell discourse ostensibly to warn against future heresy; in actuality he combats dangers of his own time. Paul predicts the advent of heretics after his departure (v. 29). Luke conceives of his era so definitively as the time after Paul's departure that he stands in the period of the heretics.[48] In the farewell discourse the problem of the heretics stands behind Paul's attempts to justify himself.[49] Their charges draw rejoinders that Paul cannot be responsible for the disintegrating situation in Asia Minor and that his gospel is complete. Because Paul responds that he has declared the entire counsel of God (vv. 20, 27), many interpreters deduce that the heretics are Gnostics who appeal to a secret teaching of Paul.[50] Paul's assertion that he has proclaimed the entire will of God would, therefore, rob the heretics of their esoteric Pauline tradition.

Such ingenious exegesis merits esteem if not approval. It runs aground because it fails to consider adequately the larger context. When we scrutinize the entire career of Paul in Acts, we discover that it is Jews who consistently raise problems for Paul. Jews plot to kill Paul in Damascus (9:23). Paul draws the wrath of Jewish Hellenists in Jerusalem (9:29).[51] The Jewish false prophet Bar-Jesus opposes Paul at Paphos on Cyprus (13:6-8). Jealous Jews in Antioch of Pisidia incite persecution against Paul and Barnabas (13:45, 50). Unbelieving Jews in Iconium stir up Gentiles against the Christian missionaries (14:2, 5). Jews from Antioch and Iconium lead a lynch mob against Paul in Lystra (14:19). Jews create an uproar in Thessalonica (17:5) and then hound Paul out of Beroea (17:13). In Corinth, Jews revile and accuse Paul (18:6, 12). In Jerusalem, Jews drag Paul out of the temple, attempt to kill him (21:30-31), and demonstrate against him when he addresses them (22:22-23). More than forty Jews plot to kill Paul in Jerusalem and take the chief priests and elders into their confidence (23:12-14). Tertullus prosecutes Paul before Felix (24:1-8), and Jews at large second his charges (24:9). The chief priests and leaders of the Jews in Jerusalem contrive with Festus against Paul (25:2-3). Later, Jews from Jerusalem go to Caesarea to testify against him (25:7).

There are two exceptions to the Jewish matrix of Paul's problems. In Philippi the owners of a slave girl seize Paul and Silas and drag them before the magistrate (16:20). In Ephesus, Demetrius the silversmith leads a riot against Paul (19:23-41). A notable coincidence between the two cases holds a clue to the way Luke views these incidents. In both instances the Jewishness of Christianity comes to the front. The slave owners accuse Paul and Silas of being Jews (16:20). And Alexander inadvertently incites the Ephesian rioters when they recognize that he is Jewish (19:34). These cases show that Luke is aware of pagan opposition to the Jewishness of Christianity, but the repeated instigation of hostility by Jews proves to be the far more serious problem for him.

Moreover, in the Miletus address Paul explicitly attributes his difficulties in Ephesus to the plots of the Jews (20:19). Shortly thereafter in the line of the narrative, Jewish accusations await Paul on his final visit to Jerusalem. Unsettling rumors that Paul teaches Jews of the diaspora to forsake the law have adverse effects on Jewish Christians there (21:21). Paul then devotes his energies to vindicating himself from such a false understanding by purifying himself in the temple (21:22-26). When that backfires, he spends significant portions of the remainder of the book defending his Jewishness. On two occasions Paul recalls his persecution of Christians as a sign of his commitment to Judaism (22:4-5; 26:9-11).[52] In four apologetic speeches he claims Pharisaic faithfulness to the law and the scriptures, and he justifies his preaching as true to Jewish tradition.[53] Furthermore, when Paul arrives in Rome, he deems it necessary to explain to the local Jewish leaders that he has not offended Jewish tradition, even though they have no reports that he has.[54]

The Miletus speech, therefore, falls in a larger context where Jews contend against Paul. The nexus of Jewish antagonism and accusations surrounding Paul's farewell discourse militates against identifying the opponents as Gnostics. Rather, the larger perspective demands that Paul's claim to have declared the whole counsel of God (20:27) be understood not as a device to deprive Gnostics of their secret Pauline tradition but as a response to charges that his gospel is incomplete.

An additional factor that links the Miletus speech to Paul's arrest in the temple corroborates this exegesis. In the farewell discourse Paul describes his encounter with Jews from Asia and warns of dangers from future opponents in Ephesus (20:29-30). Then in Jerusalem it is precisely Jews from Asia acquainted with Trophimus the Ephesian who incite Paul's arrest (21:27-29).[55] The Miletus speech could hardly have anticipated more accurately Paul's own accusers. The content of their accusation is that Paul teaches against the people, the law, and the temple. It is this kind of indictment that compels Luke to defend Paul's gospel from its alleged incompleteness.

Luke nowhere delineates Paul's gospel, but the so-called Apostolic Decree, Paul's sermons, and his apologetic speeches reveal at least some of its features. The Apostolic Decree (15:20-29) validates Gentile Christianity without invalidating nomistic Jewish Christianity and even enjoins Gentiles to keep the Noachian prescriptions which the law demanded of them.[56] Luke returns to the Apostolic Decree in Acts 21:25, where it is actually linked with the remark of James that Paul himself lives in observance of the law (21:24). Elsewhere Paul reiterates his claim to be innocent of offenses against the Jewish law (25:8; 28:17).

In Paul's preaching, the resurrection of Jesus receives major attention before Jews (13:28-37) but surprisingly little emphasis before

Gentiles (17:31). This unexpected imbalance betrays a Lucan concern, because in the defense speeches Paul describes the resurrection as the pivotal point of his conflict with Jews (23:6; 24:15, 21; 26:8; 26:23).

Paul's acceptance of the Apostolic Decree and his declarations of faithfulness to the law commit him to a gospel that provides room for Jewish Christians to keep the law as well as for Gentile Christians to live free from it, provided they observe the four basic prohibitions of the decree. Furthermore, when Paul makes the resurrection the crux of the dispute, he specifies that it is the Jewish hope. When these features of Paul's gospel are conjoined with the objections of his opponents, a gospel emerges that is complete specifically with regard to the Jewish law and the resurrection of Jesus. Paul's universalism is no rejection of Judaism.

It is noteworthy that throughout Paul's mission in Acts, Jewish opponents stir up both Jews and Gentiles. Luke, therefore, is concerned with the impact of the opponents on both groups. James expresses Luke's anxiety in order to counteract the rumors that Paul encouraged Jews of the diaspora to forsake the law because of the deleterious effects on Jewish Christians (Acts 21:20-21). But Luke has a similar uneasiness about the effects of Jewish propaganda on Gentiles. Elymas the magician seeks to turn the proconsul Sergius Paulus away from the faith (13:8), and incredulous Jews in Iconium spread anti-Christian propaganda among the Gentiles (14:2). This means that Luke probably targets Jewish opponents of his own day who seek to influence both Jews and Gentiles by maligning Paul and his message.

But the problem goes beyond Jewish propaganda. The Miletus speech recognizes threats to the congregation both from outside (Acts 20:29) and from inside (v. 30).[57] The Jewish critics of Paul correspond to the outsiders, but there is also an internal division over the alleged Pauline gospel. Although it is tempting to identify the internal heretics as Jewish Christians, the evidence is insufficient to do so. They may be Gentiles who lean toward the synagogue[58] and who find Pauline universalism inconsistent with Christianity's origins in Judaism. At any rate Luke fights on a double front against Jewish propaganda and schismatic anti-Paulinism.

IV. Conclusion

Luke's portrait of Paul is an attempt to defend and to legitimate Paul and his gospel. The vindicating force of Luke's explanation of Paul's Gentile mission and of the Pauline defense speeches is seconded by conventional legitimating techniques. In the text of Acts

Paul is presented as completely Jewish and his gospel as Jewishly complete over against Jews and Christians who oppose Pauline universalism. The failure among scholars to regard the Lucan Paul in this way can be attributed to three primary misplays. (1) The second half of Acts has been read as an account of the Gentile mission per se rather than as an account of the Pauline Gentile mission. (2) Acts has been read as a reflection of Luke's repudiation of the Jews. (3) The seminal proposals that Acts is either apologetic or irenic have been taken as mutually exclusive. What has been interpreted as Luke's rejection of Jews is actually his explanation of the Pauline Gentile mission. And the Lucan portrait of Paul is both apologetic and irenic. Against Jewish detractors and sympathetic Christian heretics alike Luke portrays Paul as innocuous to genuine Judaism as he understands it.

NOTES

[1] E. Haenchen (*The Acts of the Apostles: A Commentary* [Philadelphia: Westminster, 1971] 16) in a comment on Karl Schrader.

[2] M. Schneckenburger (*Apostelgeschichte: Zugleich eine Ergänzung der neueren Commentare* [Bern: Chr. Fischer, 1841] 52-58, 92, 221-22) suggests that Acts is an apology against anti-Pauline Judaists. F. C. Baur (*Paulus, der Apostel Jesu Christi: Sein Leben und Wirken, seine Briefe une Seine Lehre* [Stuttgart: Becher und Müller, 1845] 5-12) argues against Schneckenburger that Acts is an attempt to reconcile opposing parties rather than to defend one against the other. J. Weiss (*Über die Absicht und den literarischen Charakter der Apostelgeschichte* [Göttingen: Vandenhoeck & Ruprecht, 1897] 55-56) proposes that Acts is an apology for Gentiles in response to criticism from Jews.

[3] H. Conzelmann, *Die Apostelgeschichte erklärt* (Tübingen: Mohr [Siebeck], 1972) 85-86, 115, 159-60. See Haenchen, *Acts*, 101, 414, 417-18, 535, 724, 729-30; Kirsopp Lake and H. J. Cadbury, *The Beginnings of Christianity* (ed. F. J. Foakes Jackson and K. Lake; London: Macmillan, 1933) 4. 348; S. G. Wilson, *The Gentiles and the Gentile Mission in Luke-Acts* (Cambridge: University Press, 1973) 138, 222-23, 232.

[4] J. Jervell, *Luke and the People of God* (Minneapolis: Augsburg, 1972) 41-74, esp. 74 n. 101.

[5] Acts 2:41, 47; 4:4; 5:14; 6:1, 7; 9:42; 12:24; 13:43; 14:1; 17:10-12; 19:20; 21:20.

[6] E.g., Adolf Harnack (*The Acts of the Apostles* [New York: Putnam, 1909] xxi) makes the justification of the Gentile mission the determining principle of Acts.

[7] Jervell (*People of God*, 153-83) has demonstrated similarly that

Paul's apologies fit him alone. Paul is no symbol for Christianity at large. For an opposing view see Heinz Schürmann, "Das Testament des Paulus für die Kirche: Apg 20,18-35," *Unio Christianorum: Festschrift für Lorenz Jaeger* (ed. O. Schilling and H. Zimmermann; Paderborn: Bonifacius-Druckerei, 1962) 109, 125.

[8]Wilson (*Gentiles*, 135, 166, 169) recognizes Jewish rejection and the command of God as dual causes for the direction of the mission, but he focuses on the Gentile mission at large rather than on the Pauline Gentile mission

[9]Acts 21:39; 22:3; 23:6; 24:14, 15; 25:8; 26:4-8, 22.

[10]H. J. Cadbury, "Dust and Garments," *The Beginnings of Christianity*, 5. 269-77.

[11]Acts 14:1. Cadbury ("Dust and Garments," 271) notes that shaking off dust was an act against an entire city. Thus, Paul's return to Antioch implies that the gesture was meant as a warning rather than as a rejection.

[12]Volker Stolle, *Der Zeuge als Angeklagter: Untersuchungen zum Paulusbild des Lukas* (Stuttgart: Kohlhammer, 1973) 85.

[13]D. Tiede, *Prophecy and History in Luke-Acts* (Philadelphia: Fortress, 1980) 121-22.

[14]J. Gnilka, *Die Verstockung Israels: Isaias 6,9-10 in der Theologie der Synoptiker* (Munich: Kösel, 1961) 17, 130-54.

[15]Stolle, *Zeuge*, 86.

[16]Odil H. Steck ("Bemerkungen zu Jesaja 6," *BZ* nf 16 [1972] 188-206) has shown that Isaiah 6 is a report of the proceedings of a heavenly council rather than a call. The reference to the death of Uzziah provides a retrospective glance to explain the failure of Isaiah's advice to catch the ear of the people.

[17]Isa 7:4-10; 8:11-18. Steck, "Bemerkungen," 200-203.

[18]B. Lindars (*New Testament Apologetic: The Doctrinal Significance of the Old Testament Quotations* [London: SCM, 1961] 159-67) correctly concludes that the early church used Isa 6:10 to justify the failure of the mission to Jews and to explain their unbelief. But he is incorrect when he says ". . . Luke has been saving up this quotation as the climax to the repeated theme that Paul was opposed by the Jews, but found a better hearing amongst the Gentiles. He has saved *this* text for the purpose, because it is now the classic passage for the rejection of the Jews." The brief survey above shows rather that it is a classic passage for explaining unbelief. Isa 6:9-10 is not quoted in Qumran literature. See Gnilka, *Verstockung*, 155-85. Rabbinic literature rarely alludes to Isa 6:9-10. According to Str-B (1. 663) the allusions that do occur show that the synagogue did not understand it as God's judgment with the purpose of hardening Israel.

[19]K. Löning, *Die Saulustradition in der Apostelgeschichte* (Münster: Aschendorff, 1973) 185, 193, 204.

[20]I am indebted to Charles Talbert for pointing out to me the significance of legitimating factors for Acts.

[21]M. Dibelius (*Studies in the Acts of the Apostles* [London: SCM, 1956] 138-91) calls attention to literary parallels in the speeches of

Acts. H. Cadbury (*The Making of Luke-Acts* [New York: Macmillan, 1927] 140-209) takes note of parallels elsewhere in Acts. Numerous scholars have followed their lead in demonstrating Luke's use of conventional literary devices. See especially E. Plümacher, *Lukas als hellenistischer Schriftsteller: Studien zur Apostelgeschichte* (Göttingen: Vandenhoeck & Ruprecht, 1972).

[22] Conzelmann, (*Apostelgeschichte*, 147) sees Acts 28:6 as the zenith of the divine man motif in Acts. Haenchen (*Acts*, 716) understands it as a part of Luke's consistent portrayal of Paul as a *theios anēr*.

[23] See the critique of *theios anēr* as a category that dictates literary portraits by D. R. Adams, "The Suffering of Paul and the Dynamics of Luke-Acts" (Ph.D. diss., Yale University, 1979) 81-83.

[24] *The Charismatic Figure as Miracle Worker* (SBLDS 1; Missoula: SBL, 1972) 5, 26, 59-61, 99, 207-37, 254.

[25] Ibid., 285-87.

[26] D. Georgi, *Die Gegner des Paulus im 2 Korintherbrief: Studien zur religiösen Propaganda in der Spätantike* (Neukirchen-Vluyn: Neukirchener Verlag, 1964) 191.

[27] A. D. Nock, *Conversion: The Old and the New in Religion from Alexander the Great to Augustine of Hippo* (Oxford: Oxford University Press, 1961) 154.

[28] Haenchen's inability to see divine activity in Paul's recovery (*Acts*, 434) hinges on his failure to regard adequately the context. Granted, Luke does not mention God in vv. 19-20. But the commissioning in Antioch (13:2-3) and the return to Antioch (14:26-27) bracket the entire section, so that everything that happens to Paul and Barnabas is to be interpreted as what God has done with them (14:27). See Adams, "Suffering," 55-56.

[29] Shipwreck and snakebite form one continuous episode in a remarkable parallel in an epitaph recorded by Statyllius Flaccus. The epitaph relates that a man who escaped shipwreck was killed by a viper on the shores of Libya (*Anthologia Palatina* 7.290).

[30] G. B. Miles and G. Trompf, "Luke and Antiphon: The Theology of Acts 27-28 in the Light of Pagan Beliefs About Divine Retribution, Pollution, and Shipwreck," *HTR* 69 (1976) 260-61.

[31] Lucian (*Peregrinus* 42-44) criticizes Peregrinus's fear in the face of a storm at sea as proof that he is a charlatan. See H. D. Betz, *Lukian von Samosata und das Neue Testament: Religionsgeschichtliche und paränetische Parallelen* (Berlin: Akademie-Verlag, 1961) 171-72.

[32] Antiphon, *On the Murder of Herodes* 82-84; Miles and Trompf, "Luke and Antiphon," 262-64.

[33] Cited by H. J. Cadbury, *The Book of Acts in History* (New York: Harper, 1955) 26.

[34] B. P. Grenfell and A. S. Hunt (eds.), *New Classical Fragments and Other Greek and Latin Papyri* (Oxford: Clarendon, 1897) 133-34.

[35] Haenchen, *Acts*, 497.

[36] Euripides *Bacchanals* 433-50; Ovid *Metamorphoses* 3.692-700.

[37]On 19:11-12 as an editorial summary, see Lake and Cadbury, *Beginnings*, 4. 239 and a related note p. 54.

[38]Josephus (*Ag. Ap.* 2.16 §§161-62) notes the value of oracles for facilitating acceptance of Greek laws.

[39]Xenophon *Memorabilia* 1.2.1; 4.8.2; *Apology* 33-34; Plato *Apology* 40C-E.

[40]F. W. Danker, "The Endangered Benefactor in Luke-Acts," *Society of Biblical Literature 1981 Seminar Papers* (ed. K. H. Richards; Chico, CA: Scholars Press, 1981) 48.

[41]Haenchen, *Acts*, 527.

[42]Dibelius, *Studies*, 47-54.

[43]Literary language accounts for the superlative *akribestatos* (26:5) and the Attic *isasin* (26:4); see BDF, 2, n. 4, 60(1).

[44]W. Nestle, "Anklänge an Euripides in der Apostelgeschichte," *Philologus, Zeitschrift für das classische Altertum* 59 (1900) 48-51.

[45]Betz, *Lukian*, 107.

[46]Ibid., 107-8.

[47]So Nock *Conversion*, passim; Georgi, *Gegner des Paulus*, 187-201.

[48]H.-J. Michel, *Die Abschiedsrede des Paulus an die Kirche Apg 20,17-38: Motivgeschichte und theologische Bedeutung* (Munich: Kösel, 1973) 82.

[49]Against Schürmann, "Testament," 126. When taken in conjunction with the defense speeches in Acts 22-26, the Miletus speech clearly functions as a Pauline apology; see Jervell, *People of God*, 153-83.

[50]So Haenchen, *Acts*, 591, 596; Conzelmann, *Apostelgeschichte*, 117-18; G. Klein, *Die zwölf Apostel: Ursprung und Gehalt einer Idee* (Göttingen: Vandenhoeck & Ruprecht, 1961) 183, 213-14; C. H. Talbert, *Luke and the Gnostics* (New York: Abingdon, 1966) 13; Schürmann, "Testament," 115-17.

[51]Haenchen, *Acts*, 332-33.

[52]Klein, (*Zwölf Apostel*, 127-30, 211) contends that Luke progressively intensifies Paul's persecution to emphasize the magnitude of his conversion. But this overlooks the fact that in Acts 22:4-5 and 26:9-11 the persecution has a relatively positive function, namely, to demonstrate how Jewish Paul is.

[53]Jervell, *People of God*, 163-64.

[54]Stolle, *Zeuge*, 84.

[55]Luke makes a close identification between Asia and Ephesus; see Acts 19:10; 20:16; 20:18; Michel, *Abschiedsrede*, 29.

[56]Haenchen, *Acts*, 450 n. 1; Jervell, *People of God*, 144.

[57]Michel, *Abschiedsrede*, 82.

[58]W. Schmithals (*Der Römerbrief als historisches Problem* [Gütersloh: Mohn, 1975]) suggests that the peculiarities of Romans may be owing to its address to God-fearers. Such a suggestion may prove fertile for understanding the audience for Acts; see Haenchen, *Acts*, 414.

Donald L. Jones

THE TITLE "SERVANT"
IN LUKE-ACTS

Did Jesus understand his mission and death in terms of the Suffering Servant of Isaiah 53? Did a primitive Servant Christology exist in the earliest Christian community? Among those who have answered these questions in the affirmative are Adolf Harnack, Joachim Jeremias, and Oscar Cullmann.[1] On the other hand, some have insisted that Jesus did not pattern his ministry on the Servant figure and that other Old Testament texts influenced him as much as, if not more than, the Servant Songs of Isaiah 40-55. Further, there was no separate Servant Christology with which to identify, and all interpretations of Jesus as the Suffering Servant, including that of vicarious suffering and atonement, were introduced later in the early church to explain his death. Advocates of this position include H. J. Cadbury, Morna D. Hooker, and J. C. O'Neill.[2]

In the New Testament the title "Servant of God" (*pais tou theou*) is expressly given to Jesus five times: Matt 12:18; Acts 3:13, 26; 4:27, 30. Likewise, in five passages, quotations from the Servant Songs are applied to Jesus' mission: Matt 8:17; 12:18-21; Luke 22:37; John 12:38; Acts 8:32-36. Six of the nine texts cited are from Luke-Acts, including two of the three New Testament passages that directly connect Jesus' passion with the Suffering Servant: Luke 22:37; Acts 8:32-36; and 1 Pet 2:21-25. These observations suggest that any conclusions reached regarding the influence of the Servant theme in Luke-Acts will be crucial for understanding that influence in the New Testament generally.[3] The purpose of this paper is to explore the question: Is there a primitive Servant Christology in Luke-Acts?

Any quest for Luke's Christology must confront the speeches in Acts. Research on the various titles applied to Jesus in these addresses contributes to the determination of Lucan Christology by enabling one to observe the manner and extent to which Luke has taken over traditional designations and integrated them with his own conceptions.[4] This procedure is particularly helpful in dealing with the inevitable question: Is the Christology exhibited in Luke-Acts that which was current in the primitive Christian community shortly after Jesus' death, that is, the middle of the first century A.D.; or is the description of Christ's person and work that of Luke's own day, that is, the late first century A.D.—indeed, of Luke himself?[5] Based on considerations of the titles *christos* and *kyrios* in Luke-Acts, I have maintained the latter.[6]

A judgment on the nature of the speeches of Acts is necessary.[7] In another place[8] I have argued that, occasional traces of older kerygmatic or liturgical material notwithstanding,[9] the evidence strongly supports the view that the speeches are of Lucan composition. For the purposes of this paper, then, we will assume that the addresses as we have them are not accurate reports of speeches actually delivered but rather products of Luke's dramatic imagination of what would have been appropriate for both the speakers and the occasions. Directed more to the reader than to the imagined audiences, the discourses possess far greater literary than historical significance. They are employed by Luke to interpret the narrative and to illuminate the meaning of pivotal situations. This practice had its genesis and development among Greek and Roman historians, Thucydides in particular.

The Title "Servant" in Pre-Christian Judaism

Before we examine the New Testament evidence concerning the Servant theme, pre-Christian Judaism, both Palestinian and Hellenistic, deserves brief notice. Since good discussions are available elsewhere,[10] we will not contribute to the protracted debate on the original identity of the Deutero-Isaianic Servant, except to say that in the Old Testament the term "Servant of the Lord" (ᶜ*ebed Yahweh*) is a common expression frequently applied to the righteous in general who are loyal to the service of Yahweh and endure suffering and humiliation for his sake. A partial list of Israelites who are so called includes Moses (Exod 14:31; Num 12:7; Deut 34:5), David (2 Sam 7:5; 1 Kgs 11:34), Isaiah (Isa 20:3), and Job (Job 1:8).[11] Nor will we search the Apocrypha, Pseudepigrapha, and other Jewish writings for Servant imagery, accepting instead Hooker's conclusion that there was no pre-Christian doctrine of a suffering messiah based on Isaiah 40-55.[12] The absence of the Servant theme from Jewish literature suggests that neither this figure nor the idea of vicarious suffering was prominent at the time of Jesus.[13] We are not convinced by Eduard Lohse's argument that the concept of vicarious atonement was widespread in first-century Judaism, but Isaiah 53 was not adduced in support of it.[14] W. H. Brownlee has suggested that the Qumran sect identified the Teacher of Righteousness with the Deutero-Isaianic Servant, but even if he is correct—and the evidence is by no means conclusive— nowhere are the alleged sufferings said to have atoning value.[15]

The importance we attach to the Servant passages depends largely on our answer to the question of how the New Testament writers used the Old Testament. According to C. H. Dodd, the quotation of a few Old Testament verses in a passage recalls the whole context of the quoted passage.[16] We maintain with Cadbury, however, that the New Testament writers utilized the Old Testament in an atomistic way.[17] When parts of Isaiah 53 are quoted, for example, we cannot assume that the whole chapter is in the quoter's mind; rather, he is calling attention to the actual verses quoted. This means that unless we can find in the New Testament specific references to vicarious suffering, we cannot assume influence from Isaiah 53. By the same token, when we find the title *pais* or other allusions to the Servant Songs, we must avoid reading vicarious atonement into those contexts.[18]

The most common rendering of ʿebed in the Septuagint is *pais*, possibly to avoid the menial word *doulos* in contexts that speak intimately of the Servant. The farther Hellenistic Jewish writers moved from the Hebrew, the stronger became the tendency to interpret *pais* as "child" or "son" rather than as "servant." Thus, *pais theou* began to merge with the Hellenistic *huios theou*, but still no trace of the vicarious atonement theme can be seen.[19]

The Title "Servant" in the Synoptic Gospels

On turning to the New Testament evidence, we note immediately that *pais tou theou* is not closely associated with the Suffering Servant passages. The nearest to a direct connection is found in the quotation of Isa 42:1-4 (MT) in Matt 12:18-21, beginning "Here is my servant, whom I have chosen" (NEB). The context is the healing on the Sabbath of a man with a withered arm and the ensuing dispute with the Pharisees (12:9-17). Jesus, aware of their plot, withdraws, continues to cure all who are ill, and admonishes his followers, "not to make him known." This is seen by Matthew as fulfillment of prophecy: Jesus is one who "will not strive" nor "shout" with the Pharisees. The quotation is related, then, to Jesus' healing miracles and his desire to avoid publicity. The atomistic exegesis of the Old Testament that was prevalent in Matthew's day precludes reading into the few verses cited the concept of vicarious suffering expressed elsewhere in the Servant Songs. Even if Isaiah 40-55 were highly regarded in the Palestinian church, this one use of *pais* is not sufficient to establish that it was the key word in that material. If it were, we would expect to find far greater utilization of Servant imagery in the New

Testament than is actually the case.[20]

In Matt 8:17, Isa 53:4a,b ("He took away our illnesses and lifted our diseases from us") is quoted and applied to Jesus' healing miracles rather than to any expiatory suffering—a theme readily available elsewhere in Isaiah 53. Once more, atomistic interpretation prevents reading atonement into this context. That an explicit identification of Jesus with the Suffering Servant was not made here suggests that it was never made, either by Jesus or his early followers. Matthew's purpose in these two passages was to demonstrate that Jesus' work was foreshadowed in the Old Testament, not to construct a doctrine of the meaning of that work.[21]

The words from heaven at Jesus' baptism (Mark 1:11 par.), "Thou art my Son, my Beloved; on thee my favour rests," widely held to be a combination of Ps 2:7 and Isa 42:1, are understood by Jeremias, Cullmann, and others to have been more influenced by the latter than the former.[22] They assume that the descent of the Spirit (Mark 1:10) depended on Isa 42:1b, and that behind Mark's later clarification "my Son" (*huios*) there stood an original "my servant" (*pais*). We have no evidence, however, that Mark reinterpreted *pais* in this way—indeed, the use of the term in Acts 3 and 4 militates against it, since we would expect a similar change in the Lucan writings.[23] Even if this theory is accepted—and the evidence is far from conclusive—it does not warrant Cullmann's conclusion that Jesus at his baptism consciously took on himself the Servant role, thereby initiating a primitive Servant Christology in earliest Christianity.[24] One should rather say that if the Servant element ever existed separately, it was so weak it was soon transformed into a Son Christology.[25] The baptism tradition as we have it is a product of the early church; it is not derived from Jesus' personal reminiscences of the event. Atomistic exegesis will not permit the general similarity in thought between Mark 1:11 and Isa 42:1 to be construed as proof that Jesus understood himself to be the Suffering Servant of Isaiah 53.

Jeremias has collected from the synoptic gospels several examples which he believes show that Jesus thought about his suffering and death in the light of Isaiah 53.[26] We will look briefly at the most important of these passages, beginning with two texts from the Marcan passion predictions: Mark 9:12 and Mark 10:45 par.

In *The Mission and Achievement of Jesus*, R. H. Fuller described Mark 9:12b ("Yet how is it that the scriptures say of the Son of Man that he is to endure great suffering and to be treated with contempt?") as an original stratum in which Jesus speaks of his suffering in terms of Isaiah 53.[27] Since then H. E. Tödt has shown that *gegraptai* and *exoudenēthē* refer not to Isaiah 53 but to Ps 118:22.[28]

The Jews' rejection of Jesus has been reversed by the resurrection. This, Tödt maintains, is the earliest interpretation of Jesus' passion and death in the post-resurrection community. Rather than reflecting Jesus' own self-understanding, the passion predictions can be used only as evidence for the kerygma of the early Palestinian church.

Tödt has also argued that *diakonēthēnai* in Mark 10:45a ("Even the Son of Man did not come to be served but to serve") refers not to Isaiah 53, but to the original version of Jesus' service at table in Luke 22:27b ("Yet here am I among you like a servant").[29] The title Son of Man in 10:45a has replaced an original "I" form and is therefore later. Only at 10:45b ("to give up his life as a ransom for many") does Tödt find, in agreement with Hahn and Fuller, an allusion to Isa 53:11 (MT).[30] We, however, support Hooker and C. K. Barrett, who see here no immediate connection with Isaiah 53.[31] The phrase can hardly be regarded as an original expression of Jesus, because the idea of atonement is omitted from the Lucan parallel.

Jeremias also regards the words over the cup ("This is my blood, the blood of the covenant, shed for many") in Mark 14:24 as a clear allusion to Isa 53:11 (MT) suggesting that Jesus' shedding of blood will be for many. But this saying over the cup is completely absent from the older and briefer text of Luke 22:17. Mark reports the words over bread (14:22) in brief ("This is my body") without any suggestion of the redemptive significance of Jesus' death. In Luke 22:19a we also have simply "This is my body," to which a later hand has added from 1 Cor 11:24-25 the words "which is given for you" and "poured out for you." Thus, the explanation of Jesus' death as having atoning, redemptive significance like that of the Suffering Servant is once again absent from Luke's account.[32]

The last of Jeremias's passages which we will discuss is Luke 22:37 ("For Scripture says 'And he was counted among the outlaws' "). Here for the first and only time in the synoptics we have a clear reference to Isaiah 53 (v. 12). There is, however, no allusion to the essential function of the Servant—the vicarious bearing of sin.[33] This must have been part of the church's theological reflection on Jesus' passion. Such reflection, however, did not concentrate on any particular Old Testament passage—in fact, the passion psalms (especially 22 and 69) were much more prominent than Isaiah ever became. It was believed that in such psalms the passion of Jesus was depicted in advance and in accordance with God's will. Passages like Luke 24:26, 44 express the divine necessity (*dei*) of the passion as foretold in scripture. We conclude, then, with Tödt and O'Neill, that Jesus never explicitly referred to Deutero-Isaiah and that the Servant Songs became popular as a proof text only rather late in the church's history.[34]   Jeremias's supposed allusions to Isaiah 53 are in fact derived from other sources.

The Title "Servant" in Acts

The best example of the use of a passage from Deutero-Isaiah to illustrate humiliation and exaltation in Acts is 8:32-36, where Isaiah 53, quoted by the Ethiopian eunuch, is applied by Philip to Jesus. For the first time in Acts we have a passage from the Servant Songs connected unmistakably with Jesus' passion.   The fact that Philip begins with this text in conveying the good news of Jesus to the eunuch suggests only that Isaiah 53 served as a good introduction to Jesus' life and death, not necessarily that it was a passage of indispensable importance.   The words quoted comprise the last three lines of Isa 53:7 (LXX) and the first three lines of v. 8, where the main themes are the Servant's humiliation and his submission to suffering. However, the idea of suffering for the sins of others, so eloquently expressed both immediately preceding and following the quoted verses, is conspicuous by its absence.   It is surprising that Luke has passed over all the passages about vicarious suffering, which abound in Isaiah 53.[35]   The chapter was significant for the author of Acts not because it connected suffering with sin but because it appropriately illustrated the humiliation theme.   It served as a proof text for the necessity of Jesus' passion, not as a treatise on its meaning.[36]

The theme of humiliation illustrated by Deutero-Isaianic texts is applied in Acts to Paul as well as to Jesus, thereby casting doubt on the possibility of a specific Servant Christology that might lie behind it.[37]   As described in Acts 26:18, Paul's mission to open the eyes of Gentiles and to "turn them from darkness to light" echoes Isa 42:7. Here Servant imagery is applied to Paul only a few verses before Isa 42:6 is applied to Jesus (Acts 26:23).   Isa 49:6, which mentions the "light for the Gentiles," is applied by Paul to himself and Barnabas in Acts 13:47.   In Acts 9:15 there may be an application of Isa 48:6-7 in the Lord's instructions to Ananias concerning the necessity of Paul's suffering.   Because of this double application of Servant passages in Acts, it is extremely unlikely that Luke intended an exclusive identification of Jesus with the figure of the Suffering Servant.

Further explication of the theme of "humiliation-exaltation" in Acts is seen in Peter's speech in chap. 3.   The association of the word *pais* in v. 13 with reminiscences (especially *edoxasen*) of Isa 52:13 (LXX), where the persecuted Servant is exalted, may have suggested it to Luke as a particularly appropriate messianic title.   However, the leading feature of the fourth Servant Song—the atoning value of vicarious suffering—is missing.   Since *edoxasen* is the natural word to

use in this context, the evidence is too weak to take this as a reference to Deutero-Isaiah and to base on this one verse, as Cullmann
does, the existence of a distinct *pais* Christology in the earliest
church.[38] We agree with Ernst Haenchen that the glorification Luke
has in mind in 3:13 is not the resurrection but Jesus' earthly ministry.[39]

Claiming Acts 3:12-26 as primary evidence, Fuller, Hahn, and
Richard F. Zehnle have interpreted Jesus' mission in terms of the
Mosaic prophet-servant.[40] The titles "Holy One" and "Righteous
One" in v. 14 are viewed as examples of prophetic-servant vocabulary. The adjective "holy," applied to Jesus as it is here and at 4:27,
30, where it modifies "servant," points to a primitive tradition; and
the title *ho dikaios* is elsewhere applied to Jesus in the Stephen
speech (7:52), which these scholars find impregnated with Mosaic
prophet-servant Christology. Moses was the "righteous one" *par
excellence*.[41] This interpretation is supposedly clinched by the
quotation in 3:22-23 of Deut 18:15, 18-19 regarding the raising up of
the prophet Moses. This prophecy is fulfilled in Jesus; "God raised up
his Servant" (v. 26). J. A. T. Robinson is correct that only here in
Acts is *anastēsas* used of Jesus' historic ministry rather than of his
resurrection.[42] The word is taken directly from Deut 18:15. However, I agree with Moule, and have furnished the argument elsewhere,
that Robinson has not established his case for two distinctly different, primitive Christologies side by side in Acts 2 and 3.[43] We
conclude, then, that the use of *pais* in Acts 3 does nothing to weaken
the evidence for the rest of Luke-Acts, as we shall demonstrate, that
Luke, rather than tapping a primitive Servant Christology, used the
title "*pais*" interchangeably with "Son of God" and "Christ."

The most significant use of *pais* occurs in Acts 4, where Luke is in
touch with traditional liturgical material. The prayer of the church
in vv. 24-30 exhibits many marks that argue against its pre-Lucan
origin and for its being a later Lucan construction. Like the Nunc
Dimittis (Luke 2:29-32), it opens with the rare liturgical address
despota. The peculiarly Lucan expression "to speak your word with
all boldness" (v. 29) reappears subsequently in narrative (v. 31).
Herod is associated with Pilate in Jesus' death and elsewhere only
at Luke 23:6-12, and the people of Israel are combined with the
"peoples" of the Gentiles—again a feature unique to Luke (Luke 2:31-
32; Acts 26:17, 23).[44] We support Haenchen that with the prayer of
Isaiah 37 as a model, Luke has recast in the form of a prayer an early
Christian exegesis of Ps 2:1-2 (LXX) and has introduced *pais* out of
dependence on 3:13.[45]

In Acts 4:25ff. both David and Jesus are called the Lord's *pais*,
suggesting that Luke intended no particular identification with the

Servant. Further support for this is found in Luke 1:54 and 69, where *pais* is used of Israel and David respectively. The combination of both David and Jesus as Yahweh's Servant occurs also in the eucharistic prayer in *Didache* 9.2-3. Jesus is called God's *pais* in the prayer of the Roman congregation in *1 Clement* 59.2-4; *Martyrdom of Polycarp* 14.1, 3 and 20.2, a doxology; *Didache* 10.2-3; *Epistle of Barnabas* 6.1 and 9.2; and *Epistle to Diognetus* 8.9, 11 and 9.1. Since all these writings are independent of one another, it is probably correct to assume dependence on a common liturgical tradition.[46]

It is striking that neither Acts 4 nor *Didache* refers to Deutero-Isaiah. In *Didache* 9.2 the vine that David speaks about is probably an allusion to Ps 80:8ff. In Acts 4:25ff. the Old Testament quotation comes from Ps 2:1-2, and the single reference in v. 27 to Isaiah (61:1) is not to a Servant passage.[47] Again, the use of Isaiah 61 here suggests to some—for example, Hahn and Fuller[48]—the appointment to prophetic office in the sense of the eschatological prophet like Moses. They see a further Mosaic association in v. 30: "Stretch out your hand to heal and cause signs and wonders." We agree with Cadbury, however, that the *iasis*, together with *kai sēmeia kai terata*, is a characteristic Lucan generalization of the sign of healing which had been central in the preceding chapters, especially 4:22.[49]

In all likelihood, Luke understood *pais theou* as simply another designation for "Messiah."[50] This is in accordance with certain old Jewish prayers wherein David is called God's ʿebed or *doulos*. In 1 Macc 4:30 and 4 Ezra 3:23 it is recalled that David slew Goliath and founded Jerusalem; "servant" is here probably nothing more than a general title of honor. In Palestinian examples "servant" occurs in parallelism with or in close proximity to "the anointed one" and probably means nothing more than "chosen by God."[51] In this context "servant" meant "Messiah" and had no specific connection with Deutero-Isaiah.

Several have seen the use of *pais* in Acts 3 and 4 as evidence for a belief in Jesus as the Servant of Deutero-Isaiah. That it is found only here in what seems to be an early source confirms for them the primitive character of the title. In 1926 Harnack argued that the appearance of *pais* in the speeches of Acts is evidence enough that the Christology is embryonic and that Luke received and passed on early material.[52] Jeremias has claimed that the application of *pais* to Jesus here "belongs to a very ancient stratum of the tradition."[53] Describing the *pais* designation as the oldest answer to the Christological question Who is Jesus?, Cullmann says: "*The Acts of the Apostles* offers us the strongest proof of the fact that in the most ancient period of early Christianity there existed an explanation of the person and work of Jesus which we could characterize somewhat inaccurately as an ʿebed Yahweh Christology—or more exactly as a 'Paidology.'"[54] Luke, according to Cullmann, preserves the memory that it was Peter who first interpreted Jesus' mission as that of the Deutero-Isaianic Servant of God and who designated Jesus as such. It is no accident that, of the four passages in Acts that call Jesus *pais*, two appear in speeches ascribed to Peter and two in a prayer spoken when Peter is present.[55] Finally, Moule sees a clear distinction between the use of *pais* in chaps. 3 and 4.[56] Whereas the context in chap. 4 is liturgical, in chap. 3 apologetic claims are made for a crucified criminal by identifying him with another who received a criminal's treatment.

We claim, on the other hand, that Luke used *pais* compatibly throughout his two volumes. Aware of the long and diverse history of the term, he appropriately confined it in Acts to the early chapters in an attempt to give that material an ancient ring. The title "Servant of God" was in use rather late in the early church, as seen from *Epistle of Barnabas*, where *pais* is inserted into two Old Testament quotations to provide an explicit reference to Christ (*Barn.* 6.1, Isa 50:8, 9 and *Barn.* 9.2, Exod 15:26). The use of the adjectives "beloved" (*agapētos*) and "only begotten" (*monogenēs*) with *pais* in the apostolic fathers reflects influence of the words from heaven in the baptism and transfiguration traditions—further evidence that *pais*, while it can mean "servant," was understood primarily to mean "son."[57] Luke treats *pais*, concludes Haenchen, as a formal expression for "Son of God."[58]

Luke's Interchangeable Use of "Servant," "Christ," and "Son of God"

We have seen that Luke uses *pais* as a synonym for both "Christ" and "Son of God." But does "Son of God" mean "Christ" in the Lucan writings? In Luke 4:41, when the demons recognize Jesus as the Son of God, he rebukes them and will not allow them to speak because "they knew that he was the Messiah." Here is perhaps the clearest illustration that for Luke "Christ" and "Son of God" are synonymous.[59] Moreover, the titles are lacking in the parallels.[60]

The trial of Jesus before the council (Luke 22:66b-71) also reveals Luke's interest in *huios theou*. Jesus is asked (v. 67): "Tell us, are you the Messiah?" He answered: "If I tell you, you will not believe me." Three verses later to the question: "You are the Son of God, then?" he responds: "It is you who say that I am." Again "Christ" and "Son of God" are used in parallelism.

In Acts, Jesus is twice designated "Son of God," in 9:20 and 13:33. In the former, following his conversion Paul proclaims Jesus such in the Damascus synagogues. Two verses later it is clear that the title was not specially chosen, because there again "Messiah" is used synonymously with "Son of God." Jesus is also called God's Son in 13:33, where Ps 2:7 is quoted. It is surprising, however, given Luke's usual "subordinationist" Christology, in which Jesus was "Son of God" from birth, that Luke should here seemingly apply this text to the resurrection, thereby giving some cause for an "adoptionist" interpretation. Our only comment is that even if Luke has cited the psalm from an earlier tradition, he is careful not to insist on an "adoptionist" concept of which he does not approve. We conclude that, since *pais* is used interchangeably with "Christ" and "Son of God" and since "Son of God" in Luke-Acts is another way to express "Christ," "Servant of God," "Son of God," and "Christ" are for Luke all synonymous. If such be the case, he could hardly be dependent upon a separate Servant Christology even if one existed.

The Title "Servant" Elsewhere in the New Testament

The relevant material elsewhere in the New Testament can be presented briefly. While Paul himself may not have employed the *pais* concept, it has been argued that the language of the Servant Songs had become so much a part of the church's vocabulary that certain words used by Paul reflected an earlier identification of Jesus with the Servant. An oft-quoted example in this regard is Rom 4:25: "For he was given up to death for our misdeeds and raised to life to justify us." However, since *paradidōmi* appears to be the natural word to use in this context, one cannot link it definitely with any particular Old Testament passage, including Isa 53:12c (LXX). Likewise, since *dikaioō* is used frequently in the Septuagint, there is no evidence either that it derived from Isaiah 53 or that it was an early Christian word that reflected the Servant concept and was taken over by Paul.[61]

1 Cor 15:3-5 also has been offered as evidence for a pre-Pauline tradition that Jesus was identified with the Servant of Deutero-Isaiah.[62] It has been supposed that the phrase "in accordance with the Scriptures" refers to the Servant Songs, but the phrase in itself is quite general and is not meant to denote any particular Old Testament passage. It may bear more connection with Ps 118:22 than with Isaiah 53. It has been further claimed that the words "for our sins" refer exclusively to Isaiah 53. However, it is as doubtful that Paul received a tradition of Christ's death for sin being foretold in the scriptures as it is that Jesus' disciples could have believed that his death procured their forgiveness or that it was necessitated by their sins. It seems more probable that the association between death and the forgiveness of sins was the result of the particular significance that Paul himself attached to the passion.[63] In sum, Paul makes no

use of the Servant figure. If he had thought of Jesus as *pais theou,* surely he would have elaborated the argument!

There can be no doubt that 1 Pet 2:21-25 interprets Christ's passion in the light of Isaiah 53. The fourth Servant Song is used to emphasize Jesus' submission to humiliation, to connect his suffering with the sins of others, and to prove the necessity of his death. The humiliation of Christ is the great example that slaves facing unjust punishment should emulate.[64]

Jeremias has suggested that indirect evidence for the antiquity of the title *"pais"* is furnished by the use of *ho amnos tou theou* in John 1:29, 36.[65] The description of the Messiah as a lamb was unknown in late Judaism; and, since the Aramaic *talya* means both "lamb" and "servant," possibly behind "the lamb of God" lies the Aramaic *talya dālaha* in the sense of *ʿebed Yahweh.* This theory, however, rests on supposition and lacks evidence. While it is improbable that the primary reference of *pais* was to Isa 53:7,[66] it is likely that the Fourth Evangelist saw a secondary allusion to that chapter since the motif of a (slain) lamb and the achievement of atonement for all are among its characteristics. In John 12:38 a quotation from the Septuagint of Isa 53:1 is applied to the Jews' failure to believe the signs Jesus performed. It is significant that the passage is not applied to Christ's death and resurrection. It has been argued that the title *arnion,* "lamb," used of the exalted Christ in Rev 5:6, 12 and 13:8 but never elsewhere, is also derived from Isaiah 53. Jeremias regards *arnion* here as the equivalent of *amnos* in John 1:29, 36 and traces them both to Isa 53:7 and the double meaning in Aramaic of *talya.* However, the complete absence of the title from other early Christian literature shows that it was not a designation taken over from tradition, and other evidence of the influence of Isaiah 53 is lacking.[67]

Finally, the words "to bear the sins of many," in Heb 9:28 seems to echo a similar phrase in Isa 53:12 (LXX). Christ is depicted not only as the great high priest for the Day of Atonement ritual but also as the victim offered for sin. This idea may be derived from Isaiah 53, which also speaks of one who "bore the sin of many," not as a priest but in his own death. Thus, while no direct identification of Jesus with the Suffering Servant is made here, the imagery of Isaiah 53 probably lies behind this passage.[68]

Conclusion

What can we conclude from the foregoing? First, the alleged references to Isaiah 53 both in the New Testament generally and in Luke-Acts in particular are, for the most part, ambiguous and inconclusive. Luke, especially in his gospel, seems deliberately to avoid the theme of atonement. We found no evidence that Jesus connected his death with the forgiveness of sin or thought of his suffering as vicarious in nature. Jesus did not regard himself as fulfilling the mission of the Suffering Servant. As O'Neill puts it, "Those OT passages which we now distinguish as 'servant' passages became available for the illustration of the theme of Jesus' humiliation and glorification after *pais* had been established as a Christological title; they did not form the starting point for a so-called Servant Christology."[69]

Second, the Christology of Luke-Acts is the "developed" Christology of Luke and the Christian church at the close of the first century A.D. The speeches of Acts represent the reading back of later Christological thinking into earlier times. The crucial question regarding the use of *pais* in Acts is whether it implied an identification of Jesus with the Suffering Servant or whether it was ascribed to Jesus in the general sense of the Old Testament concept of ᶜ*ebed Yahweh*, that is, as a title of honor with no particular reference to Deutero-Isaiah. We have concluded the latter.[70] Luke applies *pais* to Jesus freely and adapts it to serve his own theological purpose. His use of the title first of David then of Jesus suggests that no particular reference is intended, and, most significantly, "Servant" is used interchangeably by Luke with two other titles—"Christ" and "Son of God."

Luke's use of *pais*, then, reveals a rather late development in Christian thought in that it is dominated by his own theological emphases and presupposes a certain amount of reflection upon Jesus' messianic mission. In short, the Lucan contexts in which Servant imagery appears reflect the Christology of Luke's own day—indeed, of Luke himself. They do not preserve from the earliest Christian community a separate and primitive Servant Christology—nor could they, since, in our judgment, such a Christology did not exist.

NOTES

[1]A. Harnack, "Die Bezeichnung Jesu als 'Knecht Gottes' und ihre Geschichte in der alten Kirche," *Sitzungsberichte der preussischen Akademie der Wissenschaften: Philosophisch-Historische Klasse* 28 (1926) 212-38; J. Jeremias, "*Pais Theou* in the NT," *TDNT* 5. 700-717; O. Cullmann, *The Christology of the New Testament* (NT Library; rev. ed.; Philadelphia: Westminster, 1963) 51-82.

[2]H. J. Cadbury, "The Titles of Jesus in Acts," *The Beginnings of Christianity. Part I. The Acts of the Apostles* (ed. F. J. Foakes Jackson and K. Lake; 5 vols.; London: Macmillan, 1920-33) 5. 364-70; Morna D. Hooker, *Jesus and the Servant: The Influence of the Servant Concept of Deutero-Isaiah in the New Testament* (London:

SPCK, 1959); J. C. O'Neill, *The Theology of Acts in Its Historical Setting* (London: SPCK, 1961) 133-39.

[3]On the Servant title in Luke-Acts, see J. A. Fitzmyer, *The Gospel According to Luke (I-IX): Introduction, Translation, and Notes* (AB 28; Garden City: Doubleday, 1981) 211-13; D. Seccombe, "Luke and Isaiah," *NTS* 27 (1981) 252-59, esp. 255-59; I. H. Marshall, *Luke: Historian and Theologian* (Exeter: Paternoster, 1970) 171-73; H. Conzelmann, *The Theology of St. Luke* (New York: Harper and Row, 1960) 175; W. G. Kümmel, *The Theology of the New Testament: According to Its Major Witnesses: Jesus—Paul—John* (Nashville: Abingdon, 1973) 108-9; J. D. Kingsbury, *Jesus Christ in Matthew, Mark, and Luke* (Proclamation Commentaries; Philadelphia: Fortress, 1981) 105-6; and B. Vawter, *This Man Jesus: An Essay toward a New Testament Christology* (Garden City: Doubleday, 1975) 79-81. On the Servant concept in general, see P. Benoit, "Jésus et le Serviteur de Dieu," *Jésus aux origines de la christologie* (ed. J. Dupont; Gembloux: Duculot, 1975) 111-40; E. Lohmeyer, *Gottesknecht und Davidssohn* (FRLANT 61; 2d ed.; Göttingen: Vandenhoeck & Ruprecht, 1953); and J. R. Michaels, *Servant and Son: Jesus in Parable and Gospel* (Atlanta: John Knox, 1981).

[4]This view is shared by Stephen S. Smalley ("The Christology of Acts Again," *Christ and Spirit in the New Testament: In Honour of C. F. D. Moule* [ed. B. Lindars and S. S. Smalley; Cambridge: University Press, 1973] 81), who sees in the titles a "vital framework" for Lucan Christology. For others, including Charles H. Talbert ("An Anti-Gnostic Tendency in Lucan Christology," *NTS* 14 [1967-68] 259-71), any who would find Luke's Christology must begin not with titles but with "the overall structure of his portrait of Christ." There is merit in each approach. Among the best recent studies in Lucan Christology are M. Rese, *Alttestamentliche Motive in der Christologie des Lukas* (SNT 1; Gütersloh: Mohn, 1969); G. Voss, *Die Christologie der lukanischen Schriften in Grundzügen* (StudNeot 2; Paris: Desclée de Brouwer, 1965); T. Holtz, *Untersuchungen über die alttestamentlichen Zitate bei Lukas* (Berlin: Akademie-Verlag, 1968); F. Schütz, *Der leidende Christus: Die angefochtene Gemeinde und das Christuskerygma der lukanischen Schriften* (BWANT 89; Stuttgart: Kohlhammer, 1969); C. H. Talbert, "Shifting Sands: The Recent Study of the Gospel of Luke," *Int* 30 (1976) 381-95, esp. 387-89; W. S. Kurz, "Hellenistic Rhetoric in the Christological Proof of Luke-Acts," *CBQ* 42 (1980) 171-95; G. W. MacRae, " 'Whom Heaven Must Receive Until the Time': Reflections on the Christology of Acts," *Int* 27 (1973) 151-65; and O. C. Edwards, *Luke's Story of Jesus* (Philadelphia: Fortress, 1981).

[5]For more general bibliography on Luke-Acts, see J. Jervell, *Luke and the People of God: A New Look at Luke-Acts* (Minneapolis: Augsburg, 1972); E. Schweizer, *Luke: A Challenge to Present Theology* (Atlanta: John Knox, 1982); C. H. Talbert, *Literary Patterns, Theological Themes, and the Genre of Luke-Acts* (SBLMS 20;

Missoula: Scholars Press, 1974); idem, "The Redaction Critical Quest for Luke the Theologian," *Jesus and Man's Hope* (ed. D. Buttrick; Perspective Books 1; Pittsburgh: Pittsburgh Theological Seminary, 1971) 1. 171-222; idem, "An Introduction to Acts," *RevExp* 71 (1974) 437-49; S. G. Wilson, *The Gentiles and the Gentile Mission in Luke-Acts* (SNTSMS 23; Cambridge: University Press, 1973); A. George, *Études sur l'oeuvre de Luc* (Paris: Gabalda, 1978); F. Bovon, *Luc le théologian: Vingt-cinq ans de recherches (1950-1975)* (Neuchâtel/Paris: Delachaux et Niestlé, 1978); A. J. Mattill and M. B. Mattill, *A Classified Bibliography of Literature on the Acts of the Apostles* (Leiden: Brill, 1966); G. Wagner, *Bibliographical Aids No. 7: An Exegetical Bibliography on the Acts of the Apostles* (Rüschlikon-Zurich: Baptist Theological Seminary, 1975); and B. M. Metzger, *Index to Periodical Literature on Christ and the Gospels* (Leiden: Brill, 1966).

[6] Donald L. Jones, "The Title *Christos* in Luke-Acts," *CBQ* 32 (1970) 69-76; "The Title *Kyrios* in Luke-Acts," *Society of Biblical Literature 1974 Seminar Papers* (ed. G. MacRae; 2 vols.; Missoula: Scholars Press, 1974) 2. 85-101.

[7] On the speeches in general, see W. W. Gasque, "The Speeches in Acts: Dibelius Reconsidered," *New Dimensions in New Testament Study* (ed. R. N. Longenecker and M. C. Tenney; Grand Rapids, MI: Zondervan, 1974) 232-50; idem, *A History of the Criticism of the Acts of the Apostles* (Grand Rapids: Eerdmans, 1975) esp. chaps. IX and X; F. F. Bruce, "The Speeches in Acts—Thirty Years After," *Reconciliation and Hope: New Testament Essays on Atonement and Eschatology Presented to L. L. Morris on His 60th Birthday* (ed. R. Banks; Grand Rapids: Eerdmans, 1974) 53-68; M. Wilcox, "A Foreword to the Study of the Speeches in Acts," *Christianity, Judaism and Other Greco-Roman Cults: Studies for Morton Smith at Sixty* (ed. J. Neusner; SJLA 12; Leiden: Brill, 1975) 1. 206-25; F. G. Downing, "Ethical Pagan Theism and the Speeches in Acts," *NTS* 27 (1981) 544-63; G. Krodel, *Acts* (Proclamation Commentaries; Philadelphia: Fortress, 1981) passim; U. Wilckens, *Die Missionsreden der Apostelgeschichte: Form- und Traditionsgeschichtliche Untersuchungen* (WMANT 5; 3d ed.; Neukirchen-Vluyn: Neukirchener Verlag, 1974); K. Kliesch, *Das heilsgeschichtliche Credo in den Reden der Apostelgeschichte* (BBB 44; Cologne and Bonn: Peter Hanstein, 1975); E. Plümacher, *Lukas als hellenistischer Schriftsteller: Studien zur Apostelgeschichte* (SUNT 9; Göttingen: Vandenhoeck & Ruprecht, 1972) passim; and J. W. Bowker, "Speeches in Acts: A Study in Proem and Yellammedenu Form," *NTS* 14 (1967) 96-110.

Among the recent contributions to the study of the individual speeches, see D. Juel, "Social Dimensions of Exegesis: The Use of Psalm 16 in Acts 2," *CBQ* 43 (1981) 543-56; C. H. H. Scobie, "The Use of Source Material in the Speeches of Acts 3 and 7," *NTS* 25 (1979) 399-421; J. Kilgallen, *The Stephen Speech: A Literary and Redactional Study of Acts 7,2-53* (AnBib 67; Rome: Biblical Institute Press, 1976) [see my review, *CBQ* 40 (1978) 639-40]; E. Richard, "Acts 7: An

Investigation of the Samaritan Evidence," *CBQ* 39 (1977) 190-208; idem, "The Polemical Character of the Joseph Episode in Acts 7," *JBL* 98 (1979) 255-67; idem, *Acts 6:1-8:4: The Author's Method of Composition* (SBLDS 41; Missoula: Scholars Press, 1978) [see my review, *CBQ* 43 (1981) 480-81]; M. Dumais, *Le langage de l'évangélisation: L'annonce missionaire en milieu juif (Actes 13,16-41)* (Recherches 16; Montreal: Bellarmin, 1976); M. F. Buss, *Die Missionspredigt des Apostels Paulus im pisidischen Antiochien: Analyse von Apg 13, 16-41 im Hinblick auf die literarische und thematische Einheit der Paulusrede* (Forschung zur Bibel 38; Stuttgart: Katholisches Bibelwerk, 1980); P. Auffret, "Essai sur la structure littéraire du discours d'Athènes (Ac xvii 23-31)," *NovT* 20 (1978) 185-202; H.-J. Michel, *Die Abschiedsrede des Paulus an die Kirche Apg 20,17-38: Motivgeschichte und theologische Bedeutung* (SANT 35; Munich: Kösel, 1973); F. Veltman, "The Defense Speeches of Paul in Acts," *Perspectives on Luke-Acts* (ed. C. H. Talbert; Special Studies Series 5; Danville, VA: Association of Baptist Professors of Religion, 1978) 243-56; and R. F. O'Toole, *Acts 26: The Christological Climax of Paul's Defense (Ac 22:1-26:32)* (AnBib 78; Rome: Biblical Institute Press, 1978).

[8] Donald L. Jones, "The Christology of the Missionary Speeches in the Acts of the Apostles" (Ph.D. diss., Duke University, 1966) 33-59.

[9] As M. Hengel puts it, "to deny in principle the presence of earlier traditions in the speeches composed by Luke makes them incomprehensible and is no more than an interpreter's whim" (*Acts and the History of Earliest Christianity* [Philadelphia: Fortress, 1980] 104).

[10] E.g., F. Hahn, *The Titles of Jesus in Christology: Their History in Early Christianity* (London: Lutterworth, 1969) 356-57; L. E. Wilshire, "The Servant City: A New Interpretation of the 'Servant of the Lord' in the Servant Songs of Deutero-Isaiah," *JBL* 94 (1975) 356-67; A. S. Kapelrud, "Second Isaiah and the Suffering Servant," *Hommages à André Dupont-Sommer* (ed. A. Caquot and M. Philonenko; Paris: Adrien Maisonneuve, 1971) 297-303; see also P.-E. Bonnard, *Le Second Isaie: son disciple et leurs éditeurs, Isaïe 40-66* (Paris: Gabalda, 1972); and A. S. Herbert, *The Book of the Prophet Isaiah: Chs 40-66* (Cambridge Bible Commentaries, NEB; New York and London: Cambridge University Press, 1975).

[11] See J. E. Ménard, "*PAIS THEOU* as Messianic Title in the Book of Acts," *CBQ* 19 (1957) 91; Cadbury, "Title of Jesus in Acts," 365-67; see also D. M. Beegle, *Moses, The Servant of Yahweh* (Grand Rapids: Eerdmans, 1972).

[12] *Jesus and the Servant*, 56-61.

[13] Rudolf Bultmann, *Theology of the New Testament* (2 vols.; New York: Scribner, 1951) 1. 31.

[14] *Märtyrer und Gottesknecht* (FRLANT 46; Göttingen: Vandenhoeck & Ruprecht, 1955) 66-78; see also R. H. Fuller, *The Foundations of New Testament Christology* (New York: Scribner, 1965) 45.

[15] "Messianic Motifs of Qumran and the New Testament," *NTS* 3 (1956) 12-30; esp. 17-20; Fuller, *Foundations*, 51-53.

[16] *The Old Testament in the New* (Philadelphia: Fortress, 1963) 12ff.

[17] "Titles of Jesus in Acts," 369-70.

[18] See Hooker, *Jesus and the Servant*, 21-23; Fuller, *Foundations*, 46.

[19] O'Neill, *Theology of Acts*, 137; Fuller, *Foundations*, 66.

[20] See Hooker, *Jesus and the Servant*, 84; O'Neill, *Theology of Acts*, 133-34.

[21] Wilhelm Bousset, *Kyrios Christos: A History of the Belief in Christ from the Beginning of Christianity to Irenaeus* (Nashville: Abingdon, 1970) 111; see also Eduard Schweizer, *Lordship and Discipleship* (SBT 28; Naperville, IL: Allenson, 1960) 50; Hooker, *Jesus and the Servant*, 83.

[22] Jeremias, "*Pais Theou*," 701; Cullmann, *Christology*, 66; Bousset, *Kyrios Christos*, 97; Fuller, *Foundations*, 169-70.

[23] Hooker, *Jesus and the Servant*, 70.

[24] *Christology*, 66-68, 73; see also Fuller, *Foundations*, 115-16.

[25] O'Neill, *Theology of Acts*, 134, 137.

[26] "*Pais Theou*," 712-13.

[27] *The Mission and Achievement of Jesus: An Examination of the Presuppositions of New Testament Theology* (SBT 12; London: SCM, 1954) 55-64.

[28] *The Son of Man in the Synoptic Tradition* (NT Library; London: SCM, 1965) 163-70; see also Fuller, *Foundations*, 118.

[29] *Son of Man*, 200-211; see also Fuller, *Foundations*, 150.

[30] Hahn, *Titles of Jesus*, 57; Fuller, *Foundations*, 118.

[31] Hooker, *Jesus and the Servant*, 74-79; C. K. Barrett, "The Background of Mark 10:45," *New Testament Essays: Studies in Memory of T. W. Manson* (ed. A. J. B. Higgins; Manchester: University Press, 1959) 1-18; see also W. J. Moulder, "The Old Testament Background and the Interpretation of Mark 10:45," *NTS* 24 (1977) 120-27.

[32] Johannes Weiss, *Earliest Christianity: A History of the Period A.D. 30—150* (2 vols.; New York: Harper, 1959) 1. 115.

[33] Cadbury, "Title of Jesus in Acts," 366; idem, *The Making of Luke-Acts* (1927; reprint, London: SPCK, 1958) 280n; see also Hooker, *Jesus and the Servant*, 86. For detailed analysis of Luke 22, see V. Taylor, *The Passion Narrative of St. Luke: A Critical and Historical Investigation* (ed. O. E. Evans; SNTSMS 19; Cambridge: University Press, 1972). According to Taylor, Luke's passion narrative "depicts Jesus as the Servant of the Lord without using the name" (p. 138). Another important work is that of H. Schürmann (*Jesu Abschiedsrede Lk 22, 21-38. III Teil: Einer quellenkritischer Untersuchung des lukanischen Abendmahlsberichtes Lk 22, 7-38* [NTAbh 20/5; Münster: Aschendorff, 1957], who has shown that elements of the Servant concept are to be found in the Lucan text of the narrative of the Lord's supper. See also D. L. Tiede, *Prophecy and History in Luke-Acts* (Philadelphia: Fortress, 1980). Luke 22-23 is the third of four sets of passages Tiede examines.

[34] Tödt, *Son of Man*, 200-211; O'Neill, *Theology of Acts*, 138.

[35]Cadbury, *The Making of Luke-Acts*, 280n.

[36]Schweizer, *Lordship*, 50; see also Hooker, *Jesus and the Servant*, 113-14.

[37]C. F. D. Moule, "The Christology of Acts," *Studies of Luke-Acts: Essays in Honor of P. Schubert* (ed. L. E. Keck and J. L. Martyn; Nashville: Abingdon, 1966) 170 n. 37; see also O'Neill, *Theology of Acts*, 134-35. *Studies in Luke-Acts* has been reprinted with a new Introduction (Philadelphia: Fortress, 1980).

[38]*Christology*, 73; see also O'Neill, *Theology of Acts*, 135.

[39]Haenchen, *The Acts of the Apostles: A Commentary* (Philadelphia: Westminster, 1971) 205.

[40]Fuller, *Foundations*, 167-69; Hahn, *Titles of Jesus*, 374-77; R. F. Zehnle, *Peter's Pentecost Discourse: Tradition and Lukan Reinterpretation in Peter's Speeches of Acts 2 and 3* (SBLMS 15; Nashville: Abingdon, 1971) passim.

[41]E. Franklin (*Christ the Lord: A Study in the Purpose and Theology of Luke-Acts* [Philadelphia: Westminster, 1975] 62) notes that Luke's use of "Righteous One" in v. 14 "refers back to the Servant in v. 13, is expanded into 'the Holy and Righteous One,' and then is paralleled by the title 'Author of Life.'" The classic work on this last title is P.-G. Müller, *Christos Archēgos: Der religionsgeschichtliche und theologische Hintergrund einer neutestamentlichen Christusprädikation* (Europäische Hochschulschriften 23/28; Bern: H. Lang; Frankfurt: P. Lang, 1973) [see my review, *JBL* 95 (1976) 305-7]. I question Müller's contention that Luke's use of the title "Servant" (along with *archēgos* and "Holy and Righteous One") reflects an "archaic Christology" behind the speech in Acts 3:12-26 (pp. 268-70). While agreeing with Müller that the title "*pais theou*" in v. 13 is to be understood "im Kontext der lukanischen Erhöhungschristologie" (p. 254), I cannot accept his implication that the title identifies Jesus with the Suffering Servant of Isaiah 53. It seems to me, rather, that the *Gottesknechtstitel* was ascribed to Jesus in the general sense of the Old Testament title of honor, *ᶜebed Yahweh*. P. Minear (*To Heal and To Reveal: The Prophetic Vocation according to Luke* [New York: Seabury, 1976] 106) comments on the link between Jesus and Moses provided by two speeches in Acts (3:12-26 and 7:2-53) and correctly notes that the designation "prophet" coalesces compatibly with other titles found in the speeches: the Holy and Righteous One, the Author of Life, God's Messiah, and God's Servant; see my review of Minear's work in *JBL* 97 (1978) 146-48.

[42]"The Most Primitive Christology of All?" *JTS* ns 7 (1956) 177ff.

[43]Moule, "Christology of Acts," 167-69; Jones, "*Christos* in Luke-Acts," 69-76, esp. 71ff.

[44]Jones, "*Christos* in Luke-Acts," 74.

[45]Haenchen, *Acts*, 228.

[46]O'Neill, *Theology of Acts*, 135-36.

[47]Ibid., 136

[48]Hahn, *Titles of Jesus*, 381; Fuller, *Foundations*, 170.

[49]Cadbury, "Titles of Jesus in Acts," 368.

[50]Note the close proximity of "Servant" in Acts 3:13, 26; 4:27, 30; to "Christ" in 3:18, 20; 4:26.

[51]See O'Neill, *Theology of Acts,* 136-37.

[52]"Bezeichnung 'Knecht Gottes.'"

[53]"*Pais Theou,*" 702.

[54]*Christology,* 73.

[55]Ibid., 74. Franklin (*Christ the Lord,* 61) contends that the close link in thought between the apostolic prayer of Acts 4 and the speech in chap. 3 suggests that the Suffering Servant is in mind and "enables the Servant idea to be something of an umbrella title which makes a link with the OT Servant figures as a whole and, more especially, throws some kind of a bridge between the Servant of Isaiah and the messianic, Davidic Servant."

[56]"Christology of Acts," 169-70.

[57]E.g., *1 Clem.* 59.2, 3; *Mart. Pol.* 14.1, 3; 20.2; *Diogn.* 8.9, 11; 9.1; see O'Neill, *Theology of Acts,* 139, 141.

[58]*Acts,* 205.

[59]Cadbury, "Titles of Jesus in Acts," 363; O'Neill, *Theology of Acts,* 139.

[60]Matt 8:14-17 and Mark 1:29-34; see also Luke 8:28 and 9:35.

[61]Hooker, *Jesus and the Servant,* 122.

[62]Jeremias, "*Pais Theou,*" 706.

[63]See Weiss, *Earliest Christianity,* 117-18; Bultmann, *NT Theology,* 1. 31.

[64]Bousset, *Kyrios Christos,* 111; see also Hooker, *Jesus and the Servant,* 125; Cadbury, "Title of Jesus in Acts," 369.

[65]"*Pais Theou,*" 708.

[66]See C. K. Barrett, "The Lamb of God," *NTS* 1 (1955) 210-18.

[67]Hooker, *Jesus and the Servant,* 126.

[68]Ibid., 123-24; Bultmann, *NT Theology,* 1. 31.

[69]*Theology of Acts,* 139.

[70]In agreement with this judgment is Emmeram Kränkl, *Jesus der Knecht Gottes: Die heilsgeschichtliche Stellung Jesu in den Reden der Apostelgeschichte* (Regensburg: Pustet, 1972) 125-29, 211; see my review of Kränkl's work in *JBL* 93 (1974) 470-71.

PART III

EXEGETICAL
STUDIES

William S. Kurz

LUKE 3:23-38 AND GRECO-ROMAN AND BIBLICAL GENEALOGIES

Introduction

Recent studies of Greco-Roman material and portions of the Bible that are similar to Luke-Acts are breaking down the old impasse in New Testament studies between Jewish and Hellenistic backgrounds. For example, the SBL Luke-Acts Seminar devoted its meeting in 1980 to the Jewish connection of Luke-Acts and in 1981 to the Greco-Roman connections.[1] This article shall study both sets of influences on the genealogy in Luke 3:23-38. The thesis is that Luke 3:23-38 plays an important role in the attempt by the author (henceforth simply "Luke") to provide a "continuation of the biblical history" in a Greco-Roman environment.[2] The genealogy especially grounds the Lucan narrative in the biblical history of God's dealings with his people since Adam. It shares the forms and functions of genealogies in Luke's Greek Bible, with Greco-Roman modifications and additions.

Because others have treated Luke's genealogy extensively, I will bypass many common considerations in commentaries and focus on the sometimes peculiar aspects which are clarified by comparison with other Greco-Roman and biblical genealogies.[3]

Greco-Roman Genealogies and Luke 3:23-38

The first striking fact about Luke's genealogy when compared with Matthew's and many in the Old Testament is its ascending rather than descending order. Wolfgang Speyer notes that the descending form was used in most Old Testament genealogies. Thus, like Matthew's genealogy, those in the early chapters of Genesis and 1 Chronicles and Ruth 4 descend from ancestor to descendants. Speyer states that the ascending form found in Luke 3 first became widespread in the Hellenistic period, and he gives Ezra 7:1-5 and Judith 8:1 as examples. In the Greco-Roman period, both kinds were available. For example, Plutarch, *Pyrrhus* 1, and *Lycurgus* 1:4 have short genealogies in descending (Matthean) order; Josephus has the ascending order in *Antiquities* 1.3.2 §79 for Noah as tenth from Adam, and 2.9.6 §229 for Moses as seventh from Abraham. Speyer speaks of the Lucan genealogy as Hellenistically fashioned.[4]

Luke uses for his ascending genealogy the genitive article *tou*, common in many Greek genealogies. Speyer claims that Luke had to use the article because of the indeclinable Semitic names, but many Greek genealogies with declinable names also use the article.[5] For example:

> *Leōnidēs ho Anaxandrideō tou Leontos tou Eurykratideō tou Anaxandrou tou Eurykrateos tou Polydōrou tou Alkamaneos tou Tēleklou tou Archeleō tou Hēgēsileō tou Doryssou tou Leōbōteō tou Echestratou tou Hēgios tou Eurystheneos tou Aristodēmou tou Aristomachou tou Kleodaiou to Hyllou tou Hēracleos* (Herodotus 7.204).

For similar examples see Herodotus 4.147; 7.11.2; 8.131. Nor does Luke 3:23 have *tou* before the name of Joseph, which is also an indeclinable Semitic name. It should be noted that in the Herodotus examples neither do the first names have *tou*. Luke's example (complicated by his parenthetical remark) reads: *ōn huios hōs enomizeto Iōsēph tou Ēli. . . .*[6]

An important Greek convention that Luke deliberately ignores in order to imitate the Greek Bible is the use of at least Greek endings on names. In the unapologetic use of barbaric names, Luke's ascending genealogy is much closer to that in Tobit 1:1 than it is even to the Greek part of a bilingual inscription. Tobit 1:1 reads: *Biblos logōn Tōbit tou Tōbiēl tou Ananiēl tou Adouēl tou Gabaēl ek tou spermatos Asiēl ek tēs phylēs Nephthalim.* The Greek part of the Palmyrene-Greek inscription has: *Aailamein Hairanou tou Mokimou tou Hairanou tou Maththa.*[7]

Whereas Luke follows the Semitic forms from the Greek Bible, Josephus follows Greek conventions and tries to put Greek endings on all the names, besides introducing some stylistic variety instead of a mere listing of names. *Antiquities* 1.3.2. §79 gives Noah's genealogy: *Nōchos . . . apo Adamou dekatos: Lamechou gar estin huios, hou patēr, ēn Mathousalas, houtos de ēn tou Anōchou tou Iaredou, Malaēlou de Iaredos egegonei, hos ek Kaina teknoutai tou Anōsou syn adelphais pleiosin, Anōsos de Sēthou huios ēn tou Adamou.* Contrast Luke's Semitic forms of the same names: *tou Nōe tou Lamech tou Mathousala tou Henōch tou Iaret tou Maleleēl tou Kainam tou Enōs tou Sēth tou Adam* (Luke 3:36-38).[8]

The length of Luke's list (more than seventy names) is most unusual for Greco-Roman writings. Herodotus tells of Hecataeus's pride in his genealogy of sixteen names back to a god, until the Egyptians told him of 345 generations of high priests (Herodotus 2.142-43).[9] Whereas Greek nobles traced their genealogies through several generations back to a god, those not of noble birth could rarely get back to the third ancestor.[10] A grave inscription of Heropythos goes back fifteen generations to the mythical Cyprios. A second-century B.C. epigram from Dodona goes back thirty generations to Cassandra. A genealogy in an inscription from Pisidia has the person forty-first after Heracles and thirty-ninth from the Dioscuri.[11] For the Romans at the beginning of the empire as well as during the republic, genealogies of many generations were very difficult and usually impossible to compile. Romans were less interested than Greeks in mythical genealogies and were more interested in historical ancestors (see the funeral praises).[12] But by the end of the Roman republic most noble houses had a genealogy going back to a hero or a god. More practically, inscriptions stressed genealogies to great-grandparents.[13]

Single linear genealogies of seventy-seven generations back to Adam are not common in the Bible either. The sheer length of Luke's list must have sounded impressive to his listeners.[14] But those familiar with the genealogies of Genesis and the first nine chapters of genealogies in 1 Chronicles would not be overawed by Luke's.

We have seen that Greeks and Romans traced genealogies back to gods. Nowhere does the Bible do this, so that Luke's tracing Jesus back to Adam and then to God sounds prima facie like the Greco-Roman custom. Speyer suggests that "Seth, Adam, God" in Luke 3:38 would jar Jewish ears.[15] However, he overlooks Luke's preparation in 3:23 for the Adam-God link: "being the son, as was thought, of Joseph." In the light of Luke's account of the virgin birth, the Adam-God relationship is like that of Jesus and Joseph.

Nevertheless, the genealogical link between Jesus and God seems more likely to have been inspired by Luke's culture than by his Bible. For the Greeks, genealogies from the gods expressed a belief in the relationship between humans and the divine. There was a wide consensus in popular belief that extraordinary humans (heroes, wonder-workers, great kings, saviors, the wise) came from gods, either from heaven or from a divine parent.[16] To be noted also is the belief, common to many Mediterranean people, in degeneration from an original golden age, as in Hesiod's *Theogony* and in Jewish apocalyptic.[17] But the Greeks did not have a common founder for all human races as in the Israelite Adam. Speyer relates the personage Adam to belief in one God.[18] Genealogical relationships and solidarity among peoples were far more important for nomads than for Greeks and Romans.[19] When the importance of genealogies (from

Israel's nomadic past) combined with the belief in only one God, a common genealogy for the whole human race from Adam resulted. This gives reason to consider further below the extension of Luke's genealogy to Adam and God.

Biblical Genealogies and Luke 3:23-38

Scholars commonly recognize that Luke locates his gospel in the context of contemporary world history (Luke 1:5; 2:1-2; esp. 3:1-2). Less universally noticed is how Luke also locates his narrative within the biblically described history of the world from Adam to the judgment day of the Lord. Luke not only showed that these events did not take place "in a corner" (Acts 26:26), but he also grounded them in God's past work and future consummation. Thus, the biblical "time line" on which Luke placed his two volumes extended from the beginning to the judgment of the world. To situate his narrative on the part of this line from Adam to "the events accomplished among us" (Luke 1:1), Luke used the form of genealogy.[20]

The following comparison of the functions of genealogies in Luke's Gospel with those in the Greek Bible will have four points: (1) the placement of the genealogy in relationship to the entire gospel; (2) the extension of the genealogy back to Adam; (3) the meaning of mentioning God at the head of the genealogy; and (4) genealogies as providing a context for the main narrative within the history of God's people.

Placement of the Genealogy Within the Entire Work

Scholars have frequently discussed the differences between Matthew and Luke in the placement of the genealogies and the question of why the genealogy in Luke appears after the infancy-youth section.[21] That the genealogy in Luke 3:23-38 is fitted into its immediate context to explain the title Son of God in Luke 3:22 and to provide an immediate backdrop for his testing as Son of God in 4:1-13 is commonly known. Not so widely recognized are the similarities in placement between Jesus' genealogy in Luke 3:23-38 and that of Moses in Exod 6:14-17.[22]

Luke precedes his genealogy with a substantial amount of introductory material. After his preface (a Hellenistic form present in later Greek biblical books like the Sirach translation and 2 Maccabees epitome), Luke begins in Greek biblical style, *Egeneto en tais hēmerais Herōdou* . . . (Luke 1:5).[23] Luke sets the stage in expectations of pious Jews before introducing the story of Jesus. Thus the story of Zachary, Elizabeth, and the conception of John precedes the parallel account of Mary's conception of Jesus (Luke 1:5-25 and 26-38).

Similarly, Exodus 1 precedes the Moses story with the transition from Joseph at the end of Genesis to the new king "who did not know Joseph" (Exod 1:8 [G], cited in Acts 7:18). His order to kill all male Israelite babies sets the stage for introducing the (unnamed) parents of Moses, both of the tribe of Levi. (One can compare the levitical priest Zachary from the division of Abijah, mentioned in 1 Chr 24:10 and Neh 12:4, 17, and Elizabeth, a daughter of Aaron.)

Both Luke 1-2 and Exodus 2 then describe the births, naming, nurturing, and growth of Moses and Jesus. Both relate an event in the youth of their heroes that foreshadowed their later work but preceded it by many years: Moses' attempt to rescue fellow Israelites, leading to his forty-year exile, and Jesus in the temple at age twelve, but subject to his parents until about age thirty.[24] Only then do the respective missions of Moses and Jesus begin. When Moses is shepherding in the desert, God reveals himself and commissions him at the burning bush (Exodus 3). The word of God coming to the Baptist in the desert begins his ministry of preaching and baptizing. When Jesus is baptized, God addresses and commissions him (Luke 3:1-22).

Because of multiple sources, of which Luke may not have been aware, Exodus 3-6 has repetitions in the commissioning of Moses to go to Pharaoh. In Exod 6:13 God again orders Moses and Aaron to Pharaoh. The genealogy of Aaron and Moses is inserted here in Exod 6:14-27. In 6:28-7:5, after the two have been "properly introduced," Moses is again told to take God's message to Pharaoh; he balks, is given Aaron as "prophet," and is further instructed in his mission. For Moses this is equivalent to one last temptation to resist his mission and clarification of what it will involve. Moses and Aaron's obedience is then reported in 7:6, and 7:7 gives their respective ages when they began their mission. Only then follows the extended narration of their rescue mission of the ten plagues culminating in the death of firstborn sons (Exod 7:8-chap. 11, followed by the Passover in chap. 12).

In a similar placement, after Jesus is named Son of God and is filled with the Spirit (Luke 3:22), his genealogy as Son of God is given (3:23-38), then the testing and clarification of his mission as Son and his obedience (4:1-13), and finally the beginning in 4:14 of the extended account of Jesus' saving mission beginning in Galilee and culminating in his own death as God's Son (23:34 and 46) at Passover time. One slight difference is that Jesus' age comes at the beginning of the genealogy, Moses' and Aaron's only after their obedience and immediately before the plague accounts.

In other words, in relationship to the overall stories of Moses in Exodus and Jesus in Luke, the genealogies occur in almost the same relative positions. They are preceded by preliminary accounts of birth, youth, and commissioning, and they are followed by detailed narratives of Moses' and Jesus' main missions.

Though such parallels can seem arbitrary, Acts 7:18-37 gives solid evidence that Luke had in mind precisely this parallelism between the structures of Jesus' career and Moses' career and that he elaborated his parallelism on the basis of the Greek version of Exodus. In a way reminiscent of Luke's use of Mark, Acts 7 retells the story of Moses with frequent quotations from the Greek text of Exodus and constant use of its language, combined with Lucan introductions, summaries, transitions, substitute favorite expressions, and interpretative comments.

The heavy use of verses, phrases, and language from Greek Exodus is quite obvious from the bold print for allusions in Nestle's 25th edition, and it is still clear in the 26th edition, which italicizes full quotations. We have room to cite only some, inviting readers who so desire to compare the Greek texts of Acts and Exodus.[25]

Acts 7:18 quotes Exod 1:7 about the new king and describes the Egyptian oppression in the same combination of words (Acts 7:19 *katasophisamenos*, Exod 1:10 *katasophisōmetha*; Acts 7:19 *ekakōsen*, Exod 1:11 *kakōsōsin*; Acts 7:19 *mē zōogoneisthai*, three forms of the verb in Exod 1:17, 18, 22). The same unusual expression is used for the baby Moses in Acts 7:20 (*ēn asteios*) and Exod 2:2 (*idontes auto asteion*; the Hebrew has the very ordinary *kî ṭôb*).[26] For Moses' adoption, Acts 7:21 has *hē thygatēr Pharaō . . . heautē eis huion*; Exod 2:10 *tēn thygatera Pharaō . . . autē eis huion*. Many other coincidences of otherwise unusual words or combinations clearly show deliberate use of Exodus by Acts 7.

Even more important is the deliberate parallelism in *structure* between the career of Moses in Acts 7 (closely based on Exodus) and that of Jesus in Luke's gospel, which has been convincingly shown by scholars.[27] Both are in times of fulfillment of promises to Abraham (Acts 7:17), both grow in wisdom (Acts 7:22 as in Luke 2:40 and 52, not in Exodus), both were "powerful in words and deeds" (Acts 7:22 = Luke 24:19). It could be said of both that "he thought the brothers would understand that God was giving salvation to them at his hand, but they did not understand" (Acts 7:25; passim for Jesus in the Gospel and the speeches of Acts). The people reject both not just once but twice. The speeches of Acts use similar expressions for the rejection and vindication of Moses and Jesus: *touton ton Mōüsēn, hon ērnēsanto . . . touton ho theos kai archonta kai lytrōtēn apestalken* (Acts 7:35 and Luke's frequent parallelism of the relative *hon* and demonstrative *touton*, as in Acts 5:30-31, *hon hymeis diecheirisasthe . . . touton ho theos archēgon kai sōtēra hypsōsen*).

Finally and conclusively, Acts 7:37 obviously parallels Moses and Jesus. "This" Moses (who worked signs and wonders [7:36] and was sent as savior [7:35]) prophesied that God would *anastēsei* ("raise up," with a pun on "resurrect") "a prophet for you . . . like me (= Deut 18:15).

Luke's effort in the speeches of Acts to show parallel structures for the careers of Jesus and Moses, while respecting differences in the details of their lives, is confirming evidence that Luke imitated the Exodus structure in the placement of his genealogy.

What can the parallel placing of the genealogies of Moses and Jesus just before the beginnings of their saving missions indicate about the narrative *functions* of each? After the introductory youth and call of Moses, the genealogy in Exod 6:14-27 situates Moses and Aaron within the priestly line of Levi, and ultimately within God's whole people, before the account of how God saved his people through them by the plagues. Unlike Luke's linear genealogy tracing just a single line of descent, the genealogy in Exod 6:14-27 is segmented to give the descendants of several sons of one father. As a result, it relates Moses and Aaron not only to direct ancestors and descendants but also to collateral priestly lines of Levi (as well as descendants of Reuben and Simeon) to which other protagonists of the desert story (like Korah, Numbers 16) belong. In fact, the genealogy focuses more on Aaron than on Moses, tracing Aaron's line through Eleazar to the priestly line of Phineas. It thus also legitimates Phineas's line by grounding it in the saving figures of the exodus.[28]

The similar placing of Luke's genealogy suggests a similar function. Supplementing the dating from contemporary rulers in Luke 3:1-2, Luke 2:23-38 gives Jesus' position within the ancestral subdivisions of God's people as well as his temporal relationship to the people's history. Thus it places Jesus in an obscure (versus the royal) branch of David's line, as Moses and Aaron belonged to Levi's. It puts Jesus at the end of God's long saving history, traced to its very beginning in Adam. Contrast the Exodus genealogy that also named Aaron's descendants and began only with the sons of Jacob. These differences are quite significant. Though Luke wrote one or two generations after Jesus, Jesus is the end of the genealogical line, unlike Aaron who was in the middle of his. The line has led to its definitive fulfillment in Jesus, and now God's people is in the eschatological age of the Spirit's outpouring, which has relativized the importance of blood relationships in God's people (Acts 10-11 and 15). Nevertheless, one function of both genealogies is to show the relationship of the saviors to their people's history.

Depth of Luke's Genealogy Back To Adam

1 Chronicles 1-9 and Luke 3:23-38 both trace their respective heroes David and Jesus all the way back to Adam through genealogies. Though the Genesis genealogies also go back to Adam, they

obviously cannot extend forward as far as David. It seems reasonable to ask whether Luke imitated Greek Chronicles in the functions to which he put his genealogy.[29] Whether the author of the genealogy in Luke 3 relied more on 1 Chronicles than on Genesis is hard to prove because of confusion in the manuscripts. In favor of Genesis is the fact that only Genesis 11:12-13 [G] agrees with Luke 3:36 in having *Kainam* (or *Kainan* in many manuscripts) between *Arphaxad* and *Sala* (Göttingen text). *Kainam* is missing in Hebrew Genesis 11 and in all but the Alexandrian manuscript of 1 Chr 1:17-24 [G].

The following considerations favor Greek Chronicles over Greek Genesis. (1) Luke 3:34 has *Abraam* with Chronicles rather than *Abram* with Genesis (Göttingen). (2) The prominent simple list form of the genealogies in Chronicles (as in Luke 3) would have been much easier to use than culling the names from Genesis 5 and 11, which have much extraneous material. (3) The likelihood that the Lucan genealogy used Chronicles for later names suggests its use for earlier ones also. Thus Greek Chronicles seems more likely than Genesis to be the source of Luke 3. But unless Codex A of 1 Chr 1:17-24 or a nonextant equivalent were used,[30] Greek Genesis would have had to be consulted for *Kainam* in Luke 3:36.[31]

The first obvious function of gathering all genealogical material from the hero back to Adam is to situate the narrative within the overall history of God's dealings with humans from the beginning. Closely related is the function of spanning gaps in the traditions narrated in the biblical context, as between creation and the patriarchal stories by the genealogies of Genesis 5 and 11, between Adam and Saul/David in 1 Chronicles, and between especially Adam and Abraham, David, and Jesus in Luke 3.[32] Another related function of the genealogical connection to Adam is to show continuity of God's people through periods of national disruption, as when the genealogies of Genesis 46 and Numbers 26 connect the sons of Judah with the exodus clans.[33] This function is less obvious between David and Adam in 1 Chronicles, but perhaps it is implied. It does seem to fit the link between Jesus and David through a Davidic line, which avoided the curses that destroyed Judah's royal line.

Genealogies can also help to show epochs in history according to a prearranged plan by God,[34] as in arrangements of names in multiples of seven[35] or the epochs marked by the flood, Abraham, exodus, etc. The Chronicler seems to have preserved this from his Genesis source, as in the separate Adam-Noah's sons and Shem-Abraham lists. It is probably clearer in Luke's source, arranged in sevens from Adam to Jesus and thus highlighting major intermediate figures, than when God has become the head of the list. Beginning from Adam, the seventh figures include Enoch, Abraham, David, Salathiel, and Jesus, which is what one would expect (cf. Jude 14, "Enoch the seventh from Adam"). With God at the head of the list, none of those names is in the seventh position, but rather Jared, Terah, Jesse, Neri, and Joseph. That would not, however, have been noticed by those listening to the reading of Luke's gospel, since the names are in ascending (reverse) order. It is quite possible that Luke reversed the order of his genealogical source to facilitate the notion of "Jesus son of . . . God," just as a copyist of manuscript D reversed Matthean royal names and substituted them into the Davidic segment of the Lucan genealogy (Nestle-Aland, 26th ed.).[36]

Another obvious function of genealogies is simply to identify the individual through his ancestry, as in 1 Sam 1:1 (Elkanah son of Jeroham son of Elihu son of Tohu son of Zuph, an Ephraimite), 1 Sam 9:1 (for Saul), 2 Sam 20:1 (for Sheba), Zeph 1:1, and Zech 1:1. Or it links the individual with well-known personages from the past.

When the genealogy proceeds through sons who were not first-born (e.g., Jacob, Judah, David, Nathan in Luke 3), the importance of being chosen by God is implied. Thus, 1 Chr 5:1-2 explains why Joseph, not Reuben, got the birthright. 1 Chr 17:7 emphasizes the free choice of David, that "I took you from the pasture from following the sheep to be leader over my people Israel." 1 Chr 2:13-15 had listed David not as first-born of Jesse but as "the seventh." The listing of Jesus' descent from David through a nonroyal line in Luke 3 may imply such free choice by God.[37]

For readers familiar with the biblical narratives, genealogies (as in Luke 3 and 1 Chronicles 1-9) also function as "encapsulated history" and a mnemonic device for quick recall of a whole sweep of history in the briefest possible way.

Why Luke Mentions God at the Head of His Genealogy

Like the Chronicler, Luke extends his genealogy back to the first man. Unlike the Chronicler, or as far as I know any other Jewish writer to his time, Luke goes even beyond Adam to God.[38] The first section of this study mentioned that Greco-Roman sources trace people back to an origin in some god. Popular Hellenistic philosophy contained the view that the whole human race is descended from the gods or divine principle. The Areopagus speech, especially Acts 17:26 and 28-29, shows that Luke was aware of such thinking. Those verses argue that all humans are descended from one man and "we" (humans) are all descendants (*genos*) of God.[39]

In argument and wording, the Areopagus speech combines Stoic, rhetorical, poetic, and biblical expressions, concepts, and allusions. It identifies the "unknown god" with the God who created and is Lord over the cosmos. God therefore does not dwell in temples made by humans; not does God need anything from humans, since "he himself gives to all men life and breath and everything" (Acts 17:25 RSV). These were important themes in popular Hellenistic philosophy and Jewish propaganda. This God made from one human (Adam) the whole race to inhabit the earth and set times and boundaries so humans would seek God (see Luke 3:38; Acts 1:7; Genesis 1-5 and 10; Deut 32:8; and Ps 74:17).

Acts 17:27b-29a are especially important for understanding Luke 3:38. They argue that God "is not far from each of us. For in him we live and move and are, as even some of your poets have said: 'for we are his [God's] *genos*.' Being there the *genos* of God. . . ." *Genos* refers to descendants of a common ancestor, and humanity as God's *genos* is found in Cleanthes and Dio Chrysostom as well as in Luke's quotation from Aratus.[40] The background for understanding how Luke 3:38 and Acts 17:28-29 relate in the context of Luke-Acts seems to be LXX Gen 1:26-27 and 5:1-3. In Gen 1:26-27 God says, "Let us make man according to our *eikona* and *homoiōsin*." They (*anthrōpos* is collective) were to rule all other creatures. "And God made man, *kat' eikona theou* he made him, male and female he made them."

The link between *eikōn* and descendants becomes clear in Gen 5:1-3. The chapter begins, "This is the *biblos geneseōs anthrōpōn*: on the day God *epoiēsen* . . . *ton Adam, kat' eikona Theou epoiēsen auton*." Gen 5:3 then uses similar expressions for Adam's begetting of Seth: *Kai egennēsen kata tēn idean autou kai kata tēn eikona autou*. The choice of words implies a careful distinction between how God is related to Adam and how gods in Greek mythology are related to heroes they beget from human partners. God made (*epoiēsen*) Adam, whereas Adam begot (*egennēsen*) Seth. God's transcendence is preserved, yet a filial relationship is implied by saying Adam was *kat' eikona Theou* as Seth was *kata tēn eikona* of Adam. The care of the Greek translators was not lost on Luke.

For on the one hand Acts 17:28-29 uses terminology from Greek literature and philosophy to say that humans are all the *genos* of God, which would ordinarily imply some kind of ancestry by God of the human race. But Acts 17:26 had said God *epoiēsen te ex henos pan ethnos anthrōpōn katoikein* . . . , although here *epoiēsen* may well be a helping verb, for Luke's Christian readers it is nevertheless allusive to the language of Genesis. We are obviously all the *genos* of God through the one man, who remains unnamed according to rhetorical style for a speech ostensibly addressed to Athenian philosophers. Especially in view of Luke 3:38, however, the allusion to Adam is obvious for Luke's readers.

Acts 17 therefore provides an explanation of Luke's affixing God to the head of Jesus' genealogy. Like Acts 17, Luke's designation of

Adam as son of God gives an *interpretatio graeca* of the biblical information. Listing a god at the head of human genealogies was pagan rather than biblical practice. But Luke's genealogy already contains hints that Adam's origin from God was not by sexual generation, hints that would be clear to readers familiar with the Bible. Two clues are his inserted phrases *hōs enomizeto* at the beginning of Luke's genealogy and "of God" at its end: "Jesus . . . being the son, as was supposed, of Joseph of Eli . . . of Adam of God" (Luke 3:23 and 38). Not only does the first phrase "harmonize" the genealogy with the virginal conception in Luke 1:26-38, but it also points to an analogy between Jesus' filial relationship to Joseph and the special kind of filial relationship of Adam to God known by anyone familiar with Genesis.

Neither Jesus nor Adam was sexually begotten by his "father" in the genealogy—Joseph and God. Rather God *made* Adam and gave him the divine prerogatives of ruling and naming the rest of creation. Luke 1:26-38 also has echoes of the creation story. Jesus is not sexually conceived but is created in Mary's womb by the Holy Spirit (Luke 1:34-35). The creative and life-giving functions of the Holy Spirit are widely attested in the Old Testament and well known among first-century Jews and Christians.[41] Nor is either of the verbs in Luke 1:35 for the Spirit's action (*epeleusetai* and *episkiasei*) used with sexual meanings in the Greek Bible or ordinary secular usage.[42] And because it is through the Holy Spirit and power of God that Jesus is created in the womb, "therefore the one to be born shall be called holy, the Son of God" (1:35).

The pericope following Luke's genealogy provides some confirming evidence for this analogy between Jesus and Adam as sons of God in a nonsexual sense, as made by God's creative power. Many have noticed an implied parallel between Adam and Jesus in Jesus' temptation (Luke 4:1-13). Jesus is tempted as Son of God, but unlike the disobedient Adam he remains an obedient Son.[43]

This evidence suggests some functions of Luke's affixing God to his genealogy. In the light of Acts 17, implying that all humans are children of God through "one man," Adam relates the biblical account to Hellenistic concerns, especially the unity of the human race and its kinship with God. Adding the phrase "as was supposed" at the beginning and "of God" at the end of the genealogy calls attention to more than one kind of sonship-paternity relationship in the genealogy. Besides ordinary generation there is also a creative fatherhood of God for Adam and Jesus, and a legal fatherhood (in terms of inheritance) of Joseph for Jesus and God for Adam. Thus, even those functions most influenced by secular Hellenistic concerns take place within the Genesis story of Adam and its perspective of God as transcendent creator of the human race.

Locating the Main Account within
the History of God's People

This function has already been implied in the earlier comparisons between Luke 3:23-38 and Exod 6:14-27 and 1 Chronicles 1-9. But those passages were compared from different perspectives, namely, the placement of the genealogy in the work and the extension of the list back to Adam. A further brief comparison with Ruth 4:18-22 G can clarify the function of showing where the story fits in the overall history of God's people. The likelihood that the author of the Luke 3 genealogy consulted Ruth for his names from Phares to David gives added reason to compare Luke 3:23-38 and Ruth 4:18-20 G.[44]

A notable similarity between Luke and Ruth is the relative independence of their main narrative from their genealogy. Both genealogies read like later insertions into a narrative that could stand without them. As in Matthew and Mark, Luke's temptation story would follow naturally upon the heavenly proclamation of Jesus as God's Son. Luke has had to insert the genealogy into his source Mark's arrangement here. Similarly, the story in Ruth is finished when the genealogy appears, which leads some even to claim it was added by a later hand.[45]

The story in Ruth reaches its climax when Ruth and Boaz preserve the name and line of Naomi's dead husband and sons through the birth of Obed. With Ruth 4:17, "A son has been born to Naomi," the plot line is resolved. But the text goes on to show the story's wider significance: "and they called his name Obed; this is the father of Jesse the father of David." This would have been sufficient to insert the story into Israel's history. The further addition of the final genealogy links the story not only with later generations up to David but also with earlier ones back to Phares the son of Judah the patriarch. In so doing, the genealogy locates the story of Ruth on the "biblical time line" from the patriarchs through the exodus generation through the judges to its "fulfillment" in David.

If so, why does the genealogy begin with Phares and not the better-known Judah? The seventh-generation emphasis may be the answer. The story's male hero Boaz is seventh from Phares but eighth from Judah.[46] Ruth 4:12 had prepared for the genealogy: "and may your house be as the house of Phares, whom Tamar bore to Judah. . . ." In both cases a dead husband's kinsman (Judah and Boaz) provides his childless widow (Tamar and Ruth) with a child on his behalf (with obvious differences!). Second, by mentioning Phares as a son of Judah the patriarch, Ruth 4:12 freed the redactor from having to begin the genealogy in 4:18 with Judah, thereby reserving the climactic seventh place in the genealogy for Boaz. This is evidence that the person responsible for the canonical version of Ruth and not some later glossarist put the genealogy at the end of Ruth.

If this is true, it follows that Luke and the redactor of Ruth have made similar adjustments in adding a genealogy to their narratives. Both genealogies are obviously insertions or additions to originally independent stories (as Luke's source Mark). Neither genealogy was needed to provide contemporary time indicators, for both stories had those already. Ruth is set in the time of the judges: *Kai egeneto en tǭ krinein tous kritas* (Ruth 1:1).[47] In accordance with Hellenistic taste, the temporal setting in Luke 3:1-2 is more detailed. Rather than providing temporal setting, both genealogies relate the story to earlier biblical accounts of God's dealings with his people. The adjustments both the author of canonical Ruth and Luke made in their genealogies were similar. The former began with Phares rather than Judah to reserve the seventh place for Boaz (4:18), preparing for this by "Phares, whom Tamar bore to Judah" in 4:12. Luke linked genealogy to narrative by inserting "as was supposed" in view of the virginal conception, and "of God" for its context between Jesus' naming and temptation as God's Son. Finally, the focus of both genealogies is the climactic figure in the history of God's people—David for the redactor of Ruth, and Jesus the Son of God, who will receive "the throne of David his father and will rule over the house of Jacob forever" (Luke 1:32-33).

Conclusions

Comparison of Luke 3:23-38 with Greco-Roman and biblical genealogies has shown that in content and function Luke's genealogy is in continuity with those in his Greek Bible, which had already been Hellenized. Some of Luke's choices among biblical options and some modifications show Greco-Roman preferences and concerns. Thus Luke's ascending format was frequent in Herodotus and inscriptions and common only in later, more Hellenized parts of the Greek Bible. Yet the closest grammatical parallel to Luke's is the ascending genealogy of Tobit 1:1 with its same use of the article and Semitic name endings.

The position of Jesus' genealogy in Luke 3 not only links his naming (3:22) and temptation (4:1-12) as God's Son but also imitates the placing of Moses' genealogy (Exod 6:14-27) between his youth, call, and mission (Exodus 2-6) and his further protest and definitive mission of the plagues (6:28-11:10). Acts 7 confirmed that Luke deliberately paralleled the structures of the career of Moses and that of Jesus, the prophet like Moses.

Luke's genealogy is biblical in many of its names and in its extension back to Adam. Its pattern of sevens confirms the continuity of God's plan from the beginning through many epochs. The mention of

God at the head of Luke's genealogy is an *interpretatio graeca* not found in Jewish sources. But modifications like *hos enomizeto* (3:22) in the light of Acts 17:26, 28-29 show that the relationship between Adam and God is seen in the light of Genesis. Neither Joseph nor God begot Jesus or Adam sexually, but God *made* Adam and treated him as a son by giving him divine prerogatives over creation.

Like Ruth 4:18-20, Luke's genealogy was added to an independent story in a source (Mark) and linked to the story through modifications in the genealogy. Both genealogies situate their stories within the history of God's people. Luke 3:23-38 links Jesus to his biblical roots and thus helps Luke provide a "continuation of the biblical history" in ways meaningful to his Greco-Roman environment.

NOTES

[1]See *Society of Biblical Literature 1980 Seminar Papers* (ed. P. J. Achtemeier; Chico, CA: Scholars Press, 1980); *Society of Biblical Literature 1981 Seminar Papers* (ed. K. H. Richards; Chico, CA: Scholars Press, 1981). F. Danker (*Benefactor: Epigraphic Study of a Graeco-Roman and New Testament Semantic Field* [St. Louis: Clayton, 1982]) says this in the conclusion of his monumental 509-page study: "For those with firm background in the Hebrew or Greek Scriptures this experience finds expression in language relating especially to the figure of the Spirit-filled 'Servant.' On the other hand, for the benefit of auditors with broad Graeco-Roman background Luke incorporates language patterns drawn from the Hellenistic semantic field of the honored benefactor. For both publics he introduces motifs that are part of the generic cultural experience."

[2]This characterization is descriptive and does not try to specify the genre of Luke-Acts, nor does it take sides among various parties trying to relate Luke-Acts to Greco-Roman history, biography, or romance. It calls attention to Luke's attempt to do in his time and culture what his Greek Bible had done earlier—narrate God's saving action for his people through chosen agents. Even his Greek Bible had such different kinds of narrative as the Elijah-Elisha cycle within Kings, 1 and 2 Maccabees, and Ruth.

[3]Extensive important recent treatments of Luke's genealogy, often in broader genealogical contexts, include M. D. Johnson, *The Purpose of the Biblical Genealogies* (SNTSMS 8; Cambridge: University Press, 1969) 229-52; W. Speyer, "Genealogie," *Reallexikon für Antike und Christentum,* 9 (ed. T. Klauser; Stuttgart: Hiersemann, 1976) cols. 1145-1268, esp. cols. 1213-34; H. Schürmann, *Das Lukasevangelium* (HTKNT 3/1; Freiburg: Herder, 1969) 1. 198-204; R. E. Brown, *The Birth of the Messiah* (Garden City: Doubleday, 1977) 57-95 (esp. tables Matt, Luke, OT, pp. 76-79); J. A. Fitzmyer, *The Gospel*

According to Luke (I-IX): Introduction, Translation, and Notes (AB 28; Garden City: Doubleday, 1981) 488-505 (esp. tables pp. 492-94); E. Klostermann, *Das Lukasevangelium* (HNT 5; 3d ed.; Tübingen: Mohr [Siebeck], 1975) 56-59; R. Hood, "The Genealogies of Jesus," *Early Christian Origins: Studies in Honor of Harold R. Willoughby* (ed. A. Wikgren; Chicago: Quadrangle, 1961) 1-15; I. H. Marshall, *The Gospel of Luke* (NIGTC; Grand Rapids: Eerdmans, 1978) 157-65; L. Ramlot, "Les généalogies bibliques: Un genre littéraire oriental," *BVC* 60 (1964) 53-70; E. Lerle, "Die Ahnenverzeichnisse Jesu: Versuch einer Christologischen Interpretation (Lk 3:23-38)," *ZNW* 72 (1981) 112-17; L. Overstreet ("Difficulties of New Testament Genealogies," *Grace Theological Journal* 2 [1981] 303-26) is a harmonizing rejection of historical criticism on them; W. S. Kurz ("Luke-Acts and Historiography in the Greek Bible," *SBL 1980 Seminar Papers*, 283-300) contains an earlier version of much of the second section of this study as well as material not treated here.

[4] Speyer, "Genealogie," ed. 1211. Note, however, that in this sense the biblical genealogies he mentioned, as well as others like Tobit 1:1, are also Hellenistic.

[5] Ibid., col. 1230.

[6] This undermines the citation of F. Godet in Overstreet ("Difficulties"); Godet argues that the absence of *tou* puts Joseph outside the genealogical list, which is therefore Mary's. See also the inscription quoted by Klostermann (*Lukas-evangelium*, 57): *Dēmētrion Hermapiou tou Hermapiou tou Hermadatou. . . .*

[7] Cited by Klostermann (*Lukasevangelium*, 56) from G. A. Cooke, *A Text-book of North Semitic Inscriptions* (Oxford: Clarendon, 1903) No. 110 (second century A.D.). Note the lack of the article on the first genitive name.

[8] See H. J. Cadbury, *The Style and Literary Method of Luke* (HTS 6; Cambridge: Harvard, 1920, repr. 1969) esp. pp. 154-58.

[9] See Speyer, "Genealogie," cols. 1158, 1169.

[10] Ibid., col. 1172.

[11] Ibid., cols. 1174-75.

[12] Ibid., cols. 1187-88.

[13] Ibid., col. 1196.

[14] For the distinction between linear and segmented genealogies, see the excellent *Genealogy and History in the Biblical World* by R. R. Wilson (Yale Near Eastern Researches 7; New Haven: Yale University Press, 1977). For the Greeks, see M. Broadbent, *Studies in Greek Genealogy* (Leiden: Brill, 1968).

[15] Speyer, "Genealogie," col 1203.

[16] Ibid., cols. 1157, 1164.

[17] Ibid., col. 1165.

[18] Ibid., col 1204.

[19] Ibid., col. 1201.

[20] For a description of Luke's biblical time line, see Kurz, "Historiography," 283-86.

[21] See Fitzmyer (*Luke*, 488-89) on the possibility that the gospel

existed at one time without the infancy narrative. C. H. Talbert ("Prophecies of Future Greatness: The Contribution of Greco-Roman Biographies to an Understanding of Luke 1:5-4:15," *The Divine Helmsman: Studies on God's Control of Human Events, Presented to Lou H. Silberman* [ed. J. L. Crenshaw and S. Sandmel; New York: Ktav, 1980] 130) challenges that hypothesis.

[22] See A. Plummer, *A Critical and Exegetical Commentary on the Gospel according to St. Luke* (ICC; New York: Scribner, 1910) 101-2; also quoted in Overstreet, "Difficulties," 314; R. E. Brown, "Genealogy (Christ)," *IDB Supplementary Volume* (ed. K. Crim; Nashville: Abingdon, 1976) 354.

[23] For biblicistic style, see judicious recent treatments by Fitzmyer (*Luke*, 109, 113-27): Luke's writings are closer than most of the New Testament to Attic writers, yet "90 per cent of his vocabulary is in the LXX, where it resembles most the vocabulary of Judges, Samuel, Kings, and above all 2 Maccabees"; and F. L. Horton, Jr. ("Reflections on the Semitisms of Luke-Acts," *Perspectives on Luke-Acts* [ed. C. H. Talbert; Special Studies Series, 5; Danville, VA: Association of Baptist Professors of Religion, 1978] 1-23), who suggests "synagogue Greek." See also standard sources like J. C. Hawkins, *Horae Synopticae: Contributions to the Study of the Synoptic Problem* (2d ed.; Oxford: Clarendon, 1909); J. H. Moulton, *A Grammar of New Testament Greek: Vol. 4, Style*, by N. Turner (Edinburgh: T. & T. Clark, 1976); H. J. Cadbury, *The Making of Luke-Acts* (1927; reprint, Naperville, IL: Allenson, 1958); idem, *The Style and Literary Method of Luke* (HTS 6; Cambridge: Harvard University Press, 1920); J. de Zwaan, "The Use of the Greek Language in Acts," and W. K. L. Clarke, "The Use of the Septuagint in Acts," *The Beginnings of Christianity* (ed. F. J. Foakes Jackson and K. Lake; London: Macmillan, 1920-1933) vol. 2. Convincing evidence of Lucan use of the Greek Bible is marshaled in E. Richard, *Acts 6:1-8:4: The Author's Method of Composition* (SBLDS 41; Missoula: Scholars Press, 1978).

[24] For Greco-Roman resonances, see Talbert, "Future Greatness," 131-37.

[25] See Richard, *Acts 6:1-8:4*, 38-140, esp. on Moses, pp. 76-102. Our two analyses were done independently and confirm each other.

[26] Compare the similar citing of *asteios* from Exodus 2 G in Heb 11:23, the only other New Testament occurrence. In the Greek Old Testament, it appears only here in Exod 2;2, in Num 22:32 (for a way acceptable to God), Judg 3:17 for Eglon, Jdt 11:23 for Judith, LXX Susanna 7, and 2 Macc 6:23 (with *logismon*). In the Stoics it seems almost equivalent to *spoudaios* (J. H. Moulton and G. Milligan, *The Vocabulary of the Greek Testament* [Grand Rapids: Eerdmans, 1949] 86).

[27] E.g., L. T. Johnson, *The Literary Function of Possessions in Luke-Acts* (SBLDS 39; Missoula: Scholars Press, 1977) 70-76. For extensive evidence of Luke's parallel structuring in general, see C. H. Talbert, *Literary Patterns, Theological Themes, and the Genre of Luke-Acts* (SBLMS 20; Missoula: Scholars Press, 1974) with references.

[28]An oddity of the Lucan genealogy is the large number of names from the priestly tribe of Levi. This is related to the peculiarity that Elizabeth, the wife of the priest Zachary and "daughter of Aaron," is called the kinswoman (*syngenis*) of Jesus' mother (Luke 1:36). All other uses of *syngenis* and cognates in Luke and Acts denote actual blood relationship (Luke 1:58, 61; 2:44; 14:12; 21:16; Acts 7:3, 14; 10:24). Therefore, besides Luke's emphasis on Jesus' Davidic ancestry, he may also be hinting at levitical connections. The same phenomenon of emphasizing one important blood line while referring to a second occurs in the genealogy in Exod 6:14-27. Exodus provides the levitical/Aaronic genealogy with Davidic connections. Exod 6:23 identifies Aaron's wife as Elizabeth (!), the daughter of Aminadab and the sister of Naasson, who are identified in Num 1:7; 7:12 and 17: Naasson is the head of the house of Judah when Moses and Aaron take the census. Compare also the Davidic genealogy in Ruth 4:20; 1 Chr 2:10; Luke 3:23-33 (and Matt 1:4). Of the four sons of Aaron and his wife Elizabeth of Judah (Exod 6:23), two died without heirs, and Eleazar and Ithamar headed the two major priestly lines. Thus, the priestly lines have connections through the wife of Aaron himself to Judah, David's tribe.

[29]Lest such imitation be rejected as too sophisticated for Luke, the widespread role of imitation as a procedure in Hellenistic rhetoric should be recalled, as well as the likelihood that Luke himself had some rhetorical training. For imitation, see E. Plümacher, *Lukas als hellenistischer Schriftsteller* (SUNT 9; Göttingen: Vandenhoeck & Ruprecht, 1972) esp. 51-69; Talbert, *Literary Patterns*, 1 and 11. For an extensive treatment of the role of rhetoric in Luke-Acts, see W. S. Kurz, "Hellenistic Rhetoric in the Christological Proof of Luke-Acts," *CBQ* 42 (1980) 171-95.

[30]Richard (*Acts 6:1-8:4*, 150-54) is helpful on textual questions in Lucan quotations from the Greek Bible. For example, he notes that the Alexandrian text, the one most in agreement with New Testament quotations, is also the one most susceptible to Christian editing.

[31]See esp. Fitzmyer, *Luke*, 488-505. With several commentators, I think Luke had among his sources a genealogy from Adam to Jesus containing seventy-seven names in eleven groups of seven. To it he himself added *tou theou* at the head of the genealogy and also the phrase *hōs enomizeto* to qualify Joseph's paternity and to harmonize the genealogy with Jesus' virginal conception in Luke 1:26-38. See Schürmann, *Lukasevangelium*, 1. 199-204; Marshall, *Luke*, 157-65, esp. 160-61; J. Ernst, *Das Evangelium nach Lukas übersetzt und erklärt* (RNT; Regensburg: Pustet, 1977) 154-57; M. D. Johnson, *Purpose*, 229-39.

[32]R. R. Wilson, "The Old Testament Genealogies in Recent Research," *JBL* 94 (1975) 172; M. D. Johnson, *Purpose*, 78. See the examples of many kinds of summaries of biblical history in G. Robinson,"Historical Summaries of Biblical History," *EvQ* 47 (1975) 195-207.

[33]M. D. Johnson, *Purpose*, 80.

[34] Ibid., 80-81.

[35] J. M. Sasson, "A Genealogical 'Convention' in Biblical Chronography?" *ZAW* 90 (1978) 171-85; see also Fitzmyer, *Luke*, 490.

[36] The reversed order meant most of the early names were unknown, so that listeners would not notice patterns of seven until later in the genealogy, if at all. Nor did Luke specify the number as Matthew did. These may help explain the widely differing number of names in important manuscripts, from about seventy-two to seventy-eight. See Speyer, "Genealogie," cols. 1230-31; Fitzmyer, *Luke*, 491-97; Brown, *Birth*, 91-92, "seventy-seven to sixty-three."

[37] M. D. Johnson, *Purpose*, 79-80.

[38] See Schürmann, *Lukasevangelium*, 1. 201-2, "ganz ungewohnlich " See Speyer, "Genealogie," col. 1203. M. D. Johnson (*Purpose*, 237) says that there is no known parallel in the Old Testament or in rabbinic texts; compare pp. 239 and 112-14 on Hellenistic and Roman practices of tracing a genealogy back to a god.

[39] For thorough discussion of these notions with their Greco-Roman and Jewish counterparts, see M. Dibelius, "Paul on the Areopagus," in his *Studies in the Acts of the Apostles* (ed. H. Greeven; London: SCM, 1956) 26-77, esp. 47-58; E. Haenchen, *The Acts of the Apostles: A Commentary* (Philadelphia: Westminster, 1971) 524-25; H. Conzelmann, *Die Apostelgeschichte* (HNT 7; 2d ed.; Tübingen: Mohr [Siebeck], 1972) 104-11; J. Roloff, *Die Apostelgeschichte* (NTD 5; Göttingen: Vandenhoeck & Ruprecht, 1981) 254-68; Speyer, "Genealogie," cols. 1147-51, 1157, 1204 and the literature they cite.

[40] BGD, p. 156, *genos*, and works cited in the preceding note.

[41] See the extensive arguments and many texts cited by Schürmann, *Lukasevangelium*, 1. 52-54; E. Sjöberg and E. Schweizer, "*pneuma*," *TDNT* 6. 386-87, 402; S. Schulz, "*skia/episkiazō*," *TDNT* 7. 399-400. See also Fitzmyer, *Luke*, 350-51; and Brown, *Birth*, 313-14. (Luke does not mention preexistence: this treatment of Jesus' being created in the womb obviously refers to the human Jesus.) Compare also Justin Martyr's explicit arguments against the pagan myths and any sexual interpretation of the Spirit's role in the virginal conception, *1 Apology* 33.3-6. The Spirit and power (which Justin identified with the Logos) *elthon epi tēn parthenon kai episkiasan ou dia synousias alla dia dynameōs enkymona katastēse* (33.6, Goodspeed, p. 49).

[42] LSJ, 618, 657; Moulton and Milligan, 231-44; J. Schneider, "*erchomai/eperchomai*," *TDNT* 2. 680-81; Schulz, "*skia*," 7. 399-400; Schürmann, *Lukasevangelium*, 1. 52-54. See Isa 32:15 G: *heōs an epelthę eph' hymas pneuma aph' hypsēlou.*

[43] In addition to commonly made comparisons between Luke 4:1-13 par. and Adam's fall and that of Israel, God's disobedient sons, in the desert, note also Jesus' prayer before his passion. In Luke 22:39-46, Jesus prays as Son to "Father," saying, "yet not my will but yours be done." See the Adam-Jesus comparisons in J. H. Neyrey, "The Absence of Jesus' Emotions—the Lucan Redaction of Lk 22,39-46," *Bib* 61 (1980) 163-65, 168.

[44]The most likely sources for the names between Judah and David are LXX 1 Chr 2:3-15 and Ruth 4:18-20. To use Chronicles here, one would have had to cull the names from among many collateral lines. Ruth 4:18-20 is a ready-made list with no extraneous material. For Luke's *Esrōm*, Ruth has *Esrōn* (Alexandrian text *Esrōm* in v. 18 only); 1 Chr 2:5 has *Arsōn*, 2:9 *Eserōn* (Rahlfs). To Luke's *Arni*, Ruth's *Arran* is closer than Chronicles' *Aram*. Luke's *Admin* seems a mistaken duplicate for the following *Aminadab* (but cf. the seventy-seven name list), which could be equally related to either list. Luke's *Sala* is closer to Ruth's *Salman* than to Chronicles' *Salmōn*. Both sources have *Ōbēd* for Luke's *Jōbēd*. In general, Schürmann (*Lukasevangelium*, 1. 201), Ernst (*Lukas*, 156-67), and Marshall (*Luke*, 164-65) prefer Ruth to Chronicles. Some suggest a Hebrew source. But because of the notorious textual difficulties with names, this explanation will have to suffice. Note the despairing comment in B. Metzger, *A Textual Commentary on the Greek New Testament* (New York: UBS, 1971) 136.

[45]See O. Eissfeldt, *The Old Testament: An Introduction* (Oxford: Blackwell, 1965) 479-80; G. E. Wood, "Ruth, Lamentations," *The Jerome Biblical Commentary* (ed. R. E. Brown, J. A. Fitzmyer, and R. E. Murphy; Englewood Cliffs, NJ: Prentice-Hall, 1968) 1. 609. O. Loretz ("Das Verhältnis zwischen Rut-Story und David-Genealogie im Rut-Buch," *ZAW* 89 [1977] 124-26) disagrees, as does A. S. Herbert ("Ruth," *Peake's Commentary on the Bible* [ed. M. Black and H. H. Rowley; London: Nelson, 1972] 316): "There is no necessity to suppose that the genealogy is a later addition to the book. . . . What the writer has done is to use this well-known and often repeated story and give it a point." I see the genealogy as inserted at the level of the canonical redaction of the story, so that, though it is not an original part of the *story*, it is an original part of the *book* of Ruth, as Luke's genealogy is an original part of his book.

[46]Cf. J. M. Sasson, "Generation, Seventh," *IDB Supplementary Volume*, 354-56; and "Genealogical 'Convention.' "

[47]Note that this typical Old Testament introduction (as in Ezek 1:1; Lamentations title; Josh 1:1; Judg 1:1; Ruth 1:1; 2 Kgdms 1:1) is an obvious mark of Luke's style: *kai egeneto en tō* plus the infinitive. It occurs in Luke 1:8; 2:6; 3:21; 5:1, 12; 8:40; 9:18, 29, 33, 51; 10:38; 11:1, 27; 14:1; 17:11, 14; 18:35, etc.

Earl Richard

THE DIVINE PURPOSE:
THE JEWS AND THE GENTILE
MISSION (ACTS 15)

The Jerusalem meeting of the apostles, elders, and community has figured prominently over the years in discussions of ecclesial structures, the Gentile mission, the church and Judaism, and a host of other topics.[1] The interest of recent scholars has been equally intense, especially in view of the alleged Pauline account of this meeting.[2] Every aspect of Acts 15, so it seems, has received considerable scrutiny, except the Old Testament citation and its function within the chapter. It is my intention, therefore, after a brief review of some of the major opinions of contemporary scholarship, to submit Acts 15 to a structural analysis in view of examining the divine purpose as it relates to the role that the Jews/Judaism played in the Gentile mission.[3] Particular attention will be paid to James's speech and the use that the author makes of the Old Testament as a vehicle of the divine will.

Contemporary Scholarship: Major Views

(1) The Jews and the Gentile mission. It is the generally accepted position of scholars that "Luke saw the reception of the Gentiles and the Gentile mission as being the result of the Jews' rejection of the gospel."[4] This interpretation is rarely questioned, although scholars often point to elements within Acts that conflict with this view. J. Jervell insists, on the contrary, that the acceptance of the good news by the Jews rather than its rejection forms the basis for the Gentile mission.[5] In reality, the two views operate with similar presuppositions based upon a chronological/geographical perspective. The Jews, first in a Palestinian and then in a diaspora setting, are the object of the Christian mission; only then the Gentiles, in a Syro-Palestinian and finally in a thoroughly pagan context, receive the

attention of the Christian missionaries. The difference lies not in substance but in emphasis; the former view sees the rejection of the Jews as *the* presupposition of the Gentile mission, while the latter position underscores the (partial) acceptance of the gospel by the Jews as *the* path that leads to the Gentiles.

(2) The Mission to the Jews in Acts and to the Gentiles in Luke. Another opinion often advanced is that the mission to Israel ceased. Relying primarily upon Acts 13:46; 18:6; and especially 28:28, some maintain that by the end of Acts the rejection of Israel is irrevocable.[6] It is also observed that there is a relative absence of the concept of a Gentile mission in Luke, a theme that appears particularly in Acts.[7]

(3) The Historical character of the Jerusalem episode. On the one hand, it is proposed that in Acts 15 "the problem of the Gentiles and the Gentile mission is once and for all decided at a meeting in Jerusalem of all the main figures in the early Church."[8] On the other, it is insisted that the principal theme of Acts 15 is a "law-free" mission to the Gentiles.[9]

The views here described have important methodological ramifications not only for the study of the Jews and their role in the Gentile mission but also for a proper understanding of the overall structure and purpose of Luke and Acts.

Structural Analysis of Acts 15:1–35

The chapter is clearly defined spatially and temporally: the action begins in Antioch with the arrival of men from Judea (v. 1) and ends there with the departure of the new Judean envoys (v. 33). While this passage is usually characterized as a Jerusalem episode (the Jerusalem council) both for geographical and theological reasons, the structural components of the introduction and conclusion require more careful analysis. The overall framework is presented in the chart on the following page.

The structural indicators are fairly clear.[10] The rhetorical elements are as follows: the problem (*zētēma*, v. 2), which discusses dissension (*stasis*, v. 2), will be resolved in the finale of the episode (*paraklēsis*, v. 31); the debate (*zētēsis*), anticipated in v. 2, is reintroduced in v. 7; and the resolution is both indicated by the approval (*dokeō* + dat., v. 22) of James's proposal (*krinō*, v. 19) and communicated in writing (*graphō*, v. 23). Further, the debate structure consists of alternating narratives and speeches. The spatial elements are equally distinct. While the starting and ending point of the episode is Antioch, thereby underscoring its spatial nature, it should not be overlooked that the impetus for the incident originated in Judea or, one should say, in Jerusalem.[11] On a strictly linear basis, the structure can be described as follows. The issue emanates from Judea, is inserted into the non-Palestinian setting of the Gentile mission, and is referred back to its source for a solution. There, after being reformulated by appropriate representatives, the issue is debated and resolved. Finally, from Jerusalem comes the remedy for the original disruption. In Acts as in the gospel, Jerusalem has spatial and rhetorical significance. Not only do all post-crucifixion events occur in or around the holy city, but also every impetus, embassy, or ideational thrust—regardless how reluctant or questionable—arises from or is related to Jerusalem. Officially and unofficially, theologically and spatially, Jerusalem is critical for an understanding of Acts 15.[12]

Introduction 1-5	the problem/dissension from Antioch to Jerusalem	—rhetorical structure —spatial structure	
Jerusalem Meeting 6-21	debate	narrative speech (Peter) narrative speech (James)	6-7a 7b-11 12 13-21
22-29	resolution	decision communique	22-23a 23b-29
Conclusion 30-35	conciliation from Jerusalem to Antioch	—rhetorical structure —spatial structure	

Of added interest are the dynamics operating within the structure outlined above, that is, the depth as opposed to the surface structure. The term "debate" occurs twice and provides the necessary clue to comprehend the dynamics involved.

```
a  statement (1)          →a' statement (5)
b  debate (2a)            →b' debate (7a)
c  report: conversion →c' speech: conversion →c" speech &
      of Gentiles (2b-3)      of Gentiles (7b-11)     sequel (13f)
d  "what God has         →d' "what God has    →d" preaching: God's
      done" (4)               done" (12)            work (34)
```

Each statement introduces a Jewish group that makes fundamental demands of Gentile converts (a), each of which provokes serious opposition (b). In the first case, unauthorized Palestinian teachers meet fierce resistance. There are considerable dissension and debate, and an official resolution of the issue is sought from Jerusalem. In the second case, members of the Jerusalem community attempt to formulate missionary policy. There follows considerable debate (nothing is said about dissension). In effect, vv. 6-12 address the issue raised by the unauthorized teachers of v. 1 (and to a lesser extent that voiced by the Pharisees), while James's speech (vv. 13-21) directs its attention to the more fundamental concern of the divine purpose (*dei*) as it is revealed in sacred scripture (v. 5). The parallel elements described above, therefore, underscore the problem of this chapter, that is, the Gentile mission and its relation to Judaism. Further, the two statements function both spatially (v. 1 introduces the issue in the context of Antioch and v. 5 in the context of Jerusalem) and thematically (first pastoral concerns are addressed and then more theological issues are interjected). Verse 1 not only acquaints the reader with the basic issue but also sets in motion the dialectical process whereby Judaism is revealed as both the source and the solution of the controversy. Verse 5 repeats the concerns of v. 1 and by its added elements carries the narrative forward and addresses a more fundamental problem. Further, the author underscores the functional significance of the debate. By merely speaking of discussion rather than providing the contents of the exchange,[13] he chooses instead to direct attention to the speeches of Peter and James, which are more closely allied to the resolution than to the discussion of the issue. The speeches, then, are structurally central, and their analysis is crucial for an understanding of the chapter.[14]

Peter's discourse tackles in fundamental terms the issue of the Gentile mission by restating the import of the Cornelius episode. On a very practical level, Peter insists that there have been Gentile converts, that this phenomenon is the result of divine initiative (himself as agent), and finally that in the realm of faith Jew and Gentile are equal. The speech states and justifies anew the conversion of Gentiles and their admission into the Christian assembly. Of further significance is the correlation of v. 10 with v. 5 (on the Mosaic law) and of v. 11 with v. 1 (on salvation), that is, Peter makes a partial response to the two Judaizing statements of the introduction. After Peter's discourse there follows a transitional narrative (v. 12), part (d) of the above schema. While its parallel (v. 4) qualifies "what God has done" by the expression "through them," v. 12 adds "among the Gentiles through them." The latter prepares for the dual character of James's speech: Judaism and the Gentile mission.

The second speech, vv. 13-21, is the center point of the entire chapter. Structurally, it is carefully related to the various parts of the episode. The two statements of vv. 1 and 5 (a) are of special interest regarding James's speech, especially the latter concerning the Mosaic law.[15] A decisive feature of the dynamics involved is the relationship of the two speeches to the Pharisees' demands: Peter (v. 10) responds in a negative way by countering the false aspect of the statement, and James (vv. 20-21) responds in a positive manner by correctly interpreting Moses. The two speeches are intentionally linked by an explicit reference to Peter/Simeon's role in the Cornelius episode (vv. 7, 14). Following the pivotal citation from Amos, James makes a proposal, which is then approved (v. 22) and expressed in writing (vv. 23-24), even to the extent of verbatim repetition (v. 29). Finally, as v. 2 emphasizes the nature of the problem (dissension, debate, issue) and as the lengthy debate underscores the unanimity of the community, so the concluding sections of the episode stress the resolution (threefold use of *dokeō*, rejoicing, conciliation, peace).

The Divine Purpose

In reading Luke and particularly in following the events of Acts, one becomes increasingly aware of the pervasive theme of the divine purpose.[16] This author, more than any other in the New Testament, is consumed by this concept, which he introduces in a variety of ways: by employing terms expressing necessity, through some type of supernatural intervention (voice from heaven, activity of the Spirit, angels, demons, appearances of the risen Christ, dreams or visions, etc.), by using various temporal expressions, or by appealing to the Old Testament and its interpretation. Of particular importance for the present study are the elements in chap. 15 that either introduce or further elaborate the divine purpose as it relates to the Jews and to the Gentile mission.

It is universally recognized that *dei* ("it is necessary" or "must") is Luke's favorite term to express necessity.[17] Its use in 15:5 along with the expression "unless you . . . you cannot . . ." (v. 1) and "these necessary things" (v. 28, *epanagkes*) leads one to expect further elaboration of God's purpose as it relates to the issue at hand. The first statement as presented by the unofficial teachers (see v. 24 for the official disclaimer) is expressly rejected by Peter, who insists that salvation for Jew and Gentile comes through faith, not circumcision (v. 11). The statement of the Pharisee believers (v. 5), however, is not so easily dismissed, nor is its function in chap. 15 very simply stated. They declare: "it is necessary to circumcise them and to command them to keep the law of Moses." Were we to conclude that the Jerusalem church decided upon a "law-free" Gentile mission, then this would be the only negative use of *dei* in all of Luke-Acts, that is, the only occasion on which the author disavows the implications of the expression.[18] Instead, since this statement expands the initial requirements of v. 1 and since the Pharisees are official members of the Jerusalem community and reputed interpreters of the law of Moses, it must be concluded that the author takes seriously the proposal of these Jewish believers and addresses the reader's attention to the resolution of the issue at hand. Moreover, it should be noted that the proposal of James, as approved and communicated by letter to the Antiochene community, is said to consist of "necessary things" (v. 28), ostensibly things required by divine revelation.

Supernatural intervention as a means of expressing the divine purpose permeates Luke and Acts.[19] In Acts 15 the action of God (vv. 4, 12) is readily invoked to justify the mission and its Gentile character. Equally significant is the role assigned to the Cornelius episode in the speeches of Peter and James, where both speakers underscore the divine initiative (vv. 7, 14).[20] Further, Peter recalls the activity of the Holy Spirit as a witness of God's action (v. 8), and, lastly, the authoritative letter unambiguously links the "necessary" character of the stipulations and the approval by the church and the Holy Spirit (v. 28).[21]

The use of temporal expressions in relation to the unfolding of the divine will is well known, particularly regarding Old Testament citations,[22] in the present case vv. 16 and 18 ("after these things" and "known from the ages"). Other such phrases that will require attention are "from the early days" (v. 7), "now" (v. 10), "first" (v. 14), and "from early generations" (v. 21). These expressions will receive further elaboration in relation to the Amos citation and the role played by Peter and James in Acts 15.

The last area of concern is Luke's use and interpretation of the Old Testament.[23] First, we must consider the Pharisees and their appeal to the law of Moses in relation to Gentile converts. Whatever may be said regarding their role in the Gospel of Luke, the situation is relatively clear in Acts. They are tolerant of, sympathetic to, or members of the Christian community.[24] In the first occurrence of the term "Pharisee" in Acts, Gamaliel is called "a teacher of the law" (5:34). In 15:5, in accordance with the Lucan perspective, even as members of the Christian assembly, they are presented as interpreters of the law. The teachers in Antioch had demanded circumcision; now the Pharisees express the logical conclusion of this requirement—not only circumcision but also full compliance with the law of Moses. Employing a literary technique similar to that used in Acts 17, where Paul and Athens typify the mission to and the world of the Gentiles,[25] Luke presents here in Acts 15 the Pharisees and Jerusalem as embodying the law and its Jewish setting.

The part played by Peter is crucial to the dialectical framework of the chapter and fundamental to Luke's point of view.[26] His speech is delineated by two temporal indicators: "from the early/beginning days" (v. 7b) and "now" (v. 10). On a pastoral level Peter counters the demands of the Judaizers by recalling that from the very beginning of the Christian era God had brought about the conversion of the Gentiles, saving them without circumcision and giving them the Holy

Spirit as sign of his approval. In the second part of the speech Peter warns against modifying the divine plan by "now" introducing new demands. If God did not require such,[27] how could the assembly "place an added[28] yoke[29] upon the neck of the (Gentile) disciples? Peter's reasoning is twofold. On the one hand, Israel (past and present) has never been very successful in its observance of the law (v. 10);[30] and, on the other, salvation is achieved not by the law (13:39) but "through the grace of the Lord Jesus" (v. 11).

The Role of James and the Old Testament

The appearance of the enigmatic James upon the scene is problematic and has occasioned discussion and harmonization of available data.[31] The identity of this individual seems intentionally omitted. That he might be a brother of Jesus, James son of Alphaeus, or some other personage named James seems of little concern to Luke. Therefore, to rely too readily upon non-Lucan sources in discussing James in Acts is methodologically questionable. Presumably, he appears three times in Acts (12:17; 15:13; 21:18), and it is from these references that we must understand his role therein. In all three instances he is located in Jerusalem and linked with its Christian community: the brothers (v. 12), the Jerusalem community (v. 15), and all the elders (v. 21). It seems, therefore, that his role here must be viewed as that of member and perhaps leader of the Jerusalem church. His discourse represents, for Luke, the thinking of that central community, a point of view that is subsequently given official status.

The entire speech would merit detailed analysis; however, it is necessary to focus upon the role played by the Old Testament. After a typical address and call for attention, James presents the theme/context of the discourse (v. 14), an Old Testament citation, and finally a proposal with a Mosaic justification (vv. 19-21).[32] Verse 14 establishes the context of the speech by referring to Peter's discourse and the paradigmatic Cornelius episode and formulates the basic twofold theme of the chapter: how God has brought about the salvation of the Gentiles. Both James's statement in v. 14 and the two parts of the Amos citation (vv. 16, 17) address themselves to this twofold motif. God's visitation has repeatedly been actualized through Jewish missionaries (vv. 3-4, 7, 12), that is, through "rebuilt" Israel (v. 16) and the synagogue (v. 21). As he visited his people Israel through the Jesus event (see Luke 1:68; 7:16), so now through reconstructed Israel he "visits the Gentiles that from among them he might form a people[33] for his name."[34] Amos 9:11-12 is cited because it agrees (*symphōneō*) with the theme just stated. The prophetic passage is taken from the Septuagint[35] but has undergone several modifications.[36] Introductory and concluding temporal formulas are either altered or added;[37] the theologically "loaded" verb *anistēmi* is eliminated twice and twice "rebuild" is substituted for it;[38] the expression "I will return" is appended to the citation;[39] and "I will raise up again" (*anorthōsō*) replaces "I will rebuild."[40] As confirmation of his initial statement James cites Amos to the effect that "from the ages" God had promised that through Israel (*hopos an*, v. 17) he would call all people to his name.

The citation functions as the centerpiece of the speech and of the Judaizing controversy. Its relation to other parts of the episode and to surrounding chapters is instructive and will be further examined in the concluding part of this study. Since, however, it is a well-known tendency of the author of the speech to write in a cumulative way so that later speeches and narratives amplify earlier themes, it is no surprise that this second Amos quotation should be closely related to the first one (7:42-43) and its context. In 7:39 the people thrust Moses aside and turn in their hearts to Egypt and to idolatry, so that in v. 42 God turns away (*strephō*, vv. 39, 42) and gives them over to the worship of the host of heaven (there follows the first Amos citation). In 15:16, the author adds to the quotation the statement that God returns (*anastrephō*) to his people. The occurrence in 14:15 and 15:19 of the related term *epistrephō*, used of conversion but without losing its spatial imagery (turn to God, from vain things) is noteworthy. The term *anoikodomeō* of 15:16 reintroduces the earlier theme of house-tabernacle-place that is prominent in chap. 7. The accumulation of detail (rebuild *twice*, fallen, destroyed parts, setting up straight again) as Cadbury notes,[41] alerts us to the significance of this theme. It is through "rebuilt" Israel (David not Solomon, as in chap. 7) that the Gentiles become a chosen people for his name. The Jews, described as the builders who rejected Jesus the cornerstone (Luke 20:17; Acts 4:11), are here in Acts 15:16 replaced by God himself as the rebuilder. No longer do humans build a house for God (Acts 7:47, 49), but God rebuilds Israel (under the image of tabernacle of David),[42] that all nations may enter.[43]

The second part of the citation also has numerous points of contact with the surrounding speeches and narratives. The themes of "seeking the Lord" and "calling/the name" will be treated later. The occurrence of the term *anthrōpos* ("the rest of humanity") is interesting in the light of its double use in 14:11, 15 (Jews state: we are *human* like you), its use in 15:26, and especially in relation to 17:26 (God has made from one every nation of humanity).[44] Related to this motif is the use of the term *ethnē*, whose distribution in each part of the episode underscores the import of this theme.[45]

The verses following the citation require particular attention. Despite the controversy regarding the relation of verse 21 to what precedes, the following parallel with the episode of the centurion's servant provides a key to the problem:

Acts 15			Luke 7 [46]
16f	[citation]	6b	[opening statement]
19	therefore it is my judgment that we not trouble those . . .	7	*therefore I do not consider myself worthy that I should come to you*
20	but that we write to them to abstain . . .		but say the word and let . . . be healed
21	For Moses from. . . .	8	For I am. . . .

Since in the healing episode v. 8 (the centurion as a man of discipline) is the justification of the *alla*-statement ("but"), a similar interpretation would seem to be required for chap. 15, whereby the stipulations of v. 20 are elucidated by reference to Moses in v. 21. The dynamics of the overall structure, however, suggest a more intricate series of relationships. In the light of the opening statement or citation the author, by means of the inferential conjunction *dio* ("therefore"),[47] introduces double conclusions: the first negative and the second positive. He then validates the crucial *alla*-statement by a final *gar*-clause ("for"). The last mentioned, therefore, serves as a pointed justification (causal conjunction) for the statement immediately preceding and, being the final element of both speeches, assumes a special relation to the entire discourse.[48]

James, on the basis of the Amos citation, submits two proposals as solutions for the problem raised by the Judaizers. The first recommends noninterference with the divine plan; Gentiles are turning to God and he is forming a people from their ranks. In effect, v. 19, along with vv. 10, 24, and 28, constitutes a formal rejection of the Judaizing demand that Gentiles become proselytes. The second proposal reveals a deeper and more radical understanding of Moses than that displayed by the believing Pharisees. Since the issue concerns Gentiles, the Mosaic law itself provides the solution; the regulations for resident aliens (Leviticus 17-18)[49] are invoked by James and approved as necessary by the assembly and the Holy Spirit. The law is not abolished but rather more correctly interpreted.

Verse 21, described by Dibelius in terms of its context and meaning as "among the most difficult in the New Testament,"[50] requires close attention in the light of the structure described earlier. The verse is certainly enigmatic, but coming at the end of James's speech it is intentionally so.[51] It confirms the Mosaic origin of the stipulations but, owing to its structural cast, relates to the dual theme of James's speech.

For Moses:

       —from early generations
              —in every city   (universal mission, v. 17)
              has had those
              who preach him   (by Jewish preachers)
       —in the synagogues
              —on every sabbath   (through Judaism, v. 16)
              being read   (divine purpose)

This verse then presents some of Luke's most basic concerns: the role of Moses, the role of the Jewish Christian preachers in relation to the Gentile mission, the role of the synagogues and Jewish assemblies, and the role of the scriptures. The law of Moses continues to be valid for Jews as Jews and for Gentiles as Gentiles. More important, Moses, as the symbol of divine revelation, "does not pass away" (Luke 16:17); instead, interpreted under the guidance of the Spirit (Acts 15:28), he remains the ultimate revelation of the divine purpose (Luke 24:44-47; Acts 26:17-18, 20, 23).

General Considerations

In view of the foregoing discussion, a reinvestigation of the opinions stated at the beginning is in order. (1) The Jews and the Gentile mission. The schema that sees the rejection of the gospel by the Jews as providing the impetus for the Gentile mission is not supported by a reading of Luke-Acts as a whole. Such a view attempts to impose upon Acts a very doubtful pattern of "rejection/Gentile-mission" by relying on surprisingly few data: the rejections at Antioch, Corinth, and Rome. To do this one must of necessity isolate the three verses (13:46; 18:6; 28:28) from their contexts. Methodologically this is suspect, since none of these occurs at the conclusion of its respective episode; this is particularly important in narrative literature. A careful reading of the context reveals a more complex situation. It is always stated that some believe and some do not (even the Gentiles of Athens are so divided, 17:32). Further, the rejection scene at Rome must be examined separately since it is different in structure and function from the other passages in question. To understand the theme of rejection in Acts one must examine the synagogue scenes from 13:1 through 19:8 (thirteen out of nineteen occurrences of the term "synagogue" in Acts). In practically every synagogue episode the outcome is negative: expulsion, persecution, or withdrawal. Equally constant are the references to successful missionary activity among Jews and Gentiles. The following pattern emerges: after the rejection in Antioch (chap. 13), Paul and Barnabas go directly to the synagogue in Iconium (chap. 14); the pattern is interrupted by a scene among Gentiles. Immediately after the "rejection" in Thessalonica (chap. 17), Paul and Silas go to the synagogue in Beroea and from there (same pattern) to Athens, where the sequence is once again interrupted by a Gentile scene. Finally, after the rebuff in Corinth (chap. 18—and eighteen months of teaching) Paul enters the synagogue in Ephesus. There is indeed a pattern of rejection in Acts, but it is not that of "rejection/Gentile-mission." Among these various scenes those of Antioch and Corinth mention specifically a turning or going to the Gentiles. A third episode should be noted, that in Ephesus (19:8-10), where, owing to the disbelief and abuse of some, Paul withdraws from the synagogue and teaches two years at the hall of Tyrannus with great success among Jews and Greeks. Not accidentally, these three scenes of rejection (chaps. 13, 18, 19) occur in each of the three journeys of Paul. One should probably relate these passages to persecution scenes throughout Acts whereby a dynamics of expansion and growth is compositionally established.[52] Preaching in the synagogues invariably leads to the Gentiles, as Acts 15 has led us to expect (through Israel salvation for the world).

Jervell's contrasting proposal, that the reception of the gospel by repentant Israel precedes and forms the basis of the Gentile mission, encounters similar objections. While he is correct in emphasizing the significance of mass Jewish conversions throughout Acts, his insistence upon the prior nature of the mission to the Jews and upon the incorporation of Gentiles as an associate people within repentant Israel is questionable at best. The theme "Israel first" is only partly temporal. The gospel is announced first to the Jews and of course early Christians were principally Jewish; however, this theme must be related to that of *how* salvation comes to the nations. It is the Jewish character and medium of salvation that is of fundamental importance here (also Acts 3:25-26). Further, his concept of the church as a "new" Israel consisting of repentant Jews and believing Gentiles rests upon very debatable and selective evidence and on too great a desire for continuity in salvation history.[53] His thesis of an Israel split by Christian preaching into repentant and irrevocably unrepentant groups represents an oversimplification of the evidence. Missionary scenes among the Jews (and Gentiles) invariably speak of believers and nonbelievers—also in Rome—but without establishing these into distinct groups. Jewish opinion in Acts regarding Christianity is divided; nonetheless, the institutionalization of this disagreement is unwarranted. Moreover, even in the rejection of the gospel, Israel continues to be called *laos* ("people," Acts 28:26-27), while converted Gentiles also constitute a *laos* (15:14). The relationship of Judaism to Christianity is considerably more complex and less defined than Jervell would have it. Neither rejection nor acceptance of the gospel is a negligible factor in Luke's scheme of things, but instead of viewing these as major agents of salvation, one should see them as facets of the gradual unfolding of the divine plan, unmistakably revealed in the sacred scriptures.

(2) The Mission to the Jews in Acts and to the Gentiles in Luke. In view of Acts 15:21, regarding Moses as preached and read, and of Luke 16:31, concerning the role played by Moses and the prophets in the understanding of the resurrection, it is hard to reconcile the often repeated conclusion that Israel as a group has been rejected for all times and the mission to it terminated. Such a thesis robs Acts 5:31 of its meaning, since "God exalted [Jesus] at his right hand . . . to give repentance to Israel." Even Paul arrives in Rome in chains "because of the hope of Israel" (28:20) and there "tries to convince them about Jesus both from Moses and from the prophets" (v. 23). Just as sight is a divine gift (Luke 8:10; 24:16, 30) especially related to an understanding of the scriptures (Luke 24:45; often in Acts— under the inspiration of the Spirit),[54] so is blindness the result of divine intervention (Luke 9:45; 18:34; 24:16) and foretold by the same scriptures. Acts 28:26-28 dwells upon this motif: the reaction of the Jews (blindness) was foretold in Isa 6:9-10, while that of the Gentiles (listening) was foretold in Ezek 3:6: "If to such [people of foreign speech] I were to send you, they would listen to you."[55] Luke reflects the situation of his time. He knows that the mission to the Jews was a mixed success (see Simeon's prophecy: "this child is set for the fall and rising of many in Israel," Luke 2:34) and is at a stalemate; however, in his composition he is careful to note that the mission to Israel is open-ended.[56] This is demonstrated by the inclusio of Acts 28:23 (testifying to the kingdom of God, about Jesus, from Moses and the prophets) and 28:30-31 (welcoming all, preaching the kingdom of God, teaching about Jesus Christ). The ears of God's people are closed and their eyes are blind, but as long as they have Moses and the prophets the mission remains possible. Moreover, it is the obligation of the Christian missionary (Paul) to preach Moses (Acts 15:21— note particularly the term *kerysso*, used also in 28:31) and thereby to open the eyes of both Jew and Gentile (Acts 26:17-18, 22-23).

While it is true that Luke avoids undisguised treatment of the Gentile mission in the gospel for historical reasons,[57] it would be misleading to overemphasize this point since this would constitute a misunderstanding of Hellenistic historiography[58] and Luke's view of mission. From the beginning of the gospel, as early as the prophetic speech of Simeon, the mission to Israel and that to the nations are interrelated as the divine purpose is revealed, particularly by appealing to the Old Testament, and actualized through the life and mission of Jesus and of the early church.[59] The salvation, which has brought forth the visitation of God to Israel (Luke 1:68-69) and was promised to all flesh (3:6), has also brought about a visitation to the Gentiles (Acts 15:14). While this same salvation finds a ready acceptance among the nations (Acts 28:28), it remains the hope of Israel (28:20).

(3) The Historical character of the Jerusalem episode. To view Acts 15 as Gentile freedom from the law is to misunderstand the purpose of the episode or, in the quest of the historical event, to "second-guess" the author and his traditions. If the analysis of the present study is correct, then the opposite obtains; the law, according to Luke, remains valid for both Jewish and Gentile Christians.[60] Moses, properly interpreted, prepares for and has his part to play within the community as Christian revelation.

A "once and for all" view of Acts 15 misrepresents the fundamental nature of Acts. The author's view of early Christianity is intimately related to the medium he chose for the presentation of his vision. Acts is episodic in character and must be read as a dynamic, dramatic whole, allowing its various parts, characters, and themes to speak as the occasion requires.[61] The Gentile mission is presented in a series of incomplete, sequential events. The Cornelius episode already points to the world mission (chaps. 10-11), as do the sequel to the Antioch speech (chap. 13) and the encounter with the Lycaonians (chap. 14). After the Jerusalem meeting the author pursues this theme in a more formal way in the Athenian speech (chap. 17) and concludes the entire book on the same theme (chap. 28). Beyond this, the episodes concerning Stephen and Philip (chaps. 6-8) as well as the conversion of Paul (chap. 9) set in motion, by Jewish missionaries, the mission announced in 1:8 and so often foreshadowed in Luke.[62] Finally, Acts 15, with its Jerusalem-Antioch setting, pays particular attention to the Jewish character of that mission and the ramifications of this for Jewish-Gentile relations.[63]

The citation of Amos 9:11-12 is pivotal in this regard. It allows the author to reintroduce his earlier statements on the role of Israel in relation to the Christian reality (chaps. 5, 7, 13). The citation also allows him to interconnect several themes involving Gentiles. The phrase "seeking the Lord" fits well into the pattern established within the principal Gentile episodes: the Ethiopian eunuch who desires understanding (chap. 8), Cornelius's openness to God (chap. 10), the Lycaonians who are anxious to see gods (chap. 14), and the Athenians who seek, feel for, and find God (chap. 17). The saying of Luke 11:9, therefore, applies to the Gentiles: "seek and you will find, knock and it will be opened" (even the gift of the Holy Spirit is forthcoming, v. 13). In addition, the expression "all the nations upon whom my name has been called" relates to v. 14 and to the interesting passage of 14:12 where the Lycaonians call Barnabas and Paul by the names of Zeus and Hermes. Like the Jews of Acts 2:21 (citation of Joel), the Lycaonians call upon the name of God (gods)—but in reality they are called by him. The theme of divine election leads the author to stress further the divine purpose by the expansion "made known from the ages." Moreover, by the addition within the quotation of "I will return," not only does he express God's presence among the Jews, but he also highlights the numerous contacts of God with the nations: God did not leave himself without witness (14:17); the Gentiles expect or imagine that the gods visit them (14:11); God visits the Gentiles to acquire a people (15:14); and, finally, he is not far from the nations of humanity (17:27).

This chapter of Acts, therefore, by its carefully chosen list of characters, geographical considerations, constant interaction of speech and narrative, interweaving of motifs, foreshadowing and recalling of episodes and themes, and conscious use and interpretation of the Old Testament, should warn us that at no single point does the author speak either definitively or in his own name. While Acts 15 plays an important part in establishing the author's view of Israel's role in the worldwide mission, it must be remembered that it is but a part and that only the whole represents his vision.[64]

As the mission to Israel has been but a partial success, so the heritage from Judaism has been but a mixed blessing.[65] While other chapters of Luke-Acts dwell upon various aspects of this heritage (e.g, Luke 11; Acts 7, 13, 26), Acts 15 makes its own special contribution to our understanding of the author's point of view. In a skillfully presented episode Luke attempts to clarify the relationship between the Jewish "mother" church and the Gentile community. What begins as an effort to assimilate Gentile Christianity into Judaism, through a dialectical process, not only arrives at a modus vivendi between the two groups (the stipulations) but also succeeds in examining the fundamental role that Judaism plays within the worldwide mission.[66]

NOTES

[1]L. Cerfaux, "Le chapitre XVe du Livre des Actes à la lumière de la littérature ancienne," *Recueil Lucien Cerfaux: études d'exégèse et d'histoire religieuse* (Gembloux: Duculot, 1954) 2. 104-24.

[2]Among others, see: M. Dibelius, *Studies in the Acts of the Apostles* (London: SCM, 1956) 93-101; W. Schmithals, *Paul and James* (London: SPCK, 1965) 38-62, 97-102; J. C. O'Neill, *The Theology of Acts in Its Historical Setting* (London: SPCK, 1970) 100-33;

E. Haenchen, *The Acts of the Apostles: A Commentary* (Philadelphia: Westminster, 1971) 440-72; S. G. Wilson, *The Gentiles and the Gentile Mission in Luke-Acts* (Cambridge: University Press, 1973) 171-95; T. Holtz, "Die Bedeutung des Apostelkonzils für Paulus," *NovT* 16 (1974) 110-48; A. Strobel, "Das Aposteldekret in Galatien: Zur Situation von Gal I und II," *NTS* 20 (1974) 177-90; M. Hengel, *Acts and the History of Earliest Christianity* (Philadelphia: Fortress, 1979) 111-26.

[3]In his excellent article "Le salut des gentils et la signification theologique du Livre des Actes" (*NTS* 6 [1959-60] 155) Dupont states: "en composant les Actes, Luc a voulu montrer comment . . . la prédication apostolique s'est tournée vers le monde païens." In effect, his analysis has shown *that* the gospel reached the Gentile world; the present study will attempt to demonstrate *how*, according to Luke, this occurred.

[4]Wilson, *Gentiles*, 227; see also F. Hahn, *Mission in the New Testament* (London: SCM, 1965) 134; Schmithals, *Paul and James*, 57; G. Bornkamm, "The Missionary Stance of Paul in 1 Corinthians 9 and in Acts," *Studies in Luke-Acts: Essays in Honor of Paul Schubert* (ed. L. E. Keck and J. L. Martyn; Nashville: Abingdon, 1966) 200-201; Haenchen, *Acts*, 100-101; H. Conzelmann, *Die Apostelgeschichte* (Tübingen: Mohr [Siebeck], 1972) 78; U. Wilckens, *Die Missionsreden der Apostelgeschichte* (Neukirchen-Vluyn: Neukirchener Verlag, 1974) 59, 70.

[5]*Luke and the People of God: A New Look at Luke-Acts* (Minneapolis: Augsburg, 1972) 43; see also O'Neill, *Theology of Acts*, 76 and L. Gaston, *No Stone on Another: Studies in the Significance of the Fall of Jerusalem in the Synoptic Gospels* (Leiden: Brill, 1970) 310, 368.

[6]See most of the works listed in n. 4; also I. H. Marshall, *Luke: Historian and Theologian* (Grand Rapids: Zondervan, 1970) 186-87; Jervell, *People of God*, 64.

[7]N. Q. King, "The 'Universalism' of the Third Gospel," *Studia Evangelica* (TU 73; Berlin: Akademie-Verlag, 1959) 199-205; H. Conzelmann, *The Theology of St. Luke* (New York: Harper & Row, 1960) 207-34.

[8]Wilson, *Gentiles*, 178.

[9]Haenchen, *Acts*, 100, 440-72; H. Flender, *St. Luke: Theologian of Redemptive History* (Philadelphia: Fortress, 1967) 15; J. J. Kilgallen, "Acts: Literary and Theological Turning Points," *BTB* 7 (1977) 178.

[10]See S. A. Panimolle, *Il discorso di Pietro all' assemblea apostolica* (Bologna: Dehoniane, 1976) 175-98, esp. 176-77.

[11]In Acts one can "go down" (*katerchomai*) from Jerusalem (8:5; 9:32?; 11:27; 15:30; 18:22?) as well as from Judea (12:9; 15:1; 21:10) with no apparent difference in meaning. Besides, from Acts 15:24 we must conclude that Jerusalem is meant; see the interesting interchange of Jerusalem and Judea in 11:1-2.

[12]On the importance of Jerusalem, see Conzelmann, *Theology*, 73-94; H. H. Oliver, "The Lucan Birth Stories and the Purpose of Luke-Acts," *NTS* 10 (1963-64) 220-21; E. Lohse, "*Siōn*," *TDNT* 7. 331-36.

[13] Dibelius (*Studies*, 95-96) expresses surprise at the minor role played by Paul (and Barnabas) in this episode. One expects this only in the light of Galatians 2.

[14] Luke, following the rules of Greco-Roman historiography, knows how to employ to advantage the various options at his disposal: speeches, summaries, and narratives; see W. C. van Unnik, "Luke's Second Book and the Rules of Hellenistic Historiography," in *Les Actes des Apôtres: traditions, rédaction, théologie* (ed. J. Kremer; Gembloux: Duculot, 1979) 36-60.

[15] The name of Moses appears three times in chap. 15: vv. 1, 5, 21. Note too that v. 3 speaks of the conversion/turning (*epistrophē*) of the Gentiles and v. 19 of the Gentiles who are turning to God (*epistrephō*).

[16] Conzelmann, *Theology*, 149-69; Jervell, *People of God*, 202. Note that C. H. Talbert does not list the divine purpose among his alternative purposes of Luke-Acts (*Luke and the Gnostics: An Examination of the Lucan Purpose* [Nashville: Abingdon, 1966] 98-110), not even P. Schubert's "proof from prophecy"; see Schubert, "The Structure and Significance of Luke 24," *Neutestamentliche Studien für Rudolf Bultmann* (Berlin: Töpelmann, 1954). But see N. A. Dahl, "The Purpose of Luke-Acts," in *Jesus in the Memory of the Early Church* (Minneapolis: Augsburg, 1976) 87-98; R. F. O'Toole, "Why Did Luke Write Acts (Lk-Acts)?" *BTB* 7 (1977) 73.

[17] We agree with H. J. Cadbury (*The Making of Luke-Acts* [New York: Macmillan, 1927] 303-6) that it is better to speak of "must" rather than "shall" when discussing Luke's use of scripture and other devices to express the divine purpose. Prophecy/fulfillment terminology is avoided, therefore, as misleading; see Schubert, "Luke," 172 n. 18. On *dei*, see W. Grundmann, *TDNT* 2. 22-24.

[18] Luke 13:14 ("there are six days on which one ought to work") presents a situation similar to Acts 15:5. Jewish interpreters of Moses cite the law in protest. Jesus does not deny the truth of the statement; instead he justifies a certain kind of work on the seventh day. So too in Acts 15, the law of Moses is not denigrated but interpreted correctly by James.

[19] On visions, voices, and angels in divine manifestations, see T. Y. Mullins, "New Testament Commission Forms, Especially in Luke-Acts," *JBL* 95 (1976) 603-14; and B. J. Hubbard, "The Role of Commissioning Accounts in Acts," *Perspectives on Luke-Acts* (ed. C. H. Talbert; Danville, VA: Association of Baptist Professors of Religion, 1978) 187-98.

[20] With these references to the Cornelius episode the audience and reader are subtly reminded of the various elements of supernatural intervention that occurred on that occasion: visions, angel, heavenly conversation, and the coming of the Spirit; see J. Dupont, "Les discours de Pierre dans les Actes et le chapitre XXIV de l'evangile de Luc," *L'évangile de Luc: problèmes littéraires et théologiques: memorial Lucien Cerfaux* (ed. F. Neirynck; Gembloux: Duculot, 1973) 366.

[21] E. Schweizer, "*pneuma*," *TDNT* 6. 407-9, rightly emphasizes the importance for Luke of visible manifestations.

[22] This phenomenon is aptly described by Cadbury (*The Making of Luke-Acts*, 305) as the "divine schedule."

[23] Whether an appeal should be made to "die lukanische LXX-Mimesis" of E. Plümacher (*Lukas als hellenistischer Schriftsteller: Studien zur Apostelgeschicht* [Göttingen: Vandenhoeck & Ruprecht, 1972] 67) remains to be seen. For an excellent survey of recent scholarship on Luke's use and interpretation of the Old Testament, see F. Bovon, *Luc le théologien: vingt-cinq ans de recherches (1950-1975)* (Neuchâtel: Delachaux et Niestlé, 1978) 89-117.

[24] O'Toole ("Why Did Luke Write," 67) concludes: "Luke holds that Christians are the true Pharisees"; see also his *Acts 26: The Christological Climax of Paul's Defense (Ac 22:1-26:32)* (AnBib 78; Rome: Biblical Institute Press, 1978) 41-44, 159-60.

[25] Dupont, "Le salut des gentils," 152-54; Haenchen, *Acts*, 517; H. Conzelmann, "The Address of Paul on the Areopagus," *Studies in Luke-Acts*, 218; Wilson, *Gentiles*, 196.

[26] Panimolle, *Discorso*, 237-65; Dupont, "Le salut des gentils," 146-49; idem, "Discours de Pierre," 365-71.

[27] The expression "put God on trial" is taken from the Old Testament (Exod 17:2; Deut 6:16) and "seems to mean acting against the declared will of God"; see K. Lake and H. J. Cadbury, *The Acts of the Apostles*, vol. 4 of *The Beginnings of Christianity* (ed. F. J. Foakes Jackson and K. Lake (London: Macmillan, 1920-33) 173; BGD, 640. Moreover, it should be interpreted in the light of Peter's statement at the end of the Cornelius episode: "who was I that I could forbid/hinder God?" (Acts 11:17).

[28] *Epitithēmi epi* should not be translated "put or place upon" but "add or place an added (burden) upon" (BGD, 302-3, 1b with Rev 22:18 given as an example). See also J. H. Moulton and G. Milligan, *The Vocabulary of the Greek Testament* (Grand Rapids: Eerdmans, 1949) 248, and more particularly the parallel of Acts 15:28: "to lay no further burden upon" (*mēden pleon epitithesthai hymin baros*), where *epi* disappears and the meaning is made clearer by the addition of *pleon* (note that the Greek idiom for "placing a yoke upon" is *epitithēmi tini zyga*). F. F. Bruce (*The Acts of the Apostles* [London: Tyndale, 1962] 293) is correct when he states: "to impose conditions in addition to the one that satisfied God would be 'tempting' Him." The emphasis is on *added* not on *burden*.

[29] The law as a "yoke" clearly is a positive concept in Judaism of the New Testament period (Lake and Cadbury, *Beginnings*, 4. 173-74), and its description here as a "burden" (see the parallel in v. 28 = *baros*) probably represents "lexical slippage" from the figurative back to the literal meaning. For another example, see Acts 13:11, where "not to see the sun" is equated with blindness; see also E. Richard, "The Old Testament in Acts: Wilcox's Semitisms in Retrospect," *CBQ* 42 (1980) 332-33.

[30] Haenchen (*Acts*, 446) states of this passage: "the law is in any case impossible of fulfillment." This is hard to believe, since there is no other such statement in Luke-Acts. "To carry/bear a yoke" seems natural enough, but does *ouk ischyō* mean "to not be able" in the sense of "to be impossible"? Commenting on the papyri, Moulton and Milligan (*Vocabulary*, 308) state: "The ordinary sense 'to be able,' without the connotation of *strength*, may be seen early in . . ."—examples from the third century B.C. through the third century A.D. are given. Further, one should relate this passage to Acts 7:53: "you received the law . . . and did not keep it." Thus, in the present case, we should read: "which neither our fathers nor we succeeded in bearing."

[31] See J. Munck's severe critique of the Tübingen legacy, *Paul and the Salvation of Mankind* (Richmond: Knox, 1959) 69-86.

[32] The divisions given above correspond to E. Schweizer's categories as follows: (a) address, (b) appeal for attention, (c) misunderstanding > theme/context, (d) quotation from scripture, (g) reply to misunderstanding > proposal, (h) call to repentance = Gentiles turning to God (v. 19b), and (i) message focused upon the particular audience = decree and its Mosaic justification; see "Concerning the Speeches in Acts," *Studies in Luke-Acts*, 208-10; E. Richard, *Acts 6:1-8:4: The Author's Method of Composition* (Missoula: Scholars Press, 1978) 254-60.

[33] Usually *laos* in Luke-Acts designates the Jewish populace, although it frequently has the meaning "chosen people or people of God." In the first instance it always refers to Jews, while in the second its range is extended to include Christians or people destined to become such (Acts 18:10) and by further extension it includes those among the Gentiles who will become Christian (Acts 15:14). It would also seem that the plural *laoi* of Luke 2:31-32, referring to both Gentiles and Jews, should be thus explained. See the discussions of N. A. Dahl, "A People for His Name (Acts XV.14)," *NTS* 4 (1957-58) 324-25; Haenchen, *Acts*, 535; and H. Strathmann, "*laos*," *TDNT* 4.29-35, 50-57.

[34] That Acts 15:14 is a creation of the author of Acts with a certain "couleur biblique," as Dupont suggests, is correct ("LAOS EX ETHNŌN [Acts XV.14]" *NTS* 3 [1956-57] 48-49), but that it is a citation of a Septuagint text (Deut 7:6 or 14:2) is too conjectural to be convincing. At the same time, Dahl's contention ("A People for His Name," 327) that the phrase is a targumic expression deriving from Zech 2:15 and therefore "must have roots which go back to early Jewish Christianity" is based on inadmissible linguistic evidence. His targumic data are now supplemented by abundant evidence from Targum Neofiti I. My conclusion, after examination of the expression "for my/the Lord's name," is that it is in fact a mark of late Aramaic (after A.D. 200), where *lšm* regularly replaces *l-* with God as object (see, e.g., *Tg. Neof. Lev.* where *lyhwh* is normally rendered *lšmh dyyy*). Luke employs the expression "the name" so often that appeal to such late sources is unwarranted.

[35]The theory of dependence upon the Hebrew text or upon some type of testimonium has often been proposed; see M. Wilcox, *The Semitisms of Acts* (Oxford: Clarendon, 1965) 49; Gaston, *No Stone on Another*, 200-204; R. Hodgson, "The Testimony Hypothesis," *JBL* 98 (1979) 368-69; R. F. Zehnle, *Peter's Pentecost Discourse: Tradition and Lukan Reinterpretation in Peter's Speeches of Acts 2 and 3* (Nashville: Abingdon, 1971) 29-31. See Richard, "The Old Testament in Acts," 339; and Dupont, "LAOS EX ETHNŌN," 47.

[36]*Contra* T. Holtz's theory that the first half of the citation, owing to its differences from the Septuagint derives from Judaizing Christians while the second half was later added by the author to support his concept of the Gentile mission (*Untersuchungen über die alttestamentlichen Zitate bei Lukas* [Berlin: Akademie-Verlag, 1968] 21-27). Equally unacceptable is O'Neill's proposal concerning Acts 15:16 that it is "a free and independent translation from the Hebrew" that was later partly "corrected" by reference to the Septuagint (*Theology of Acts*, 122-23).

[37]*Meta tauta*, a favorite expression of this author and one he omitted in his citation of Joel 3:1 (= Acts 2:17), is here considered more appropriate. At the same time, the ending of the Amos quotation leads him to a similar passage in Isa 45:21. Since both formulas are standard prophetic phrases, the observation of Lake and Cadbury (*Beginnings*, 4. 176) is apropos: the author "rounds out his Biblical quotations in Biblical style."

[38]The transitive use of *anistēmi* (nine occurrences in Acts— fourteen in the entire New Testament) is reserved by Luke for the resurrection of Jesus (six times). On three occasions this construction involves the citation of Deut 18:15 (raising up a prophet like Moses). See further E. Richard, "The Creative Use of Amos by the Author of Acts," *NovT* 24 (1982) 47. R. F. O'Toole ("Some Observations on *anistēmi*, 'I Raise,' in Acts 3:22, 26," *Science et Esprit* 31 [1979] 85-92), in an otherwise interesting article, omits discussion of the term's relation to Deut 18:15 (citation in Acts 3:22 and 7:37) and its omission in Acts 15:16 (another citation) and so fails to treat the whole issue.

[39]Just as there is a visitation of the Gentiles (15:14; contrast 14:11-18), so God returns to his people Israel in order that the Gentiles may turn to him (*anastrephō* and *epistrephō*).

[40]*Anorthoō*, only here in Acts, is employed to underscore the raising up *once more* (*ana-*) of fallen Israel, in contrast to the raising up (*orthos*—only there in Acts) of a Gentile cripple from birth (14:8, 10).

[41]*The Making of Luke-Acts*, 35-36. See further Dupont, "Le salut des gentils," 151-52; H. J. Cadbury, "Four Features of Lucan Style," *Studies in Luke-Acts*, 88-102.

[42]The *skēnē* of Acts 15:16 (= Amos 9:11) recalls the *skēnōma* of 7:46 (= Ps 131:5)—both favorably associated with David. On the role of David, see Richard, *Acts 6:1-8:4*, 337-38; E. Lohse, "*huios David*," *TDNT* 8. 482-87.

[43] See the intriguing image of 14:27: "they declared . . . how [God] had opened a door of faith to the Gentiles."

[44] Note also Acts 10:26. On the theme of the two Adams, see M. Bornkamm, "Faith and Reason in Paul's Epistles," *NTS* 4 (1957-58) 95; Dupont, "Le salut des gentils," 154.

[45] For a more extended study of the citation, see my "Creative Use of Amos," 44-52.

[46]

Acts 15		Luke 7
19	dio egō krinō	7	*dio oude emauton ēxiōsa*
	mē parenochlein tois . . .		*pros se elthein*
20	alla episteilai autois		alla eipe logō
	tou apechesthai		kai iothētō . . .
21	Moysēs gar ek. . . .	8	kai gar egō. . . .

[47] Note that the italicized passage is peculiar to Luke (not in Matthew) and therefore ought to be attributed to Lucan editing.

[48] The author has a penchant for concluding speeches with pithy statements or citations with carefully chosen endings (so Dupont ["Le salut des gentils," 136], who calls Luke's introductions and conclusions "endroits privilégiés"). Note that for the healing episode (Luke 7:1-10) the centurion's statement in v. 8 provides the rationale for the entire story (the opening declaration, the *alla*-statement, and also Jesus' reaction in v. 9). Other examples of this construction are found in Luke 1:35-36; Acts 26:26-27; 27:25-26, 34-35.

[49] So Haenchen (*Acts*, 450-51) and most recent commentaries.

[50] *Studies*, 97.

[51] In Luke 1:37, a text with a structure comparable to the one under discussion, note Gabriel's final statement, which seeks to justify all that precedes: "For with God nothing will be impossible."

[52] The persecution resulting from the Stephen episode is a good example of this process (a fact referred to several times in Acts). The rejection episodes seem to serve different functions in the narrative of Acts. In 13:51 shaking off the dust from the feet and the departure must be viewed as an enactment of Luke (9:5). This episode also signals an increased concern for the Gentile mission (chap. 14) with no change in missionary procedure. Acts 18:6-11, which should be studied with an eye on Luke 10:10-12, points to a new type of missionary approach (see the ending of the episode). In presenting Paul as separating from the synagogue and moving to a public forum, 19:9-10 also breaks new ground (note especially the following "civic" episodes). One can infer only that the complexity of Luke's traditions and vision required a multiplicity of compositional devices. For interesting attempts to balance these rejection texts with equally important acceptance passages, see L. T. Johnson, *The Literary Function of Possessions in Luke-Acts* (SBLDS 39; Missoula: Scholars Press, 1977) 54-58; E. Franklin, *Christ the Lord: A Study in the Purpose and Theology of Luke-Acts* (Philadelphia: Westminster, 1975) 113-15.

[53]Jervell, *People of God*, 44-49, 53-55, 62-64, 147. See also Wilson, *Gentiles*, 227-33; M. Moscato ("A Critique of Jervell's *Luke and the People of God*," *Society of Biblical Literature 1975 Seminar Papers* [Missoula: Scholars Press, 1975] 2. 161-68) for extended criticism of Jervell's proposals.

[54]On the concept of sight, particularly "to open the eyes" (Acts 26:18), see O'Toole, *Acts 26*, 70-81.

[55]Both reactions were foreshadowed in Luke 4:14-30; see D. R. Miesner, "The Circumferential Speeches of Luke-Acts: Patterns and Purpose," *Society of Biblical Literature 1978 Seminar Papers* (Missoula: Scholars Press, 1978) 2. 233-37; the parallels between Luke 4 and Acts 28 are compelling but the conclusion less so.

[56]So also Franklin, *Christ the Lord*, 78; A. George, "Israël," *Etudes sur l'oeuvre de Luc* (Paris: Gabalda, 1978) 87-125; P. G. Müller, "Die jüdische Entscheidung gegen Jesus nach der Apostelgeschichte," *Les Actes des Apôtres*, 523-31.

[57]Wilson, *Gentiles*, 229; Franklin, *Christ the Lord*, 122.

[58]Cadbury, *The Making of Luke-Acts*, 184-209; idem, "The Speeches in Acts," *Beginnings*, 5. 402-27; idem et al., "The Greek and Jewish Traditions of Writing History," *Beginnings*, 2. 7-29; M. Dibelius, "The Speeches in Acts and Ancient Historiography," *Studies*, 138-85; Schweizer, "Concerning the Speeches," 186-93; C. K. Barrett, *Luke the Historian in Recent Study* (Philadelphia: Fortress, 1970); C. H. Talbert, *Literary Patterns, Theological Themes, and the Genre of Luke-Acts* (Missoula: Scholars Press, 1974); V. K. Robbins, "By Land and by Sea: The We-Passages and Ancient Sea Voyages," *Perspectives on Luke-Acts*, 215-42; E. Plümacher, "Die Apostelgeschichte als historische Monographie," *Les Actes des Apôtres*, 457-66; W. C. van Unnik, "Luke's Second Book," 37-60; W. S. Kurz, "Hellenistic Rhetoric in the Christological Proof in Luke-Acts," *CBQ* 42 (1980) 171-95.

[59]Hahn, *Mission*, 128-32, 136; Oliver, "Lucan Birth Stories," 215-26; Jervell, *People of God*, 56; Franklin, *Christ the Lord*, 119-24; Dupont, "Le salut des gentils," 139, 141 (critique of King, 138 n. 2); and P. S. Minear, "Luke's Use of the Birth Stories," *Studies in Luke-Acts*, 111-30 (*contra* Conzelmann).

[60]So also Jervell, *People of God*, 144; Franklin, *Christ the Lord*, 125; *contra* Conzelmann, *Theology*, 145-49, 211-13; and S. G. Wilson, *Luke and the Pastoral Epistles* (London: SPCK, 1979) 96-97. Others allow that the law remains valid for Jewish Christians, e.g., P. Vielhauer, "On the 'Paulinism' of Acts," *Studies in Luke-Acts*," 41.

[61]Cadbury, *The Making of Luke-Acts*, 302; C. K. Barrett, "Paul's Speech on the Areopagus," *New Testament Christianity for Africa and the World* (ed. M. E. Glasswell and F. W. Fasholé-Luke; London: SPCK, 1974) 69-77.

[62]Hahn, *Mission*, 128-36. On Luke's "forward and backward" technique as a literary and theological device, see Schubert, "Luke 24," 185.

[63] Mention should be made of the interesting proposal of L. C. Crockett ("Luke 4:25-26 and Jewish-Gentile Relations in Luke-Acts," *JBL* 88 [1969] that as early as the Nazareth episode "Luke's use of the OT was dominated by the Jewish-gentile question."

[64] On reading Luke-Acts as a whole, see the observations of W. C. van Unnik, "The 'Book of Acts' the Confirmation of the Gospel," *NovT* 4 (1960) 34-38; Barrett, "Paul's Speech on the Areopagus," 69-71; Cadbury, *The Making of Luke-Acts,* 299-316.

[65] E. Richard, "The Polemical Character of the Joseph Episode in Acts 7," *JBL* 98 (1979) 262-67; idem, *Acts 6:1-8:4,* 319-52.

[66] For a convenient analysis of major views on "Israël et l'Eglise: Mission et Extension," consult Bovon, *Luc le théologien,* 342-61.

Jerome Neyrey

THE FORENSIC DEFENSE SPEECH
AND PAUL'S TRIAL SPEECHES
IN ACTS 22-26:
FORM AND FUNCTION

Interest in forensic aspects of Acts of the Apostles has not been lacking in the past. Various legal issues surrounding Paul's trials in Acts 21-26 were studied by H. J. Cadbury and more recently by A. N. Sherwin-White and J. Dupont.[1] The apologetic character of Paul's defense speeches was the subject of a recent dissertation by F. Veltman;[2] and the forensic aspect of *martyrein* and its compounds has been treated in many recent studies.[3] Even the form of argumentation used in Acts, the syllogism known as the enthymeme, has been discussed.[4] A general survey of the forensic terminology in Acts was presented by Trites in a recent article.[5] There has been, therefore, no lack of interest in the forensic aspect of Acts.[6]

We regularly give special attention to the speeches of Acts, either the missionary character and kerygmatic structure of chaps. 2, 10, and 13,[7] or the Areopagus speech and Jewish propaganda,[8] or the *apologia* character of Paul's defense speeches.[9] I suggest that for the defense speeches of Paul in Acts a new descriptive category and a new literary form are appropriate—the forensic defense speech. My hypothesis is that the trial speeches of Paul in Acts 22-26 are formally structured according to the profile of forensic defense speeches as these are described in the rhetorical handbooks. According to Quintilian, a forensic defense speech consists of five parts: "Most authorities divide the forensic speech into five parts: the exordium (*prooemium*), the statement of facts (*narratio*), the proof (*probatio*), the refutation (*refutatio*), and the peroration (*peroratio*)" (*Inst.* 3.9.1). In this study I will pay particular attention to the first three structural parts of a typical forensic speech: (1) the exordium, in which the character of the speaker or witness if favorably presented, (2) the statement of facts, in which the true issue, the real charges and the appropriate defense are stated; and (3) the proof or evidence for the defense.

I

The opening part of a forensic speech is called the exordium or *prooemium*.[10] Its sole purpose is to prepare the audience in such a way that they will be disposed to lend a ready ear to the rest of the speech,[11] in short, to render them "well disposed, attentive, and receptive."[12] It may happen in an honorable case that the speaker already enjoys favor; but in difficult cases, where sympathy is alienated, the speaker must practice "insinuation" to win good will and hence a receptive hearing.[13] Good will comes from four quarters: from the person of the speaker, from the person of the opponent, from the person of the judge, and from the case itself.[14] The way in which an exordium may try to win good will from the judge by flattering him has been amply studied in regard to the *captatio benevolentiae* in Acts 24: 1-4.

Good will can and must also be won by the proper presentation of the person of the speaker or defendant, that is, by presenting the ethos or character of the speaker in the most favorable light.[15] As Quintilian said, "if he is believed to be a good man, this consideration will exercise the strongest influence at every point in the case" and lead the hearers to accept him as an absolutely reliable witness (*Inst.* 4.1.7). Hence, orators were instructed in the exordium to develop the ethos of the pleader or defendent, "to paint their characters in words as being upright, stainless, conscientious, modest, etc.,"[16] which is done by telling of their "merits, achievements or reputable life."[17]

Specific instructions are given in Cicero's *De Inventione* for developing the ethos of a person. Nine attributes are listed as topics for development:

1. *Name:* proper and definite appellation
2. *Nature:* sex, age, race, place of birth, family
3. *Manner of Life:* with whom he was reared, in what tradition and under whose direction, what teachers . . . what instructors in the art of living, with whom he associates on terms of friendship, in what occupation, trade or profession he is engaged
4. *Fortune:* slave or free, rich or poor, private citizen or official with authority, whether he acquired his position justly or unjustly
5. *Habit:* stable or absolute constitution of mind or body
6. *Feeling:* temporary change in mind or body
7. *Interest:* unremitting mental activity ardently devoted to some subject and accompanied by intense pleasure

8. *Purpose:* deliberate plan for doing or not doing something

9. *Achievements, accidents, speech:* what he did, what happened, what he said (*Inv.* 1.24.34–25.36).[18]

In Acts, two of Paul's forensic speeches begin with an exordium in which Paul's ethos is elaborately presented in such a way as to win him a good hearing. Both exordia contain to an exceptional degree the nine attributes that rhetorical tradition indicates ought to be developed relevant to the ethos of the speaker.

1. *Name:* Paul asserts that he is *not* the Egyptian revolutionary but Paul of Tarsus (21:38–39).

2. *Nature:* By race Paul is a Jew; his place of birth is Tarsus in Cilicia (22:3).

3. *Manner of Life:* He was reared in Jerusalem (22:3; 26:4), educated by the eminent teacher Gamaliel (22:3), instructed in the tradition of the Pharisees (26:5); his modus vivendi was according to the strict manner of the law; with regard to piety, he was zealous for God (22:3; 26:5). His associates were the leading religious figures of Jerusalem (22:5). With regard to occupation, he spent his time persecuting the heterodox Way, deputized by the Jerusalem clergy (22:4; 26:9–11).

4. *Fortune:* Paul claims to be an authorized official, deputized in Judea and Damascus by Jerusalem's "high priests and the whole council of elders" (22:5; 26:9–12).

5. *Habit:* During all of his early life he was steadily "zealous for the law according to the strict manner of the Pharisees" (22:3).

6. *Feeling:* He experienced a strong and unusual change in mind and body in the theophany on route to Damascus, from confident hostility to the Way to acceptance of it (22:7-8; 26:14-15), from sight to blindness to sight again (22:11).

7. *Interest:* Either in persecuting the Way or in preaching it, Paul displays unremitting mental activity ardently devoted to religion.

8. *Purpose:* In persecuting the Way he acted according to a deliberate and approved plan, duly authorized (22:15; 26:16-18).

9. *Achievements, accidents, speech:* Paul tells us in detail what happened on route to Damascus, what he said, and what Jesus said, and what he did (22:6-11; 26:12-18).

The exordia of Paul's two speeches, then, contain all of the vital information that pertains to a favorable portrayal of the *ethos* of a defendant or witness in a difficult case. On the basis of Paul's education, piety, and authorization, he is shown to be a witness of reputable social standing, upright, stable, and pious, whose testimony deserves a fair hearing in court. The correct formal understanding of the exordium helps us to appreciate the function of Paul's autobiographical statements in the first part of his defense speeches.

One can grasp the importance of this item in a forensic defense speech by contrasting the presentation of Paul as an educated and socially respectable person with the way Peter and John are treated in their trial in Acts 4. What makes a good witness? Or who may give testimony? In general Greek and Roman courts excluded as witnesses women, slaves, and children;[19] only adult males in full possession of civic rights were acceptable as witnesses in court.[20] According to Josephus, slaves may not give testimony "because of the baseness of their souls since they will not attest the truth whether from cupidity or fear" (*Ant.* 4.8.15 §219). Women, he continues, are unacceptable because of the "levity and temerity of their sex" (ibid.). Jewish laws proscribed as witnesses "usurers, dice-players, pigeon-flyers, etc."—in short, anyone considered wicked or lawless.

The social status of the witness, however, was of considerable importance in Jewish as well as in Greco-Roman courts. A. E. Harvey stated the issue most succinctly: "Whose word can we trust? If a citizen who enjoyed the respect of society solemnly affirmed that something was the case, this was all one could ask for . . . the all-important question was the character of the witnesses."[21] Josephus's remarks illustrate this point: ". . . had my case against John been tried and had I produced some two or three excellent men as witnesses to my behavior, it is evident that you would have been compelled, after inquiries into their character, to acquit me of the charges brought against me" (*Vita* 49 §256). Respectable social status, then, was a prerequisite for the acceptance of a witness's testimony.

Conversely, low social standing radically depreciated a witness's testimony. Paul claimed respectable social standing in the presentation of his ethos, but the testimony of Peter and John is dismissed in their trial largely on the basis of their low social standing: "they saw that they were common, uneducated men" (Acts 4:13), that is ʿammê hā-āreṣ.[22] The Talmud records a statement about the legal status of an ʿam hā-āreṣ: "Our rabbis taught: six things were said of an *am ha-aretz:* we do not commit testimony to them; we do not accept testimony from them" (*b. Pesaḥ.* 49b). The presentation of Paul's ethos in the exordia of his speeches, then, was calculated to prevent his dismissal as a "common, uneducated" person, as was the case with Peter and John. In Luke's eyes, it was necessary to secure a good hearing for Paul's testimony by presenting his ethos favorably, especially his education and piety.

II

The second structural part of a forensic speech is called the statement of facts or *narratio.*[23] It is the part of a forensic speech to the court "as to the nature of the case under dispute,"[24] whose purpose is "to prepare the mind of the judge."[25] Four aspects of the statement of facts are traditionally listed: (a) the main question, (b) the line of defense, (c) the point for the judge's decision, and (d) the foundation or basic argument for the defense.[26] The main question (quaestio/ ζήτημα) is the chief subject of the debate: whether a thing has been done, what it is that was done, whether it was rightly done.[27] The line of defense (ratio/αἴτιον) contains the defendant's motive or justification for the act in dispute.[28] The point for the judge's decision (iudicatio/κρινόμενον) is that which arises from the assertion or denial of the reason and motive.[29] The judge must finally rule on the defendant's argument and statements. Finally, the foundation (firmamentum/συνέχον) is the strongest argument of the defense and the one most relevant to the point for the judge's decision.[30]

The traditional case of Orestes illustrates these four points.[31] (a) The main question in this case does not involve a question of fact; Orestes killed Clytemnestra. The main question is, rather, "was he justified or not?" He is charged with matricide, but he claims to be avenging a patricide. The proper definition of the act under judgment is the paramount question. (b) His line of defense consists of his motive, namely, vengeance for Clytemnestra's murder of his father. (c) The point for the judge's decision, then, is whether it was right that even a guilty mother be slain by her son. (d) The central argument or foundation for the defense, according to Cicero, is Orestes' avowal that "the disposition of his mother toward his father, himself and his sisters, the kingdom, the reputation of the race and the family was such that it was the peculiar duty of her children to punish her" (Inv. 1.14.19).[32]

Appreciation of this structural part of a forensic defense speech has bearing on our understanding of certain parts of Paul's defense speeches. (a) The main question of his trial is a point of considerable elaboration. In 21:38 he is charged with "teaching men everywhere against the people and the law and this place," charges implying heresy or apostasy from Jewish religion. Paul attempts to show that he is not against Israel's scriptures or its God (24:12-13). On the contrary he admits that "according to the Way, which they call a sect, I worship the God of our fathers, believing everything laid down by the law or written in the prophets" (24:14). The question for Paul is not heresy or apostasy but the true understanding of the law, which is faith in the resurrection.

In the course of Paul's trials it becomes clear that the main question is not the charges alleged against Paul in 21:38 or 24:5-8 but entirely other issues.[33] The tribune Claudius Lysias remarked, "I found that he was accused about questions of their law (ζητημάτων), but charged with nothing deserving death or imprisonment" (23:29). Festus tells Agrippa that the main question is not the alleged charges but a question of religion: "when his accusers stood up, they brought no charge in his case of such evils as I supposed; but they had certain points of dispute (ζητήματα) with him about their own superstition and about one Jesus, who was dead, but whom Paul asserted to be alive" (25:18-19).

In his own defense speeches, Paul repeatedly insists that the main question is the resurrection of Jesus—as a fact, as God's doing, and as the point of the scriptures. In the trial before the Jewish court in chap. 23, he insists that the main question is the resurrection: "with respect to the resurrection I am on trial" (23:6). In the trial before Felix in chap. 24, even as Paul dismisses the charges that Tertullus brought against him (24:10-13, 17-20), he admits that the issue is the orthodoxy of his faith, "I admit that according to the Way I believe everything laid down by the law or written in the prophets, having a hope in God which they themselves accept that there will be a resurrection of both the just and the unjust" (24:14-15). The main question, he tells the court, is "with respect to the resurrection" (24:21). Finally, in the trial before Festus, Paul once more defines the main question of the forensic proceedings, "I stand here on trial for hope in the promise made by God to our fathers, to which the twelve tribes hope to attain. And for this hope I am accused by the Jews" (26:6-7). The main question according to the defense, then, is the issue of Jesus' resurrection[34] and the orthodoxy of this belief as the point of the Jewish scriptures (see 26:22-23).

(b) Concerning the second part of the statement of facts, the justifying motive, a dishonorable motive for Paul's actions is imputed to him by Tertullus in the charges made against him in 24:5-6. His preaching of the resurrection is portrayed by the prosecution as an act of agitation or sedition, a point fully in accord with instructions for plaintiffs in rhetorical handbooks.[35] But in his own defense Paul puts forward the true and justifying motive for his preaching of the resurrection.[36] He tells us of a heavenly command to preach (26:16-18), a solemn authorization to speak, similar to the commissioning of Israel's prophets.[37] His motive for preaching is identical to that of Peter in 5:29, namely, obedience to heavenly directives: "wherefore I was not disobedient to the heavenly vision, but declared first to those at Damascus, then at Jerusalem, and throughout all the country of Judea" (26:19-20). Heavenly help, moreover, sustained Paul throughout his commission to preach, "to this day I have had the help that comes from God" (26:22). Just as the motive for his preaching is obedience to a heavenly command, so the substance of his preaching is not sedition or heresy but the truth of God's scriptures, "saying nothing but what the prophets and Moses said would come to pass" (26:22; see 24:14). The main question is the resurrection, and the justifying motive for preaching it was a heavenly command.

(c) The point for the judge's decision is clearly brought out in Paul's defense speeches. What must be judged by Jewish and Gentile judges alike is the legitimacy of Paul's main question, the resurrection of Jesus by God. The defense speeches call attention to this point when they note that what must be judged (κρίνεται, κρινόμενον) is the issue of the resurrection:

23:6   "With respect to the hope of the resurrection
         of the dead *I am on trial* (κρίνομαι)"
24:21   "With respect to the resurrection of the
         dead *I am on trial* (κρίνομαι)"
26:6-7   "*I stand on trial* (κρινόμενος) for hope in
         the promise made by God to our fathers"
26:8   "Why is it *judged* incredible (κρίνεται) by
         any of you that God raises the dead?"

III

The third structural part of a forensic defense speech is called the proof (*probatio/πίστις*), in which witnesses, arguments, and evidence are marshaled.[38] Rhetorical handbooks advise the orator how to organize proofs in accord with forensic procedure. "First among the proofs," according to Quintilian, "must be placed the evidence of witnesses and confessions that are obtained by torture."[39] In the proof sections of Paul's defense speeches, the prime evidence in support of the main question (i.e., the resurrection) is the testimony of the witness Paul. Paul indicates that he is a valid legal witness to the resurrection, duly authorized to preach this; he repeats on trial the authorization that came to him through the heavenly vision, "I have appeared to you for this purpose: to appoint you to bear witness to the things of which you have seen me" (26:16; see 22:15). The authorized testimony of a valid witness is the first among proofs. Yet, if such testimony is not convincing, say the handbooks, it needs confirmation from "probability, examples, tokens, signs and maxims."[40] The best evidence is testimony confirmed by tokens (τεκμήρια) and signs (σημεῖα).

Confirmation of Paul's testimony about the resurrection comes from the appearances of Jesus of which Paul was an eyewitness.[41] The importance of the appearances of Jesus precisely as forensic evidence can be brought out by reference to Luke's own terminology in regard to this phenomenon. As far back as Aristotle, two types of proof were distinguished: (a) necessary proof, from which a definite conclusion could be drawn; and (b) credible proof, from which no necessary conclusion can be drawn. The former is called an irrefutable proof (τεκμήριον) and the latter probably proof (εἰκότα/ σημεῖα/ *signa*).[42] The necessary proof (τεκμήριον) is one that cannot be refuted; from it a cogent and logical syllogism can be constructed. Credible or probable proof (εἰκότα), however, is of great value when taken in conjunction with other proofs, for they enable one to infer that something has happened.[43]

Luke designates the appearances of the risen Jesus as irrefutable and necessary proofs: "to them he presented himself alive after his passion by many proofs (τεκμηρίοις), appearing to them forty days" (Acts 1:3). In another place Luke bolstered the testimony of a preacher of the resurrection by mention of special evidence or proof of the resurrection of Jesus: "God raised him up and made him manifest; not to all the people but to us who were chosen by God as witnesses, who ate and drank with him after he rose from the dead" (Acts 10:41). This recalls the proof of the resurrection offered to the eleven when the appearing Jesus proved that he was no ghost by eating with the witnesses (Luke 24:37-43).[44] This irrefutable evidence serves as the basis for a more formal argument which concludes that Jesus is "Lord and Christ" (2:36), the author of life (3:15), and the savior of the world (4:10-12). The appearances are proof that God raised him from the dead and enthroned him as Lord and Messiah.[45]

With regard to his forensic defense in Acts 22 and 26, Paul testifies about the resurrection of Jesus. As we saw earlier, he focused the main question of the trial on the resurrection. Yet his testimony is not entirely convincing to this court, so he must confirm it. Hence, Paul recounts in considerable detail in 22:6-12 and 26:12-16 the irrefutable proof (τεκμήριον) of his testimony, the appearance of Jesus to him on route to Damascus. According to Acts, then, the narrative of the appearance of Jesus functions as the irrefutable proof of Paul's defense concerning the resurrection.[46]

Besides this necessary and irrefutable proof of Paul's testimony, there is further confirmatory evidence. Under this category we can consider probable or credible signs. These are the εἰκότα of Aristotle, the signs that allow us to infer that something has happened. As the handbooks say, "one thing is a sign of another—not any casual thing of any other casual thing, nor everything whatever of everything whatever, but only a thing that normally precedes or accompanies or follows a thing."[47]

With regard to the signs that confirm Paul's testimony, the incidents accompanying the heavenly revelation of the risen Jesus while on route to Damascus may be treated as εἰκότα, probable signs. First, the appearance of Jesus was accompanied by a great heavenly light (22:6, 9; 26:13). The light was admittedly an extraordinary phenomenon, "brighter than the sun"; it was seen by Paul "and by those journeying with me" (26:13). It has been noted that the Damascus appearance is form-critically described as an epiphany from heaven, typical motifs of which are heavenly lights, mighty voices, and fallings to the ground.[48] The light from heaven, then, is perceived as a typical sign that regularly accompanies a heavenly revelation, which sign functions forensically in Paul's defense speeches as evidence that Paul was receiving a heavenly revelation. From it we infer that something has happened. This is a sign that, according to rhetorical handbooks, normally accompanies another thing. Second, Paul's blindness and subsequent cure are still another sign (22:11, 13; see 9:7-9, 17). This may be taken as a prophetic symbol of Paul's enlightenment about Jesus. Of themselves these two phenomena do not necessarily involve Jesus' resurrection; revelatory lights flashed around Daniel (Dan 10:5-9) and Aseneth (14:1); Tobit was blinded and subsequently healed (Tob 11:11-13). They are signs, however, enabling us to infer that something else has happened, namely, that Paul was receiving a heavenly revelation, itself an irrefutable proof of his testimony about the resurrection.

A speaker's testimony can be corroborated by witnesses who can confirm all the relevant aspects of his testimony. Witnesses can confirm every point of his exordium: his orthodox upbringing and education "is known by all the Jews" (26:4); his zeal as a Pharisee can be verified by local witnesses, "if they are willing to testify" (26:5). His initial hatred of the Way can be corroborated by excellent witnesses, "the high priest and the whole council of the elders bear me witness" (22:5). And his authorization for persecuting the Christians in Damascus can be supported by written documents, "from them I received letters to the brethren" (22:5).

Paul's experience on route to Damascus can also be confirmed by corroborating witnesses. The traveling companions of Paul also saw the light (22:9; 26:13); they too fell to the ground (26:14). They can verify the extraordinary light, as well as Paul's blindness and cure (22:11), credible signs (εἰχότα) from which one can infer a heavenly revelation to Paul. These events have still another witness who can confirm them, Ananias. He is a trustworthy witness whose standing in the court is unimpeachable, "a devout man according to the law and well spoken of by all the Jews who lived there" (22:12). He too received a heavenly revelation in a dream about the events on the way to Damascus; he can verify that Paul experienced the risen Jesus, "the God of our father has appointed you . . . to see the Just One and hear a voice from his mouth" (22:14). After miraculously healing Paul of his blindness, Ananias confirmed Paul's authorization to preach about the resurrection, "for you will be a witness for him to all men of what you have seen and heard" (22:15). Thus Ananias can corroborate Paul on every point of his testimony about the risen Jesus and the events on route to Damascus. According to correct forensic procedure, then, there are two witnesses to these events.

In an excellent study of this material, A. Wikenhauser called attention to the motif in Acts of "double dreams," a motif common in pagan and Jewish literature.[49]   This motif consists of a heavenly revelation to a principal figure and a simultaneous parallel revelation to a friend or relative who can corroborate the main revelation. Such a motif, which occurred in the case of Peter and Cornelius in Acts 10, is found also in the appearances of Jesus to Paul and Ananias in 9:3-6, 10-16 and 22:6-10, 12-16. And so the appearance to Ananias functions as confirmation of the appearance to Paul.

Still more confirmatory evidence in support of Paul's testimony comes from proofs that the handbooks call "probabilities." In setting forth a statement to judge and jury, an orator should "pay attention to the question of whether he will find his hearers possessed of a personal knowledge of the things of which he is speaking, as that is the sort of statement they are most likely to believe."[50] Is there a common experience to which the orator can appeal?[51]   Will the audience understand? This type of proof, "probability," seems to have been taken into consideration in the composition of the proof section of Paul's forensic speeches in the narration of Jesus' appearance to Paul. In the first place, the revelation of the risen Jesus is recounted according to the typical form that G. Lohfink has described as an epiphany account. Comparing the appearance accounts in Acts 9, 22, and 26 with Old Testament examples such as Gen 31:11-13; 46:2-3; Exod 3:2-10, Lohfink suggested the following formal elements:[52]

A1	introductory formula	. . . saying to him
A2	address: double vocative	Saul! Saul!
B1	introductory formula	but he answered
B2	question	who are you, Lord?
C1	introductory formula	But he . . .
C2	self-presentation of appearing figure	I am Jesus, whom you are persecuting
C3	commission	But rise and go . . .

A court familiar with Old Testament materials would presumably understand the traditional form of Paul's account of Jesus' appearance and his "probable" claim to have received a heavenly revelation.[53] Similarly, Lohfink has shown that the account of Paul's commissioning to preach the resurrection in 26:16-18 is modeled on a mosaic of citations from the prophets about their vocation commissionings, as the following synopsis indicates:[54]

(a)	Acts 26:16	"Stand on your feet"
	Ezek 2:1	"Stand on your feet"
(b)	Acts 26:17	"delivering you from the people and the nations"
	Jer 1:8	"be not afraid of them, for I am with you to deliver you"
(c)	Acts 26:17b	"from the nations to whom I send you"
	Jer 1:7	"to whomever I send you, you shall go"
(d)	Acts 26:18	"to open their eyes that they may turn from darkness to light"
	Isa 42:6-7	"a light to the nations, to open the eyes that are blind"

Again the form and content of Paul's testimony about his commission to preach the resurrection are phrased in such a way as to appear "probable" to a court familiar with the Old Testament, suggesting a prophetic commissioning.

Paul is appealing to what is common or "probable" in the experience of his audience when he maintains over and over that the resurrection is not a novel or heterodox doctrine. He insists that it is a "probability," a statement fully in accord with the views of his hearers. For example, he confesses in his defense in 24:14-15 that he "believes everything laid down in the law or written in the prophets," which includes "the hope in God which they themselves accept that there will be a resurrection of both just and unjust." In 26:6-7, he insists again that his hope in the resurrection is the same thing "to which our twelve tribes hope to attain." He remarks that in testifying to the resurrection he is "saying nothing but what the prophets and Moses said would come to pass" (26:22). The resurrection, then, is a "probable" phenomenon to Paul, indeed, a longstanding tradition in Jewish religion.

IV

In conclusion, what I hope to have shown in this brief study is that the trial speeches of Paul in Acts deserve to be described formally as forensic defense speeches according to the models presented in the rhetorical handbooks. The forensic defense speech is an appropriate form for appreciating the structure of Paul's speeches and for grasping the function of the individual items in those speeches. Knowledge of forensic speeches and forensic procedure is indispensable for understanding Acts. The following synopsis conveniently summarizes the data of this study:

		ACTS 22:	23:	24:	26:
A.	***Exordium***				
	1. appeal to judge	—	—	—	2-3
	2. ethos of speaker	4-5	1	—	4-5
B.	***Statement of Facts***				
	1. main question	—	6	10-20	6-7
	2. justifying motive	10,14-15	—	—	16-20
	3. point for judge's decision	—	6	14-15, 21	6-8
C.	***Proof***				
	1. μαρτυρία	15	—	—	16
	2. τεκμήριον	6-10	—	—	12-18
	3. σημεῖον	6, 9 (light) 11, 13 (blindness)	—	—	13 (light) —
	4. corroborating witnesses	5,9 12-15	—	—	5,12-13
	5. probabilities	7-10 (epiphany)	—	—	14-16 (epiphany)
		—	—	—	16-18 (prophetic commissioning)

NOTES

[1] H. J. Cadbury, "Roman Law and the Trial of Paul," *The Beginnings of Christianity* (ed. F. J. Foakes Jackson and Kirsopp Lake; 1920-1933; reprint, Grand Rapids: Baker, 1979) 5. 297-338; A. N. Sherwin-White, *Roman Society and Roman Law in the New Testament* (Oxford: Clarendon, 1963) 48-70; J. Dupont, *Études sur les Actes des Apôtres* (Paris: Cerf, 1967) 527-52.

[2]Fredrick Veltman, "The Defense Speeches of Paul in Acts" (Th.D. diss., Berkeley Graduate Theological Union, 1975); idem, "The Defense Speeches of Paul in Acts," *Perspectives on Luke-Acts* (ed. C. H. Talbert; Danville, VA: Association of Baptist Professors of Religion, 1978) 243-56.

[3]H. Strathmann, "μάρτυς," *TDNT* 4. 474-514; J. Beutler, *Martyria* (Frankfurt: Josef Knecht, 1972); A. A. Trites, *The New Testament Concept of Witness* (Cambridge: University Press, 1977).

[4]William S. Kurz, "The Function of Christological Proof from Prophecy for Luke and Justin (Ph.D. diss., Yale, 1977); idem, "Hellenistic Rhetoric and the Christological Proof of Luke-Acts," *CBQ* 42 (1980) 171-95.

[5]A. A. Trites, "The Importance of Legal Scenes and Language in the Book of Acts," *NovT* 15 (1974) 278-84.

[6]For example, Stephan Lösch, "Die Dankesrede des Tertullus: Apg 24, 1-4," *TQ* 112 (1931) 295-319; J. M. Gilchrist, "On What Charge was St. Paul Brought to Rome?" *ExpTim* 78 (1967) 264-66; Mark Black, "Paul and Roman Law in Acts," *RQ* 24 (1981) 209-18.

[7]See C. H. Dodd, *The Apostolic Preaching and Its Development* (London: Hodder and Stoughton, 1936); J. Dupont, "Les discours missionaires des Actes des Apôtres," *RB* 69 (1962) 37-60; Eduard Schweizer, "Concerning the Speeches in Acts," *Studies in Luke-Acts* (ed. L. E. Keck and J. L. Martyn; London: SPCK, 1966) 208-16; and U. Wilckens, *Die Missionsreden der Apostelgeschichte* (WMANT 5; 3d ed.; Neukirchen-Vluyn: Neukirchener Verlag, 1974).

[8]Bertil Gärtner, *The Areopagus Speech and Natural Revelation* (ASNU 21; Lund: Gleerup, 1955).

[9]In his doctoral dissertation, F. Veltman ("The Defense Speeches in Acts") surveyed defense speeches in ancient literature, examining whether there existed a typical form of ἀπολογία. The application of this material to Paul's speeches in Acts was inconclusive, according to Veltman, because the correspondence between classical examples and Paul's defense speeches tended to be found basically in the narrative framework around the speeches rather than in the speeches themselves (p. 251). My study disagrees with Veltman because the classical sources used for this comparison include much more material from rhetorical handbooks than Veltman considered.

[10]*Her.* 1.4.6; Cicero *Inv.* 1.15.20, and Quintilian *Inst.* 4.1.1-4. My interest in the exordium extends beyond the traditional but narrow understanding of it as a *captatio benevolentiae* in regard to the judge's favor; for this, see Lösch, "Die Dankesrede des Tertullus," 295-319.

[11]Quintilian *Inst.* 4.1.5.

[12]Cicero *Inv.* 1.15.20; *Top.* 97.

[13]*Her.* 1.6.9; Cicero *Inv.* 1.15.20-16.21 and 17.23-25; Quintilian *Inst.* 4.1.45-50.

[14]Cicero *Inv.* 1.16.22.

[15]See Philo *Spec. Leg.* 4.43; W. M. Sattler, "Conceptions of *ethos* in Ancient Rhetoric," *Speech Monographs* 14 (1957) 55-65; George

Kennedy, *The Art of Rhetoric in the Roman World* (Princeton: University Press, 1972) 100-101.

[16]Cicero *De Or.* 2.43.184.

[17]Cicero *De Or.* 2.43.182 and 79.321.

[18]See also *Her.* 2.6.9 and Quintilian *Inst.* 5.10.23-29.

[19]Robert J. Bonner, *Lawyers and Litigants in Ancient Athens* (Chicago: University of Chicago Press, 1927) 185-88; A. H. J. Greenidge, *The Legal Procedure of Cicero's Time* (Oxford: Clarendon, 1901) 482-83.

[20]Robert J. Bonner, *Evidence in Athenian Courts* (Chicago: University of Chicago Press, 1905) 27-28, 32.

[21]A. E. Harvey, *Jesus on Trial* (Atlanta: John Knox, 1976) 20; see also H. F. Jolowicz, *Historical Introduction to the Study of Roman Law* (Cambridge: University Press, 1967) 462.

[22]See G. F. Moore, "The Am ha-areṣ (the People of the Land) and the Ḥaberīm (Associates)," *Beginnings,* 1. 439-45; H. Schlier, "ἰδιώτης," *TDNT* 3. 215-16.

[23]*Her.* 1.3.4; Quintilian *Inst.* 3.9.1.

[24]Quintilian *Inst.* 4.2.31.

[25]Quintilian *Inst.* 4.2.4-5.

[26]Quintilian *Inst.* 3.11.6-7.

[27]Cicero *Inv.* 1.13.18; Quintilian *Inst.* 3.11.2.

[28]Cicero *Inv.* 1.13.18; Quintilian *Inst.* 3.11.4.

[29]Cicero *Inv.* 1.13.18; Quintilian *Inst.* 3.11.5-6.

[30]Cicero *Inv.* 1.14.19; Quintilian *Inst.* 3.11.9.

[31]The case of Orestes was the handbook model for explaining this material: see *Her.* 1.10.17; Cicero *Inv.*1.13.18-14.19; and Quintilian *Inst.* 3.11.4-13.

[32]See also Quintilian, *Inst.* 3.11.12.

[33]See Robert J. O'Toole, *The Christological Climax of Paul's Defense* (AnBib 78; Rome: Biblical Institute Press, 1978) 40.

[34]Compare this with the reasons stated for Peter's arrest in Acts 4:2.

[35]See *Her.* 2.2.3-3.4; Cicero *Inv.* 2.5.16-8.28.

[36]*Her.* 1.16.26; see Acts 19:40, where αἴτιον is used for the justifying motive.

[37]For example, G. Lohfink, *The Conversion of St. Paul* (Chicago: Franciscan Herald Press, 1976) 70-71.

[38]Cicero *Inv.* 1.24.34; Quintilian *Inst.* 5, pr. 3-5; see n. 23 above.

[39]*Rh. Al.* 36 (1442b37); Isocrates (17.54) claims that such testimony has the highest value in a court of law: "I see that in private and public causes you judge that nothing is more deserving of belief or true than testimony given under torture." Concerning testimony extracted under torture, Acts 22:24 states that the arresting officer intended "to examine him (Paul) by scourging" to obtain Paul's testimony, "to find out why they shouted thus against him."

[40]*Rh. Al.* 36 (1442b39-1443a6).

[41]Eyewitness testimony was always demanded; no ancient court ever accepted hearsay evidence. Demosthenes' remark is typical in

this regard: "It was fitting . . . to state only things of which they have accurate knowledge and to bring forward no hearsay in a trial of this sort. Such a procedure has from time immemorial been recognized as so clearly unjust that the laws do not admit the production of hearsay testimony even in the case of the most trifling charges" (57, "Against Eubulides," 4). Philo, in discoursing on Exod 23:1, remarked that Jewish judges likewise did not accept hearsay evidence (*Spec. Leg.* 4.59); in another place he notes that hearsay testimony was prohibited by law (*Conf.* 141); see *t. Sanh.* 8.3.

[42] Aristotle *Rh.* 1.2.16-17 (1357b1-9).

[43] Quintilian *Inst.* 5.9.3-9.

[44] See H. J. Cadbury, "Rebuttal, A Submerged Motif in the Gospels," *Quantulacumque* (ed. R. P. Casey; London: Christophers, 1937) 99-108.

[45] On the construction of a valid syllogism from evidence in Acts, see William S. Kurz, "Hellenistic Rhetoric," 172-84.

[46] In still another speech in Acts the resurrection of Jesus is cited as a formal proof of something. Paul was persuading the Athenians to accept his testimony about God. Besides arguing that God is one and is creator of the world (17:24-29), Paul affirmed God's eschatological role, how he will "judge the world in righteousness by a man whom he has appointed" (17:31a). The proof of this latter assertion is the fact that this same God raised Jesus from the dead: "of this he has given proof (πίστιν) to all by raising him from the dead" (17:31b). Πίστις (proof) is the technical rhetorical term for forensic proof; see *Rh. Al.* 7 (1428a17) and Quintilian *Inst.* 5.10.8.

[47] *Rh. Al.* 12 (1430b30).

[48] Lohfink, *Conversion of St. Paul*, 61-68.

[49] A. Wikenhauser, "Doppelträume," *Bib* 29 (1948) 100-111.

[50] *Rh. Al.* 7 (1428a32); Quintilian *Inst.* 5.10.16-19; see Aristotle *Rh.* 1.2.15 (1357a35-40), 1.15.17 (1376a18-24), and 2.25.8 (1402b13-20).

[51] *Rh. Al.* 7 (1428b4).

[52] Lohfink, *Conversion of St. Paul*, 62-66.

[53] See also Benjamin J. Hubbard, "The Role of Commissioning Accounts in Acts," *Perspectives on Luke-Acts*, 187-98; idem, "Commissioning Stories in Luke-Acts: A Study of Their Antecedents, Form and Content," *Semeia* 8 (1977) 103-26; T. Y. Mullins, "New Testament Commission Form, Especially in Luke-Acts," *JBL* 95 (1976) 603-14.

[54] Lohfink, *Conversion of St. Paul*, 70-71; see also Otto Betz, "Die Vision des Paulus im Tempel von Jerusalem. Apg 22,17-21 als Beitrag zur Deutung des Damaskuserlebnisses," *Verborum Veritas* (ed. O. Boecher and K. Haacker; Wuppertal: Rolf Brockhaus, 1970) 113-23.

G. W. Trompf

ON WHY LUKE DECLINED TO RECOUNT THE DEATH OF PAUL: ACTS 27-28 AND BEYOND *

The present conclusion to the book of Acts calls for an explanation. One particular puzzle it presents concerns the fate of Paul. A modern reader would like to learn how long Paul dwelt in Rome, whether he lived there for a considerable period, was tried, imprisoned or acquitted, whether he died there of "natural causes" or was put to death, or whether he subsequently journeyed to other parts of the Mediterranean world. The same reader has reason to suspect that his ancient counterpart would have put the book down with a similar set of unanswered questions. The possibility even presents itself that the author would have been sorry to leave matters at Acts 28:31 and would have wished his prospective audience to learn much more.

The conundrum has prompted a number of explanations. Some attempt to satisfy the current curiosity about "what actually did happen" afterward, and some try to explain, even to justify Luke's dénouement as it stands by imagining the responses of his Hellenistic readership and (more commonly) by attempting to reconstruct the author's intentions. In recent literature it has been maintained that a further phase of Paul's ministry saw the production of the Pastorals and even of those epistles that issued from a captivity in Ephesus that is not mentioned in Acts.[1] To envisage these subsequent developments, however, is not to deny both the ancient tradition and archeological indications that Paul died in Rome,[2] nor to shelve questions about why Luke's volume goes no farther than it does. Any one of a number of special historical circumstances, of course, could have determined the present ending: Luke may have died; if he was a companion of Paul, he may have left Rome either during or not long after his friend's "two years' detention" had elapsed;[3] he may have intended to write a third volume but did not fulfill his hopes; he may actually have written more, but death may have cut short his endeavors or his manuscripts may have been lost.[4]

Interesting though all such possibilities may be, certain scholars have set them aside as sheer speculation and uphold the view that the present conclusion conforms to Lucan theological or historiographical preoccupations as assessed by redaction-critical techniques. The final chapter takes both Paul and the reader to Rome; that is significant enough in itself when one considers how this extraordinary traveler, who has already managed to wander around half the Mediterranean region, is providentially transported to the hub of the then-known *oikoumenē*.[5] Then there are the solemn pronouncements of 28:25-28. The Isaianic passage that was important enough in earliest Christianity to be used in all three other evangelists' works (Isa 6:9, 10; see Mark 4:12; Matt 13:14-15; John 12:40) stands at the end of Luke-Acts as a final justification of the mission to the Gentiles. For the third time it is made clear that, because many Jews will not accept the Christ, salvation is sent τοῖς ἔθνεσιν instead (28:28; cf. 13:46; 18:6).[6] With a somewhat idiosyncratic yet related hermeneutic, M. D. Goulder has suggested that Luke consciously made this arrival and teaching in Rome parallel to the resurrection at the end of the gospel; Paul overcame the powers of chaos and death by being saved from shipwreck.[7] There is enough in the text itself of such moment and finality that it was hardly necessary for Luke—or perhaps it was not in his historico-theological interests—to take the narrative any further.

Not satisfied with the way redaction-criticism has tried to account for the precise forms and content of Luke's concluding chapters (esp. chaps. 27-28), I have sought to explain them by a fresh appraisal of Luke's method as a "Christian Hellenistic" historian. G. B. Miles and I have proposed the thesis (developed further by D. Ladouceur) that Luke declined to recount Paul's trial in Rome (whatever its outcome, or even quite apart from whether it happened), because Paul had been "acquitted by a tribunal no less formidable than the divinely controlled ocean itself." The higher decision implicit in Paul's escape from the sea—in the fact that he was not a man of pollution or guilt who would bring loss of life to anyone on board ship, in his utter imperviousness to the sting of a serpent, and even in his final safe sea passage to Ostia under the sign of the Dioskouroi (the pagan "patron saints of sailors")—simply renders an earthly judgment irrelevant.[8] Although bound by a chain (28:20b), Paul proceeds along the via Appia usually taken by visitors and is even received by a special welcoming party (vv. 14-16). The judgment at the climax of the work is not delivered by the Roman power but by Paul himself, and in a way that clinches Luke's important theme that Christianity has moved beyond Judaism and is now in the extraordinary position of capturing the attention of the whole Roman Empire. Luke takes pains to point out that Paul is well treated as a highly respected prisoner (vv. 16b, 30), and one is tempted to suggest that Luke did so to please defenders of imperial justice among his readers. After all, the Romans had already been preparing to release Paul at Caesarea (26:30–32; 28:18). Yet with his final comments on the heroic missionary's relative freedom and with the parting (dare I say democratic?) allusion to *parrēsia* (v. 31),[9] Luke also constructs a conclusion that is refined according to the best standards of biblical historiography. Scholars have missed the fascinating similarity between the final two verses of Luke's work and the conclusion to the Deuteronomic history at 2 Kgs 25:28–30. Both King Johoiachin and Paul were captives far from the homeland of Israel, but they were permitted room to maneuver and the economic means to live comfortably. "The strange ending of Acts is no longer strange; it has the special touch of Old Testament history upon it."[10]

Luke's concluding sequence, running from Caesarea to Rome, nicely illustrates his ability to exploit an interest held in common by both biblical and Hellenistic historiographers and to play on a crucial theme that not only endowed his work with a singular unity but also met the needs of both a Jewish and a Gentile readership. I refer here to the interest in the principles of retribution, which I have already documented in detail from the extant Israelite and Greco-Roman histories that preceded Luke's writing.[11] Put simply, most ancient historians were bent on demonstrating how the affairs they recounted had moral meanings: that Xerxes, for instance, was justly punished for his *hybris* in attempting to conquer Hellás (Herodotus); that post-Periclean Athens overstepped the mark when it sent out the Sicilian expedition and so brought disaster upon itself (Thucydides); that the sins of Israel eventually brought exile to Babylon (the Deuteronomist); that the moral superiority of Rome over its opponents justified its victories (Polybius); that the righteousness of restored Israel under Ezra and Nehemiah merited the return of architectural and liturgical achievements known in Davidic-Solomonic times (the Chronicler). In Israelite historiography Yahweh was always the Master and Dispenser of rewards and punishments; in the Greco-Roman tradition matters were not so simple. Although some writers were happy to talk of the intervention of the divine, others alluded to impersonal or quasi-hypostatized governing principles. Educing significances from human affairs, however, invariably meant evoking the same basic issue, that is, whether the nations, groups or individuals being treated achieved remarkable success or suffered misfortunes, or whether they experienced "salvation" or death.[12] The outcome of events for better or worse led to reflection upon possible moral meanings. Indeed, the outcome of a whole complex of events could be the very factor that propelled a would-be historian to undertake the task in the first place. In the course of the narrative, in any case, the historian was to highlight special developments—including the manner in which great figures overcame adversity, for instance, or the nature and implications of deaths among the *dramatis personae*—either to edify the audience or to teach "lessons for future behavior."[13]

A whole complex or contour of events is obviously important for Luke's raison d'être as an author. Being a Christian (now ranked among the evangelists), he believed he was writing about happenings of universal rather than merely regional or parochial significance. Self-consciously adopting the role of a historian (unlike Mark, Matthew, and John), Luke sought to account for the remarkable and rapid emergence of Christianity, "characterizing" rather than "preaching" the life of Jesus,[14] and demonstrating how the new message came to be spread from the extreme edge of the Roman Empire to its very hub. The theme of retribution or the concern to show the rewards and punishments of God in history is conspicuous in Luke-Acts and is reflected above all in the second of the two volumes. Leaving readers an overall impression, Luke shows that the righteous succeed despite adversity and that the gospel is indeed taken "to the end of the earth" (Acts 1:8b).[15] Those who unjustly oppose the new movement, in contrast, are not only requited for being unable to suppress it but (in the case of unbelieving Jews) are also rejected by God, whose oracles are quoted against them by Lucan heroes.[16] The ruin of the Jewish nation had already been forecast by Jesus, and the New Testament nowhere more clearly pronounced this awesome fate than in Luke's works.[17] If, as I have argued, there are important general themes binding together Jesus' teaching in the central section of Luke's gospel, "retribution" and "discipleship" are two of them,[18] and it is not asking much to believe that, for Luke, Jesus' sense of disobedient Israel's doom and his encouragement of the disciples set the stage for what transpired in Acts. Jesus' message is not simply left sufficient unto itself; it is made to make sense by historical eventualities. It does so because the new order of faith, power, and the Spirit produce endurance and ultimate victory, while the opponents of the message find themselves running at their peril against God himself.[19]

It is precisely because Luke was aware that Jewish and Greco-Roman readers shared common general presuppositions about a "moral order" in human affairs that he handled the issue of death very carefully in his two volumes. How a person died, it was held in both cultural complexes, would tell something significant about the quality of that person's life. For example, a doughty warrior killed on the field of battle was to be extolled as courageous, heroic, or perhaps as a martyr;[20] those who died ignominiously were to be suspected of receiving their just deserts,[21] while special admiration could be reserved for those who (like Cato Minor or the Zealots at Masada) took their own lives rather than be put to death by their enemies.[22] Now if Luke's approach to the general consequences of accepting or rejecting the divine will is rather more distinctively Jewish than Greco-Roman in flavor, he is evidently more eclectic, or more concerned with accommodating pressures from both traditions in his handling of individual deaths. One is tempted to believe, in fact, that Luke sensed how a *diēgēsis* of Jesus' life without a sequel would have seemed insufficient to those who had popular preconceptions about a "moral order." Jesus may have overcome death, but it remained to be shown that his apparent post-resurrection "departure" did not leave his followers utterly vulnerable and without sustenance. Jesus had been subjected to trials by Jews, Herodians, and Romans, and he had even been betrayed by one of his own close followers. Did those responsible for the crimes against the bringer of God's *sōtēria* and against "the light for revelation to the nations" (Luke 2:31-32) escape the recompenses they deserved? It is hard to believe, even if Luke may have anticipated an extraterrestrial judgment, that the evangelist himself had been no less troubled about this question than the audience he now sought to satisfy in his writing.

Acts indicates how justice is done to evildoers. If Matthew related how Judas "repented," returned the blood money, and hanged himself in remorse (27:3-5), the first chapter of Luke's second volume shows how Judas bought a field from the reward of his *adikia* and then unwittingly died a hideous death (Acts 1:18). Luke's account would have been far more striking for both Jews and Greeks: the Jews would have recognized its basis in biblical prophecy (2:16, 20), and the Greeks would have seen the foreshadowing of it in ancient "oracles" and by Jesus himself (v. 20; cf. Luke 22:22b). Thus both groups would be in a position to acknowledge it as a fitting end to the betrayer.[23] The death of Herod (Agrippa I) as recounted in Acts 12:20-23 is another case in point, and because the Herod who dies eaten by worms is not specifically identified, his ugly end stands as implied retribution against "Herodianism" in general.[24] Josephus, for his part, tried to excuse the dying Agrippa he admired by noting his last-minute self-reproachfulness (*Ant.* 19.8.2 §§343-350; cf. 19.1.17 §144; 19.2.4 §200; 19.7.2-19.8.1 §§328-342), but for Luke there is no excuse. Thus, sudden extinction comes at the hand of the Lord's angel (a very

Jewish touch; see 2 Kgs 19:35; Isa 37:36; 1 Chr 21:7-16) to an impious monarch, whom most Gentile readers would have been excused for confusing with the taunting Herod of Luke 23 (esp. v. 11).[25]

Divine rejection of rebellious Jews as a whole group is accentuated by Paul's prophecy of Ananias' assassination (Acts 23:2-3), which implicitly requites the Jewish high priesthood in particular for its part in the crucifixion of Jesus and in the martyrdom of Stephen. By not specifying the key role of Caiaphas in the notorious sanhedrin hearing (see Matt 26:57, 59-68; John 18:13-14), Luke leaves the impression that Annas was the high priest of Jesus' time (Luke 3:2; Acts 4:6; 5:21b, 27)—thus a man whose name was barely distinguishable from that of the doomed Ananias.[26] The fact that Luke elsewhere refers to the seven sons of a τινος Σκευᾶ 'Ιουδαίου ἀρχιερέως (19:14), who are all overcome by evil power(s), suggests much subtler tilting against the Jewish hierarchy, as well as the choice of an episode to illustrate Jesus' warning to the Jews about the strength of evil spirits as unexpected oppressors (Luke 11:24-26).[27] The story of the seven sons, however, is probably more comparable to Luke's approach to the cases of Ananias and Sapphira and to the two magicians Simon and Elymas. The two betrayers of a sacred trust fall dead at Peter's feet (5:5, 10), the archfiend of "simony" is left in fear of Peter's imprecations (8:24), while Elymas is struck blind for undermining the faith of a new convert (16:11-12). Elymas's loss of sight reminds us how even Saul's temporary blindness emerges as an appropriate recompense for one who had approved the stoning of Stephen and persecuted the church (8:1-3; 9:1-2, 5, 8-9).

In the book of Acts, indeed, nothing falls out of place in terms of normative expectations about retributive principles in the two great ancient historiographical traditions familiar to Luke. Allusions are made to Jewish movements—the insurrections of Theudas and Judas the Galilean, the Sicarii revolt under the "Egyptian" (5:35-39; 21:38)—which arose at the same time as Christianity, but it is left clear that they come to nothing and, given the purport of Gamaliel's significant speech, are not "from God" (5:39). As for the Romans, although they and their prisons might impede the path of the Christians (16:19-24; 17:9; 18:2; 23:35; 24:23; 28:17b, 20), provincial intervention, and especially Roman legal institutions, invariably enable the bearers of the new message to proceed with their work a step farther (e.g., 16:39-40; 18:12-18; 19:35-20:1; 25:10-12) or to find new opportunities for conversions (e.g., 16:29-34; 21:39-22:21; 24:24; 26:1-28; 28:31; cf. 10:1-38). Luke anticipated that his readers would perceive it as fitting that God had not designed to bring punishment upon Rome; Rome was God's tool in bringing the ἡμέραι ἐκδικήσεως on Israel (as suggested by Luke 21:20-22), and Rome's representatives were plainly reluctant to condemn either Jesus or Paul as guilty parties (23:4, 14b, 22; Acts 13:28; 25:14-19; 26:30-32, yet cf. 2:23b; 4:27).[28] Thus Luke was undoubtedly very concerned with demonstrating that the unfolding of events conformed to the will of God and could be seen to do so above all because the whole of history, as well as the significant upshots within it, carried with it a paradigmatic moral congruity. This concern is nowhere more clearly evinced than in Luke's treatment of certain unpleasant deaths as the deserved chastisements of Yahweh.

Must one not concede, however, that there are two highly unpleasant deaths recounted in Luke-Acts that run counter to these conclusions? I refer, of course, to the crucifying of Jesus and the stoning of Stephen. These exceptions are all the more important for the special relationship they bear to each other. That they are meant to stand as exceptions, though, is evident enough, and one could hardly conclude that either figure deserved his affliction. That the innocent could experience unmerited suffering and even murder, in any case, was clearly a commonplace among Jews and pagans, and in fact it was precisely the spilling of innocent blood that seemed to cry out for morally fitting retribution.[29] One of Luke's crucial points about Jesus' death is made when the centurion declares not that this man was "a son of God" as in Mark (15:39) and Matthew (27:54) but "truly this man was innocent" (*dikaios*) (Luke 23:47), the palpable injustice of the crucifixion already having been argued out by the penitent thief (23:40-41; *dikaios* is omitted by Mark and Matthew). Stephen's death, in comparison, although it was similarly that of a righteous man (Acts 6:5b, 8, 15b) who was "done away with" on the first day of a great persecution (8:1; 22:19-20),[30] partly hinged on his final accusations against the Jewish leaders that they were the culprits who had betrayed and killed the "Innocent (or Righteous) One" (*Dikaios*) (7:52; cf. v. 54).[31] Both the deaths, nonetheless, reflect the qualities of endurance, piety, and magnanimity which were designed to evoke admiration from Luke's readers. That both victims, quite astoundingly, show themselves able to forgive their murderers is deliberately emphasized (Luke 23:34, omitted in Mark and Matthew; Acts 7:60), and the sense of deathlessness conveyed even from the cross (Luke 23:43, omitted in Mark and Matthew) (though only fully clinched by the resurrection) is also present in Stephen's final vision of the Son of Man (Acts 7:56). Stephen's vision, in fact, is the first crucial post-resurrection experience of Jesus in particular, and it anticipates similar encounters that both establish Christ's continuing life and special authority, and confirm that the message is meant for believing Gentiles rather than for disbelieving Jews (9:5, 10-15; 22:17-21; 23:11; cf. 10:9-35).

Thus, these are the lamentable deaths of the virtuous, not welcome repayments exacted from the guilty, and although Stephen's martyrdom is clearly developed as a reenactment of his Lord's suffering,[32] Jesus' death remains very special indeed. It is an occurrence which the Christ himself foretold (Luke 9:20-22; 9:44-45; 13:32-33; 18:31-33) and which was predetermined by the divine will (2:35a; 22:22; Acts 2:23; 4:28; 13:29, cf. 8:32-35). There is a notable attempt to prepare Jewish readers for the horrors of the cross by reminding them of the killing of the prophets (Luke 4:24; 6:23, 26; 11:50-51; 3:33; cf. 16:31), and there is evidence that Luke organized his material concerning the Last Supper and Gethsemane to educate Gentiles who were not prepared to consider any such extremity as crucifixion nor any punishment accepted by the Roman administration, as the conditions for an honorable demise. There is sufficient evidence to have persuaded me, moreover, that Jesus' Last Supper with chosen companions and his manner of foreshadowing "death inevitable for him during a discourse at table," were consciously set parallel to the last hours of Cato Minor, who carried out the most celebrated personal suicide in Roman history.[33] At the stage when Luke begins unfolding his passion narrative, many Gentile readers would have been as confused as the disciples themselves about Jesus' attitude to his own death. By employing the *logia* that deprecated Gentile attitudes to greatness (Luke 22:25-27; cf. its context in Mark 10:42-45), however, and by playing on the ambiguity about how the two swords offered to Jesus are to be used (Luke 22:37b, omitted by Mark and Matthew), Luke shows how his hero comes to make the hardest decisions in the greatest agony (Luke 22:41-44, yet cf. Mark, which is not parallel to Matthew) and goes to his destiny with astounding equanimity (Luke 22:51, 53, 61, 67-70; 23:3, 9, 28-31).[34]

All this being the case—at least the arguable one—how does it relate to the question of Paul's death? It is related in a number of significant respects, which can be placed under three headings to conclude this contribution. First, there is literary artistry to consider. Luke was no mean littérateur and his subtle, often quite uncanny means of bringing unity to his history cannot be underestimated.[35] The question arises, then, whether Luke's work would have lost something in terms of aesthetic balance if the second volume had ended with a death as the first had done (and with a death which, not being followed by the unique resurrection of the Christ, might have left the reader lacking that sense of power and hope Luke believed commensurate with the whole story of Christianity as he conceived it). The use of the shipwreck motif (which Luke might have exploited elsewhere in his account, if he had had more traditions; cf. 2 Cor 11:25) was a brilliant alternative. It sufficed to say that, whatever happened to Paul, the ocean itself and thus the Lord of the waters (see Luke 5:4-8; 8:22-25) declared Paul's innocence and allowed Luke to round off his creation on an optimistic note.[36]

Second, if, as nonbiblical tradition has it, Paul was beheaded, dying as a victim like his master (in all likelihood during the emperor Nero's reign),[37] then Luke had another ignominious (and therefore "problematic") death on his hands—and one that was not going to present the new faith as an attraction. Quite apart from the fact that Luke was probably trying to gauge the conversion potential of his attempt at "accurate" historiography, there also remained the anomaly that the very Roman administration that deemed Paul undeserving of imprisonment eventually did away with him. It was awkward enough for Luke to have to admit that a Roman procurator had sent Jesus to the worst of deaths (note Acts 2:23b; 4:27) (and it is hard to believe Luke did not learn how cruel and arrogant Pilate really was),[38] but to finish with an account of blatant imperial hypocrisy was yet another thing. Here I assume, and I believe quite justifiably, that the ἐνέμεινεν δὲ διετίαν ὅλην of Acts 28:30a is an ominous indication that he was allowed two years of freedom before something more taxing (20:25, 38; 27:24; 28:26; 2 Tim 4:16-18),[39] and that the time between his potentially exonerative trial (ca. A.D. 62) and any *volte face* which brought about his death (in ca. A.D. 63) was rather less than some have alleged.[40] It was certainly too small an interval to prevent Luke's offending the sensibilities of influential Romans who were intended to make up part of his readership.

Finally, to recount Paul's unfortunate end would have only raised those very doubts that Luke apparently presumed to be lurking in the minds of readers who appealed to traditional retributive logic. The hero, after eluding so many near-fatal mishaps, was eventually subjected to a ghastly disgrace, and, even were he to have endured it stoically, such circumstances did not provide a useful moral to round off the career of Paul. One must concede here, of course, that there is only a prima facie case for presuming that Luke felt constrained to end his work still following the adventures of Paul, but, notwithstanding the eleven chapters devoted to other matters in the book of Acts, this inference is hardly unwarranted. It requires only an analysis of Luke's approach to the grisly death of another hero to appreciate that the evangelist did not wish to detail an issue already envisaged to have a large amount of space. I refer to the fate of John the Baptist. It is significant that Luke omits the lengthy account of the Baptist's death and the display of his head upon a platter (Mark 6:17-29 ≠ Matt 14:3-12). He simply refers to John's imprisonment by Herod (= Antipas) in Luke 3:19, to the exchange of messages between John and Jesus (7:18-22), and then, through allusions in others' speeches, to his beheading (9:8-9) and completed *dromos* (Acts 13:25).[41] In this he is as passing in his treatment as he was with the death of James the son of Zebedee (12:2); he is probably more interested in annotating the Herodian threat to Christianity (Luke 9:10b; 13:31; 23:6-12; Acts 4:27), which results in the chastizing affliction on Herod (= Agrippa) at Caesarea (12:23). In the case of Paul's end, even though "Paul's whole progress from Corinth to Jerusalem reads in Luke's account like a march to martyrdom" (see esp. 20:23-24, 38), considerations counted against yet another description of an ugly execution.[42]

We can suggest good reasons, then, why Luke finished his second volume at a point in the story before Paul's beheading. It did not suit his artistic, political and historico-theological intentions to go further. This is not to state a truism nor an *argumentum ex silentio*, for we have good cause to contend that the general issue of the nature of individual deaths has affected his presentation of events in many significant respects. When one accounts for his examples of divine retribution upon evildoers, furthermore, one might well be persuaded that reflection upon this issue was vital in propelling Luke to write a second volume and thus to organize material in the gospel commensurately.

NOTES

*In Memoriam: Robert Maddox (1931-1982), valued friend and scholar. Dr. Robert Maddox, who lectured in Divinity at the University of Sydney, was Australia's foremost scholar in the study of Luke. I cite his major works below (n. 6).

[1] J. N. D. Kelly, *A Commentary on the Pastoral Epistles* (Black's NT Commentaries; London: A. and C. Black, 1963) 26, 30; D. Guthrie, *New Testament Introduction* (Downers Grove, IL: Inter-Varsity, 1970) 598-99; see also E. E. Ellis, "The Authorship of the Pastorals: a résumé and assessment of current trends," *EvQ* 32 (1960) 151-61. For background, see Eusebius *Hist. eccl.* 2.22.1-2; W. M. Ramsay, *St. Paul the Traveller and the Roman Citizen* (London: Hodder and Stoughton, 1920) 360-61. On the Ephesus captivity theory, see, for background, G. S. Duncan, *St. Paul's Ephesian Ministry* (London: Hodder and Stoughton, 1929); for a list of Duncan's supporters, see Guthrie, *NT Introduction*, 531 n. 2; against Duncan, see J. L. Houlden, *Paul's Letters from Prison* (Pelican NT Comm.; Harmondsworth: Penguin, 1970) 42-44.

[2] Eusebius *Hist. eccl.* 2.22.2-8; *Acta Pauli* 10.1-7; see E. Kirschbaum, *The Tombs of St. Peter and St. Paul* (trans. J. H. Murray; London: Secker and Warburg, 1959) 165-213.

[3] The term διετία in Acts 28:30 could be translated "two year jail sentence" (cf. 24:27) or "two years detention before trial" (Philo *In Flaccum* 128) or even "two years grace before trial" (or after which no trial is necessary) (see BGU.628 = *Aegyptische Urkunden aus den Königlichen Museen zu Berlin: Griechische Urkunden* [Berlin: Weidmannsche Buchhandlung, 1895-1933]; Pliny *Epist.* 10.56). It does not have to be a technical term, however (see Arndt and Gingrich, 194a), and the use of the qualifier ὅλην counts against a technical usage here. Lake wishes to argue (on the basis of BGU.628) that Paul won his case by default for lasting out two years without being brought to trial (under pre-Neronian legal conditions) (quoted at length in H. J. Cadbury, "Roman Law and the Trial of Paul," *The Beginnings of Christianity* [ed. F. J. Foakes Jackson and K. Lake; London: Macmillan, 1933] 5. 335), but we must ask why nothing is made of Paul's freedom after this term was up and why Luke is more concerned with showing Paul's continuous preaching of the kingdom during it. If something better rather than worse (or more difficult) was to come, it is extraordinary that Luke should not have been at least slightly more optimistic than he was in his closing verses.

[4] See, e.g., J. de Zwaan, "Was the Book of Acts a Posthumous Edition," *HTR* 17 (1924) 95-98; for the theory that Luke died, see H. Lietzmann, *The History of the Early Church* (trans. B. Lee Woolf; London: Lutterworth, 1961) 2. 78; for Luke's ignorance of the outcome, presumably because he was not in Rome, see F. J. Foakes Jackson, *The Acts of the Apostles* (MNTC; London: Hodder and Stoughton, 1931) 236; I. H. Marshall, *St. Luke: Historian and Theologian* (Exeter: Paternoster, 1970) 220; on Luke's finishing his work just after the events he last recounted, see J. Munck, *The Acts of the Apostles* (AB 31; trans. W. F. Albright and C. S. Mann; Garden City: Doubleday, 1967) 260 (with background in von Harnack); on Luke's planning a third volume, see Cadbury, "Roman Law," 5. 327 (with background in Ramsay). On Luke's wrestling with the unfulfilled prophecy of Acts 27:24 yet remaining true to the facts, see T. Zahn, *Die Apostelgeschichte des Lukas* (Kommentar zum Neuen Testament 5; Leipzig and Erlangen: Deichert, 1921) 718; and for a criticism of all the above views (and some others), see S. G. Wilson, *The Gentiles and the Gentile Mission in Luke-Acts* (Cambridge: University Press, 233-38 (Wilson presumes that Luke's readers already knew the rest of the story).

[5] E. Haenchen, *Die Apostelgeschichte* (Kritisch-Exegetischer Kommentar über das Neue Testament; Göttingen: Vandenhoeck & Ruprecht, 1965) 86-87, 643-55; F. F. Bruce, *The Acts of the Apostles* (New London Commentary on the NT; London: Marshall, Morgan and Scott, 1965) 535-36. See also, G. W. Trompf, *The Idea of Historical Recurrence in Western Thought* (Berkeley, Los Angeles, and London: University of California Press, 1979) 1. 149-50, 155.

[6]See R. Maddox, *The Purpose of Luke-Acts* (FRLANT; Göttingen: Vandenhoeck & Ruprecht, 1982) chap. 2, section 5; see also his *Witnesses to the End of the Earth; the pattern of mission in the book of Acts* (Sydney: UTC, 1980) 73. Luke makes conspicuously little of the fact that there were Christians already in Rome; see Wilson, *Gentiles*, 237.

[7]M. D. Goulder, *Type and History in Acts* (London: A. and C. Black, 1964) 62-63.

[8]G. B. Miles and G. W. Trompf, "Luke and Antiphon: The Theology of Acts 27-28 in the Light of Pagan Beliefs about Divine Retribution, Pollution and Shipwreck," *HTR* 69 (1976) 267, cf. 265 (mainly using Antiphon's *Peri tou Herodou phonou*); D. Ladouceur, "Hellenistic Preconceptions of Shipwrecks and Pollution as a Context for Acts 27-28," *HTR* 73 (1980) 435-49 (especially on Andocides, *De mysteriis*; and the Diaskouroi). C. H. Talbert has kindly pointed out other relevant references closer to Luke's time: Chariton *Ta peri Chairean kai Kalliroēn* 3.3.10; 3.3.18; 3.4.9-10, etc.; Tacitus *Historiae* 1.38; and the Talmudic tractates *b. Ber.* 5.1; *Baba Meṣia* 58b-59.

[9]On *parrēsia* in the language of Greek democracy, see esp. Euripedes, *Hippolytus* 422; Aristophanes *Thesmophoriazusae* 541; Plato *Republic* 557B; Demosthenes *Orationes* 6.31; Polybius *Historiae* 2.38.6.

[10]Trompf, *Idea*, 145; see also Jer 52:31-34.

[11]Trompf, *Idea*, 93-106, 155-70; idem, "Notions of Historical Recurrence in Classical Hebrew Historiography," *Studies in the Historical Books of the Old Testament* (ed. J. A. Emerton; VTSup 30; Leiden: Brill, 1980) 219-29.

[12]See, e.g., H. R. Immerwahr, *Form and Thought in Herodotus* (Philological Monographs 23; Cleveland: Western Reserve University Press, 1966) 306-26; J. H. Finley, "The Unity of Thucydides' History," *Athenian Studies (to W. S. Ferguson)* (Cambridge: Harvard University Press, 1940) 284-89; C. North, *The Old Testament Interpretation of History* (Fernley Hartley Trust Lectures; London: Epworth, 1946) 85-118.

[13]Trompf, *Idea*, 3, 60-61, 66, 70, 74-75, 81, 97-98, 101, 105-6, 111, 158-60, 165, 178.

[14]Trompf, "La section médiane de l'Évangile de Luc: l'organisation des documents," *RHPR* 53 (1973) 144, 154.

[15]Acts 4:21-24; 5:19-23; 8:4; 9:23-27; 12:7-17; 14:19-20; 15:1-3; 16:19-34; 17:6-10; 19:29-20:1; 21:30-23:11. On the significance of 1:8, see esp. Wilson, *Gentiles*, 122-25, 228-38.

[16]Acts 13:47; see also 4:1-7, 21-22; 5:17-28, 40; 7:51-8:2; 9:23; 13:45-46, 50; 14:2-6; 17:13; 18:6, 12-16; 19:9; 20:3, 29-30; 21:27-36; 23:2-22; 24:1-9; 25:2-3; 28:24-27.

[17]For an important discussion, see Maddox, *Purpose*, chap. 2 section 6.

[18]Trompf, "La section," 145-53, s.vv. "acceptation/reject," "apostolat."

[19]In this respect Acts 9:5, on "kicking against the goads" (cf.

διώχεις) must be seen as theologically or apologetically paradigmatic, not simply as a plain historical statement of how a persecutor joined the persecuted.

[20] E.g., Herodotus *Historiae* 1.31: Polybius *Hist.* 3.116.9-13; 16.9.1-2; 30.7.3-4; 38.1.7; Arrian *Anabasis* 7.17; Seneca *De tranquillitate animi* 16.1-4; 1 Macc 1:1-2; 2 Macc 7:20-37; 4 Macc 16:12-18:24. See F. G. Downing, "Jesus and Martyrdom," *JTS* 14 (1963) 279-94.

[21] E.g., Theognis 197-208; Herodotus *Hist.* 4.79; Timaeus, Frgs. 19 (23), 119a, 155 (*Die Fragmente der griechischen Historiker* [ed. F. Jacoby; Berlin: Weidmann, 1926-58] IIIB:585, 634, 644); Xenophon *Anabasis* 5.3.13; Polybius *Hist.* 4.81.5; 87.10-11; 5.27.5-9; 15.26a.1-2; 18.54.6-12; 23.10.2-4, 12-15; Diodorus Siculus *Bibliotheke* 16.61.1-4 etc.

[22] Plutarch *Vit. Cat. Min.* 68.1-71.1; Josephus *J.W.* 7.8.1-7.9.1 §§ 268-401 (even if Josephus was against the Zealots' actions and reckoned them as deserving of retribution, as in 7.6.5 §§ 211-12, the room he allows for Eleazer the Zealot's final and partly self-reproachful speeches permits the premeditated suicidalism familiar to his Greco-Roman readership to be fully aired, in 7.8.6-7 §§ 323-88); see also 1 Sam 31:4-6; Josephus *Ant.* 18.1.6 §23; *J.W.* 1.2.4 §58; 2.8.10 §151. On persons braving their fates stoically, see Plutarch *Vit. Brut.* 52.1-53.5 (Brutus and Porcia); *Vit. Cic.* 48.1-4 (Cicero); Seneca *Epistulae morales* 102.26ff., etc.

[23] To corroborate the more distinctly Greco-Roman touch here, see Polybius on the hanging of Archias, the betrayer of Cyprus (*Hist.* 33.5.2-4).

[24] On anti-Herodianism in the gospels, see esp. H. Braunert, "Der römische Provinzialzensus und der Schätzungsbericht des Lukas Evangeliums," *Historia* 6 (1957) 192ff.; see also Trompf, *Idea*, 173 and n. 263.

[25] See Acts 25:13, 23-26, 26:1-3, 27-32, on the naming of Agrippa (II) coupled with a more sympathetic treatment.

[26] The gospels differ about whether Annas or Caiaphas was the high-priest in Jesus' time; see Matt 26:57 (Caiaphas); John 18:22-24 (both Annas and Caiaphas!). The problem is best solved by supposing that the Jewish leaders never accepted the Roman annulment of Annas's position in A.D. 15 (yet see S. Sandmel ["Annas," "Caiaphas," *IDB* 1. 138, 481-82] for an unnecessarily skeptical interpretation).

[27] Luke includes 11:24-26 in a whole section related to retribution —or to the consequences of accepting or rejecting the message— (11:14-12:12), but unlike Matthew, Jesus (to 11:36 in any case) speaks to Israel in general and not just to the Pharisees (see Matt 12:22-50, esp. 12:45b; omitted by Luke). See Trompf, "La section," 146-47.

[28] The use of the term ἀνόμων in 2:33 is definitely pejorative but deliberately vague in its reference. The naming of Pontius Pilate in conjunction with Herod and both the "Gentiles and peoples of Israel" (4:27) is not to be taken lightly (and it anticipates late creedal statements!), but the emphasis on divine foreknowledge in v. 28 nevertheless softens the criticism. The presence of these anti-Roman

sentiments suggests a source, albeit one still subject to Luke's wary editorship.

[29] See, e.g., Num 35:16-30; 2 Sam 11:2-12:15; 1 Kgs 16:9-19; 21:1-29; 2 Kgs 12:16; 23:26; Ps 10:8, 12; 94:6-7 (for Old Testament perspectives); Theognis 315-18; Polybius *Hist.* 8.30.1-9; Diodorus *Bibliotheke* 16.61.1-4; Cicero *Pro Sestio* 67.40; Plutarch *De sera numinis vindicta* 548C-549D (for important texts on Greco-Roman attitudes).

[30] The terms ἀναιρέσις and οἱ ἀναιροῦντες in 8:1 and 22:20 primarily denote "murder, murdering" in Koine Greek (Arndt and Gingrich, 54a), though other usages are evident in classical Greek.

[31] The point applies whether we capitalize the delta or not; more authoritative manuscripts were transcribed in upper case letters.

[32] See Trompf, *Idea*, 123. The term *martyr* is used of Stephen only in Acts 22:20.

[33] Plutarch *Vit. Cat. Min.* 62.1-71.1; see Trompf, *Idea*, 153-54.

[34] The differences between these last cited verses and comparable passages in the other three canonical gospels are subtle but significant. According to Luke, Jesus actually heals the high priest's slave whose ear is severed (22:51b, omitted by Matthew and John), while still being able to remonstrate against the violence of his disciples (v. 51a, some ≠ Matt 26:52-54; John 18:11) and those who arrested him (52-53, some ≠ Mark 14:48-49; Matt 26:55-56, omitted by John). In contrast to the other evangelists, Luke has Jesus' words to his captors highlight injustice and iniquity, without the reflection on scripture or prophecy fulfillment (cf. Mark 14:49; Matt 26:56; John 18:9). After Peter's denials, Jesus is in a position to single him out as if to confirm his control over proceedings (22:61, omitted by Mark, Matthew, and John). Jesus is more remonstrative against his Jewish judges in Luke's gospel than in the other synoptics (22:67-69, cf. Mark 14:62; Matt 26:63a; 64), but in this respect Luke's account shares a touch of reality in common with John 18:20, 23. In Luke, Jesus' answer Σὺ λέγεις to Pilate's question about whether he was king of the Jews (23:3) comes as an assured answer that leaves the procurator no course except to declare his innocence (23:4, cf. Mark 15:2-5; Matt 27:11-14) (John 18:33b, 38 is again closer to Luke's account, but the fourth evangelist has much more detail and sustains the realism more ably here). In Luke 23:28-31, Jesus, even while he is carrying the cross, is able to comfort mourners and utter an oracle (omitted by Mark, Matthew, and John).

[35] Authors who have been most helpful in bringing out this aspect of the Lucan achievement include H. J. Cadbury, *The Making of Luke-Acts* (1927; reprint, London: SPCK, 1958) esp. part 2; Goulder, *Type and History*; E. Plümacher, *Lukas als hellenistischer Schriftsteller: Studien zur Apostelgeschichte* (SUNT 9; Göttingen: Vandenhoeck & Ruprecht, 1972); C. H. Talbert, *Literary Patterns, Theological Themes, and the Genre of Luke-Acts* (SBLMS 20; Missoula: Scholars Press, 1974).

[36] And thus also on a note of "activity" rather than "passivity"; see Haenchen, *Apostelgeschichte*, 654.

[37]G. H. C. Macgregor (*IB*, 9. 351) thinks that all the evidence points to a death before Nero's reign; but see n. 40 below. On the beheading, see Eusebius *Hist. eccl.* 2.25.5; *Acta Pauli* 10.4.

[38]Note Josephus's account, in contrast, in *J.W.* 2.9.2–4 §§169–77; *Ant.* 18.3.1–18.4.2 §§55–89.

[39]Note esp. 20:25, 38; 27:24; cf. also 28:16. The Western text of Acts 28:16 has Paul under the charge of "the prefect of the Emperor's bodyguard," who evidently took charge of political prisoners from the Province before their trials. Whether such an office existed before Trajan, however, remains problematic. See Pliny *Epist.* 10.57; see also Haenchen, *Apostelgeschichte*, 642.

[40]The choice of chronologies is important here. I am tied neither to Eusebius (*Chronica* [ed. Jerome, Bodleian MS. Fol.116; reproduced, with introd. by J. K. Fotheringham; Oxford: Oxford University Press, 1905]; see *Hist. eccl.* 2.26.1; 3.5.1), who put Paul's death in Nero's fourteenth year (= A.D. 67–68), nor to the fourth-century Liberian Catalogue of Saints, which puts it as early as A.D. 55. Of the various modern alternatives I prefer a date of arrival in Rome ca. A.D. 60 (following esp. H. Metzger, *St. Paul's Journeys in the Greek Orient* [trans. S. H. Hooke; Studies in Biblical Archaeology 4; London: SCM, 1955] 74) but take seriously the possibility of Nero's change of face toward Christians, as Eusebius (albeit rather cautiously) suggested (2.22.8). Hence, when Paul eventually faced a second hearing (see 2 Tim 4:16–18), Luke still being with him (4:11), Christians had become a far less acceptable breed. Here I take 2 Tim 4:6–21 to be an authentic "last-minute" fragment of Paul, around which a pastoral was constructed (see C. K. Barrett, *The Pastoral Epistles* [Oxford: Clarendon, 1963] 10–11). For my own attitudes to the authenticity of the Pastorals, see "On Attitudes toward Women in Paul and Paulinist Literature: 1 Cor. 11:3–16 and its Context," *CBQ* 42 (1980) 205–15.

[41]The fact that John's birth and ministry are given a comparatively large amount of attention (Luke 1:5–25, 57–80; 3:2–20) makes it all the more important that Luke does not relate his death. The additional data revealing Luke to have conceived John as the last of the prophets (7:24–35; 16:16) and one who does not necessarily baptize Jesus (3:21–22; John 1:32–34; yet cf. Mark 1:9–11; Matt 3:13–17; see also H. Conzelmann, *The Theology of St. Luke* [London: Faber and Faber, 1964] 21) do not explain why he should have glossed over John's death so rapidly.

[42]Macgregor, *IB* 9. 350 (for the quotation); see also Haenchen, *Apostelgeschichte*, 654–55.

INDEX OF MODERN AUTHORS